Sδ̃τ̃ω̃
2Sℓ̃ω̃

D1617487

JOSEPH CONRAD'S LETTERS TO
R. B. CUNNINGHAME GRAHAM

R. B. Cunninghame Graham (1923)
by Jacob Epstein

JOSEPH CONRAD'S
LETTERS TO
R. B. CUNNINGHAME GRAHAM

EDITED BY

C. T. WATTS

Lecturer in English
University of Sussex

CAMBRIDGE
AT THE UNIVERSITY PRESS
1969

Published by the Syndics of the Cambridge University Press
Bentley House, 200 Euston Road, London N.W.1
American Branch: 32 East 57th Street, New York, N.Y. 10022

Introduction and notes © Cambridge University Press 1969
The letters of Joseph Conrad are included by arrangement
with J. M. Dent and Sons Ltd, and the Trustees of the
Joseph Conrad Estate

Library of Congress Catalogue Card Number: 69–16288
Standard Book Number: 521   07213   1

Printed in Great Britain
at the University Printing House, Cambridge
(Brooke Crutchley, University Printer)

Contents

Acknowledgements

This volume is based on a large part of the Ph.D. thesis on which I worked at Cambridge from 1961 to 1964. My supervisor for that period was the late Mr Douglas Brown, to whose kindness, encouragement and wisdom I remain permanently indebted. I am also particularly beholden to Admiral Sir Angus Cunninghame Graham, who answered numerous written and oral enquiries and gave me free access to his uncle's books and papers. Mr Richard Curle gave me useful advice and permitted me to read many letters sent to him by Cunninghame Graham. Lady Jean Halsey generously gave me access to the collection of letters to her grandmother, the Ranee of Sarawak, Lady Margaret Brooke. The late R. E. Muirhead, Secretary of the Scottish National Party, kindly lent me papers by and about Cunninghame Graham. Mrs Violet Tschiffely gave patient answers to numerous enquiries, as did Professor Herbert Faulkner West, who helped in many ways. I am also grateful for the information or other help given by: Mr Jocelyn Baines, whose critical biography of Conrad was my prime reference book; Mr John Conrad; Mr David Garnett; Professor F. R. Karl; Mr René MacColl; Mr Marischal Murray; Señor Felipe Pérez; and the staffs of the Baker Library, Dartmouth College; the British Museum; the Corporation of Lloyd's; Illinois University Library; the London Library; London University Library; the National Library of Scotland; New York Public Library; and Sussex, Texas and Yale University Libraries.

For permission to use copyright material I am grateful to Messrs J. M. Dent and Sons and the Trustees of the Joseph Conrad Estate; Admiral Sir Angus Cunninghame Graham; Mr David Garnett; Lady Jean Halsey; Señor Felipe Pérez; Mr Innes Rose; the Baker Library; Manuscript Collections, Carnegie Library, Syracuse University; the Academic Center Library, Texas University; Yale University Library; The University of Chicago Press; Laurence Pollinger Ltd. and the Estate of the late Mrs Frieda Lawrence; and the Public Trustee and the Society of Authors. The Clarendon Press, publishers of the *Review of English*

Studies, and Oxford University Press, publishers of *Notes and Queries*, kindly permitted me to use material (specified later in this volume) which I first published in those periodicals.

The frontispiece is by courtesy of Manchester City Art Gallery and Lady Epstein.

Abbreviations

AFT   A. F. Tschiffely, *Don Roberto* (Heinemann, London, 1937).

ASA   The manuscript collection of Admiral Sir Angus Cunninghame Graham.

Aubry   G. Jean-Aubry or G. Jean Aubry.

Baines   Jocelyn Baines, *Joseph Conrad: A Critical Biography* (Weidenfeld and Nicolson, London, 1960).

Blackburn   W. Blackburn (ed.), *Joseph Conrad: Letters to William Blackwood and David S. Meldrum* (Duke University Press, Durham, North Carolina, 1958).

DG   David Garnett, *The Golden Echo* (Chatto and Windus, London, 1953).

ECB   *The English Catalogue of Books.*

EGL   Edward Garnett (ed.), *Letters from Conrad, 1895 to 1924* (Nonesuch Press, London, 1928).

EKH   E. K. Hay, *The Political Novels of Joseph Conrad* (University of Chicago Press, Chicago and London, 1963).

Gordan   J. D. Gordan, *Joseph Conrad: The Making of a Novelist* (Harvard University Press, Cambridge, Mass., 1941).

Graham   R. B. Cunninghame Graham.

GTK   G. T. Keating, *A Conrad Memorial Library* (Doubleday, Doran, New York, 1929).

HFW   Herbert Faulkner West, *A Modern Conquistador: Robert Bontine Cunninghame Graham: His Life and Works* (Cranley and Day, London, 1932).

JEC   Jessie Conrad, *Joseph Conrad and his Circle* (Jarrolds, London, 1935).

KRZ   L. Krzyżanowski (ed.), *Joseph Conrad: Centennial Essays* (Polish Institute of Arts and Sciences in America, New York, 1960).

LFR   G. Jean-Aubry (ed.), *Joseph Conrad: Lettres Françaises* (Gallimard, Paris, 1929).

LL   G. Jean-Aubry (ed.), *Joseph Conrad: Life and Letters*, 2 vols. (Heinemann, London, 1927).

Mogreb   R. B. Cunninghame Graham, *Mogreb-el-Acksa: A Journey in Morocco* (Heinemann, London, 1898).

MPL   J. A. Gee and P. J. Sturm (tr. and ed.), *Letters of Joseph Conrad to Marguerite Poradowska, 1890–1920* (Yale University Press, New Haven, 1940).

NLS   The National Library of Scotland.

Notes   Joseph Conrad, *Notes on Life and Letters* (Uniform Edn., Dent, London, 1924).

RCL   Richard Curle (ed.), *Conrad to a Friend: 150 Selected Letters from Joseph Conrad to Richard Curle* (Sampson Low, Marston, London, 1928).

SR   The *Saturday Review* (London).

TJW   T. J. Wise, *A Bibliography of the Writings of Joseph Conrad (1895–1921)* (privately printed, London, 1921).

WHH   Richard Curle (ed.), *W. H. Hudson's Letters to R. B. Cunninghame Graham* (Golden Cockerel Press, London, 1941).

Editorial Note

Of the eighty-one letters from Conrad to Graham in this volume, seventy-nine have been edited from photocopies of the originals now in the United States, and the remaining two have been edited from the Ardoch manuscripts. Fifty-two of the letters, and part of a further one, have been previously published in *LL*. The remaining twenty-eight are previously uncollected ones, though I have given the texts of three of them (letters 10, 13 and 66) in periodical articles. This edition therefore includes twenty-five letters which as far as I have been able to ascertain are unpublished.

I have been unable to find any of Graham's letters to Conrad, though I have made many enquiries. Possibly these letters were destroyed by Conrad. None of them has been quoted in any relevant work that I have seen; and as early as 1932, Herbert Faulkner West reported a similar lack of success in his search (*HFW*, pp. 109–10). With one exception (noted here on p. 182) this collection represents, I believe, all the surviving letters of this exchange; but it may still represent less than two-thirds of Conrad's side of the original correspondence. It seems unlikely that Conrad should have written nothing to Graham in the years 1913, 1916 and 1918, for example; and Conrad's remark to Edward Garnett on 29 March [1898] that 'Graham.....has been in bed since but writes every second day' (*EGL*, p. 129) indicates other gaps in the sequence of extant replies. Fortunately, however, Conrad's most fruitful years as a writer, from 1897 to 1904, are also the years during which the available correspondence is most prolific. It can be seen how Conrad struggles to define his philosophical and political beliefs, and some of his literary views, in relation to (and at times in opposition to) Graham's, without disrupting their friendship; how that friendship matures from the early enthusiasm into an enduring trust and affection; how Graham becomes a central figure in Conrad's attempt to write for the *Saturday Review*, followed by the attempt to escape from the desk to the capstan; and how Graham helps to sustain Conrad in some of his most strenuous literary struggles.

Apart from the convenience of arranging the Conrad-to-Graham letters in one volume, my reasons for re-presenting the letters which have previously appeared in G. Jean-Aubry's invaluable *Joseph Conrad: Life and Letters* are as follows. First, Jean-Aubry's annotations and chronological arrangement of the material were corrigible at several points. Secondly, he omitted, without indication, parts of many of the letters; and some of the omitted passages are of considerable interest. Thirdly, he made running corrections and alterations to Conrad's spelling, punctuation, and capitalisation. A closer approximation to the original seemed to me to be generally desirable, particularly in view of the exegetic attentions which letters like that of 8 February 1899 have attracted; and as Conrad was usually a careful letter-writer, it seemed that a high degree of fidelity would not entail a series of petty textual annoyances for present readers. In my footnotes I indicate the more significant differences between the *LL* text and the original, but not the numerous trivial differences whose pattern is shown in appendix 1.

My aim, then, has been to preserve Conrad's text without correction or omission. I have not inserted the editorial *sic* into the body of each letter: Conradian errors which might be mistaken for misprints or editorial slips are listed in footnotes in addition to being preserved in the text, except for the least important idiosyncrasies of punctuation which are kept in the text but not listed separately.

Where Conrad has clearly inserted a word as an afterthought, and where he has cancelled a word and written a correction above or upon it, I have in all save the most trivial cases indicated this fact in a note and have given there the cancelled word when it has been decipherable.

I have neither supplied omitted accents nor corrected wrong accents, but where Conrad has made a random stroke which might equally well be a *grave*, an acute or a circumflex, I have given the appropriate correct accent.

I have maintained Conrad's capitalisation: but inevitably there have been borderline cases where it has been impossible to decide with certainty whether a capital or small letter was intended.

Printed or embossed letterheads are enclosed in angle brackets, thus:

⟨OSWALDS,

BISHOPSBOURNE.⟩

The openings of some paragraphs, as in their originals, have not been indented.

The number of each footnote refers to the line number of the transcript.

In the commentary, where I have omitted part of a quotation, I indicate this deletion by means of a group of 5 dots (.....); a group of three dots is used for a non-editorial hiatus.

The sources of the letters from Conrad to Cunninghame Graham are as follows: letter 31, Yale University Library; letters 56 and 79, the collection of Admiral Sir Angus Cunninghame Graham at Ardoch, Cardross, Dunbartonshire; letter 64, the Carnegie Library of Syracuse University, New York; all others, the Baker Library of Dartmouth College, Hanover, New Hampshire.

The letters to Cunninghame Graham from S. P. Triana are at Ardoch, as were until recently those from Edward Garnett, which have now joined Cunninghame Graham's letters to Edward Garnett in the Academic Center Library of the University of Texas.

Quotations from Conrad's works are, with a few indicated exceptions, from the Uniform Edition (Dent, London, 1923–8).

INTRODUCTION

'In our activity alone do we find the
sustaining illusion of an independent
existence.....'   *Nostromo*

Conrad and Cunninghame Graham

In November 1885, ninety-six years after the storming of the Bastille, four years after the founding of *Tit-Bits*, and twelve years before the vulturine Donkin was to tell the crew of the 'Narcissus' about the days when all seamen would be well-fed skippers, a General Election took place in Great Britain. The Social Democratic Federation optimistically and unsuccessfully entered candidates, including John Burns, an unemployed engineer; and Gladstone's Liberals profited from the extension of the franchise under the Third Reform Act by defeating the Conservatives. Even Gladstone, observing the competition between the main parties for the new democratic vote, had talked of the 'leaning of both parties to socialism, which I radically disapprove';[1] and in the month following the Election, a man who signed himself 'K. N. Korzeniowski' (and not yet as 'Joseph Conrad') wrote to Spiridion Kliszewski:

the International Socialist Association are triumphant, and every disreputable ragamuffin in Europe feels that the day of universal brotherhood, despoliation and disorder is coming apace, and nurses daydreams of well-plenished pockets amongst the ruin of all that is respectable, venerable and holy. The great British Empire went over the edge, and yet on to the inclined plane of social progress and radical reform.....

England was the only barrier to the pressure of infernal doctrines born in continental back-slums. Now, there is nothing!.....

Socialism must inevitably end in Cæsarism.....

The whole herd of idiotic humanity are moving in that direction at the bidding of unscrupulous rascals and a few sincere, but dangerous, lunatics.[2]

The following year—the year in which Gissing published *Demos*—was one of severe unemployment as a cyclical depression reached its worst point. In February, crowds looted shops in Mayfair and smashed the windows of clubs in Pall Mall, and John Burns at Hyde Park told a demonstration of the unemployed:

We are not strong enough at the present moment to cope with armed force, but when we give you the signal will you rise? [Loud cries of 'Yes'.][3]

---

[1] J. Morley, *Life of William Ewart Gladstone* (Macmillan, London, 1906), II, 461. [2] *LL*, I, 84.

[3] *Democrat* (13 Feb. 1886), quoted by H. Pelling, *The Origins of The Labour Party 1880–1900* (Oxford, London, 1965), p. 42.

Five months later R. B. Cunninghame Graham, whom *The Times* called a 'cow-boy dandy',[1] was elected to parliament; and *Hansard* reported thus the conclusion of his maiden speech, which referred to the recent Irish evictions:

The homes destroyed in Glenbeigh were, no doubt, as dear to the poor peasant, in his lonely village on the stony mountain side in the far west, as was the shoddy mansion in South Kensington to the capitalist, as was Haddon Hall to its owner, or as was Buckingham Palace to the absentee owner of that dreadful building. Who could say that the affairs of this handful of obscure tenants in a wind-swept and rain-bedewed, stony corner of Ireland, might not prove to have given the first blow to that society in which one man worked and another enjoyed the fruit—that society in which capital and luxury made a Heaven for 30,000, and a Hell for 30,000,000—that society whose crowning achievement was this dreary waste of mud and stucco—with its misery, its want and destitution, its degradation, its prostitution, and its glaring social inequalities—the society which we call London—that society which, by a refinement of irony, had placed the mainspring of human action, almost the power of life and death, and the absolute power to pay labour and to reward honour, behind the grey tweed veil which enshrouded the greasy pocket-book of the capitalist.[2]

In 1897 this defiant speaker wrote to Conrad; and in 1925 Arthur Symons recorded:

Conrad said to me once, in a tone of tragic and almost passionate pathos I shall never forget: 'Could you conceive for a moment that I could go on existing if Cunninghame Graham were to die?'[3]

Conrad's friendship with Cunninghame Graham, which lasted from 1897 until Conrad's death in 1924, could be called an expanding paradox. On the strength of his maiden speech alone it will have been seen that Graham qualified as one of Conrad's 'sincere, but dangerous, lunatics'. If Conrad wished to preserve all that was 'respectable, venerable and holy', Graham on the other hand was to declare himself the enemy

not only of the State and all its works, political and economical, but of the Churches and their moralities and faiths;

and he explained:

There is no other halting place for Socialists: either they must reject the whole, or swallow all—or not be honest.[4]

---

[1] Quoted in *AFT*, p. 212.
[2] *Hansard's Parliamentary Debates*, 3rd series, vol. cccx, col. 445 (1 Feb. 1887).
[3] *Notes on Joseph Conrad* (Myers, London, 1925), p. 31.
[4] 'The Enemy' in *Justice* (London, 3 May 1913), p. 5.

Conrad could write of

liberty, which can only be found under the English flag all over the world,[1]

whereas Graham asserted that

It needs nothing but the presence of the conquering white man, decked in his shoddy clothes, armed with his gas-pipe gun, his Bible in his hand....., his merchandise (that is, his whisky, gin and cotton cloths) securely stored in his corrugated iron-roofed sheds, and he himself active and persevering as a beaver or red ant, to bring about a sickness which, like the 'modorra', exterminates the people whom he came to benefit.[2]

And fifteen years before the author of *The Secret Agent* was to begin his analysis of anarchism ('a brazen cheat exploiting the poignant miseries and passionate credulities of a mankind always so tragically eager for self-destruction'),[3] Graham, who had spoken alongside the anarchist Kropotkin and the assassin Stepniak at open-air demonstrations in London,[4] told trade unionists this:

Our Parliament is All Fools Paradise. Those who make safe speeches, the lawyers, guinea pigs, and others, get quiet hearing. Why? Because the place wants a purge. Some say force is no remedy. Was their [sic] then no use of it in '93. [sic][5]

What is the outlook?
A general strike on May 1st, you say, for the Eight Hours' Day.
A general strike! That means a revolution. You cannot leave the towns in darkness.....without a revolution, for the Whigs and Tories would coalesce to coerce you.
Well, let it come; it cannot come too soon, with butchering Stanleys held in high renown, with cheating and extortion rife amongst us, with sweaters in high places.....[6]

While Conrad in England was reserved, reticent, and reluctant to appear before the public, Graham was a flamboyant public figure who by 1890 had already been the subject of magazine profiles and political cartoons, and whose desire to offer his opinions

[1] Letter to Aniela Zagorska dated 25 December 1899. Z. Najder, *Conrad's Polish Background* (Oxford, London, 1964), p. 232.
[2] 'Higginson's Dream' in *Thirteen Stories* (Heinemann, London, 1900), p. 181.
[3] 'Author's Note' to *The Secret Agent* (Dent, 1923), p. ix.
[4] *People's Press* (London, 10 May 1890), p. 6; and G. Woodcock and I. Avakumović: *The Anarchist Prince* (Boardman, London, 1950), pp. 225, 231-3.
[5] *People's Press* (21 June 1890), p. 3. Urge a man to fight, and he may at least clench his fist: such is Graham's testy logic. He continues: 'Think not, sweet Oxonian juvenal, I wish the mob to try conclusions with the Maxim gun. I only state a fact....., that People's Parliament is a ship of fools.....Surely it is getting almost time to take to boarding-pikes (by ballot, if you will) and capture it.'   [6] *Ibid.* (22 Nov. 1890), p. 7.

5

to the public seemed to be curbed only by the physical difficulty of simultaneously haranguing a crowd and composing a letter to the press (therefore he compromised by reporting his own public appearances). Conrad, plagued by gout, 'nerves', debt and doubt, 'almost needed a Caesarean operation of the soul', Graham remarked, 'before he was delivered of his masterpieces';[1] whereas Graham uttered with comparatively cornucopian profusion, and left others to scratch their heads over the uncorrected proofs which his hasty and atrocious handwriting had proleptically sabotaged.

Nevertheless Conrad had more in common with Graham, temperamentally and ethically, than with Garnett, Wells, James, or any of his other literary correspondents; and Richard Curle describes a meeting between the two men, late in Conrad's life, as though it were a meeting between two brothers, commenting:

In each other's company they appeared to grow younger; they treated one another with that kind of playfulness which can only arise from a complete, unquestioning, and ancient friendship. I doubt whether the presence of any man made Conrad happier than the presence of Don Roberto.....
(*HFW*, p. 114.)

Conrad's exultant reply to Graham's first letter is partly a cry of recognition: for in a sense Graham was Conrad's 'secret sharer', whose conflicting political conclusions derived from similar moral premises within a similar vision. Both men were described as 'aristocratic' in their bearing, appearance, and in their sense of chivalry, honour, and justice; and their related contempt for the arrogant materialism of their era was founded on retrospection, on a personal and historic nostalgia, which had been leavened by the accumulated experience, the problems and disillusions, of their youthful years of travel, labour and adventure, until irony (the natural recourse of those who doubt the general contemporary validity of their positions) had become for both a principal mode of thought and expression. Between themselves the masks of irony could be lowered, if not entirely laid aside; as when Conrad told Graham:

I think that we do agree.....You are a most hopeless idealist—your aspirations are irrealisable. You want from men faith, honour, fidelity to truth in themselves and others.....What makes you dangerous is your unwarrantable belief that your desire may be realized. This is the only point of difference between us. I do not believe. And if I desire the very same things no one cares.[2]

[1] Introduction to *Lord Jim* (Dent, London, 1935), p. ix.   [2] Letter 5.

Yet Graham knew that the days of cavalry were as numbered as the days of the clippers. In Conrad, he heard the monitory echo of his own pessimism; and in Graham, Conrad saw the melodramatic extension of his own Quixotism.

Cunninghame Graham...a figure slightly absurd and slightly pathetic: or so we may feel, perhaps in reaction against the uncritically romantic presentation of a critically romantic figure, as we turn the pages of photographs in Tschiffely's biography of him. Nevertheless many of his contemporaries saw the singularity rather than the absurdity, and glamour rather than pathos. Shaw remarked that he had refrained from making him the hero of *Captain Brassbound's Conversion* only because 'so incredible a personage must have destroyed its likelihood';[1] Chesterton claimed that

Nothing could prevent Balfour being Prime Minister......; but Cunninghame Graham achieved the adventure of being Cunninghame Graham;[2]

and John Lavery, before explaining how Graham had helped to establish him as an artist, said: 'I think I did something to help Graham in the creation of his masterpiece—himself'.[3] He was variously traveller, cattle-rancher and horse-dealer, fencing-master, Liberal M.P., pioneer socialist, Mohammed el Fasi,[4] demagogue, convict, begetter of the Sergius Saranoff in *Arms and the Man*,[5] political columnist, essayist, critic, story-writer, historian,

[1] *Three Plays for Puritans* (Richards, London, 1901), p. 301.
[2] *Autobiography* (Hutchinson, London, 1936), p. 269.
[3] *The Life of a Painter* (Cassell, London, 1940), p. 92.
[4] See *Mogreb*. Ocular proof also in *AFT*, facing p. 294.
[5] In the Notes to *Captain Brassbound's Conversion* Shaw states merely that he had taken one of Graham's parliamentary exclamations and given it to Saranoff, the hero of *Arms and the Man*: 'The House, strong in stupidity, did not understand him [Graham] until in an inspired moment he voiced a universal impulse by bluntly damning its hypocrisy. Of all the eloquence of that silly parliament, there remains only one single damn......The shocked House demanded that he should withdraw his cruel word. 'I never withdraw', said he; and I promptly stole the potent phrase for the sake of its perfect style, and used it as a cockade for the Bulgarian hero of Arms and the Man. The theft prospered; and I naturally take the first opportunity of repeating it.' (*Three Plays for Puritans*, p. 302.) However, Sergius Saranoff's theatrical quixotism, his aristocratic scorn for modern warfare, and details of Shaw's account (in the stage-directions) of his personality and physical appearance, suggest that the debt to Graham was a slightly more substantial if satiric one. Shaw's private secretary wrote: 'Shaw once described Cunninghame Graham as "a story writer of genius: he figures in my play Arms and the Man with Webb

translator, Scottish Nationalist, 'the curly darling' to factory-girls,[1] and withal 'a first-class shot with pistols';[2] but unlike Dryden's 'Chymist, Fidler, States-Man and Buffoon' he acted his rôles with panache and accomplishment—he understood his lines and manifested a consistent style which was more than a series of poses.

Shaw records:

He is, I regret to add, an impenitent and unashamed dandy: such boots, such a hat, would have dazzled D'Orsay himself. With that hat he once saluted me in Regent St. when I was walking with my mother. Her interest was instantly kindled; and the following conversation ensued. 'Who is that?' 'Cunninghame Graham.' 'Nonsense! Cunninghame Graham is one of your Socialists: that man is a gentleman.' This is the punishment of vanity[3]

—but a venial vanity, perhaps: if he sat scores of times for artists, Lavery, Rothenstein, Epstein and the others could hardly have asked for a more striking subject; and since the vanity of his conduct expressed itself most notably in his defence of underdogs, of the exploited, and of humane but unpopular causes, it was scarcely more to be condemned than the roar and fume of an ambulance engine.

In *Return to Yesterday*, Ford Madox Ford gives an anecdote which deserves to be true:

Once, driving with Mr. Graham to Roslyn Castle from Edinburgh I heard a politically minded lady say to him:

'You ought, Mr. Graham, to be the first president of a British Republic.'

'I ought, madam, if I had my rights', he answered sardonically, 'to be the king of this country. And what a three weeks that would be!'[4]

in strong contrast".' (Blanche Patch, *Thirty Years with G.B.S.*, Gollancz, London, 1951, p. 69. Webb provided the basis for Bluntschli.)
   Of *Captain Brassbound's Conversion*, Shaw wrote: 'I claim as a notable merit in the authorship of this play that I have been intelligent enough to steal its scenery, its surroundings, its atmosphere, its geography, its knowledge of the east, its fascinating Cadis and Krooboys and Sheikhs and mud castles from an excellent book of philosophic travel and vivid adventure entitled Mogreb-el-Acksa (Morocco the Most Holy) by Cunninghame Graham.' (*Three Plays for Puritans*, p. 301.)
[1] In a letter to Graham dated 2 January 1898 Garnett wrote: 'I will try to get Unwin to be definite about the portrait for *The Ipané* this week. By the way, Madame Stepniak to whom I showed it, exclaimed in horror "But where are the *curls*? I have heard the factory girls at a meeting call him 'the curly darling!'"
   I explained that the curls were probably abandoned in the prison where you sojourned—but she is dissatisfied.'
[2] Letter to me from John Conrad (7 Jan. 1963).
[3] *Three Plays for Puritans*, p. 303.
[4] Gollancz, London, 1931, p. 38.

8

Graham was five years older than Conrad, having been born into the Scottish landed aristocracy on 24 May 1852, as the eldest son of Major William Bontine, a wealthy officer in the Scots Greys, and the Hon. Mrs Bontine, formerly Anne Elizabeth Fleeming: her mother was Spanish, her father was the Admiral Fleeming who met and impressed Bolivar.[1] On his father's side, Graham could trace his descent from King Robert II.[2] His family were claimants to the Earldoms of Strathearn, Menteith and Airth;[3] and his ancestors included Robert Graham, the poet and radical who was Rector of Glasgow University in 1785 and M.P. from 1794 to 1796,[4] and the William Graham of Gartmore who, enlivening Boswell's visit to Switzerland, 'raged against the Scots Parliament House, and a man's passing his whole life in writing "d-mned papers"'.[5]

Between 1869 and 1884, after schooling at Harrow and in Brussels, Graham made repeated journeys to South and Central America, living among gauchos, llaneros and cattle-ranchers, and making attempts to establish a career as a cattle- and horse-dealer which were frustrated partly by the revolutionary upheavals in Paraguay and Argentina and partly by his inexperience.[6] This period provided not only the raw material for many of his later writings but also one of the main ostensive bases for his moral outlook in politics and literature. In later years he said in parliament,

Let hon. Members remember that I came into this House, not from the merchant's office or the lawyer's court, but straight from the prairies of America, where want is unknown, so that the sight of such misery as exists in London was brought home to my mind with exceptional force.[7]

In 1878 he met, eloped with, and married, Gabriela—Gabrielle de la Balmondière, Yeats's 'little bright American',[8] who was born

1 This meeting with Bolivar is described in the appendix to Graham's *José Antonio Páez* (Heinemann, London, 1929).
2 Graham's *Notes on the District of Menteith* (Black, London, 1895), pp. 25–33; and *AFT*, p. 4.
3 *Notes on the District of Menteith*, pp. 33–57.
4 The subject of Graham's *Doughty Deeds* (Heinemann, London, 1925).
5 F. A. Pottle (ed.), *Boswell on the Grand Tour: Germany and Switzerland 1764* (Heinemann, London, 1953), p. 264.
6 Graham's letters to his mother, 1870–83 (ASA). Many are quoted in *AFT*, chapters 3–9.
7 *Hansard*, vol. CCCXXXIII, col. 1070 (6 March 1889). Graham, of course, knew Edward Carpenter, the author of *Civilisation: Its Cause and Cure*.
8 Allan Wade (ed.), *The Letters of W. B. Yeats* (Hart-Davis, London, 1954), pp. 63–4. See also my note, 'A Letter from W. B. Yeats to R. B. Cunninghame Graham', *Review of English Studies*, N.S. XVIII (Aug. 1967), 292–3.

in Chile of French and Spanish parentage. In private her personality was contemplative: she painted vague water-colours and, chain-smoking, was to write sentimental poems, tales like 'The Christ of Toro' in *The Yellow Book*, and a study of St Teresa. In public life she became a working associate of Morris and the Socialist League,[1] giving lectures and later (in the words of *The Times*)[2] 'running all over Spain making socialist speeches'. Hers was an industrious but childless partnership with Graham.

He was elected to parliament as Liberal member for North-West Lanark in July 1886 (after standing unsuccessfully in 1882 and 1885) and remained an M.P. until 1892. His Liberalism was nominal: with reason he was described by the *People's Press*[3] as 'the only member of Parliament who can really be called a Socialist'. He condemned British imperialism, corporal and capital punishment, profiteering landlords and industrialists, child labour, the House of Lords, and religious instruction for school-children; and he advocated the eight-hour day 'in all trades and occupations', free education, home rule for Ireland and Scotland, and nationalisation—in 1887 he urged the government to 'take possession of the mines and machinery of this country, and work them for the benefit of the country, and not in the selfish interest of capitalists'.[4] His speeches were characteristically impetuous, forceful and ironic: on two occasions he was ordered by the Speaker to withdraw,[5] and the retort 'I never withdraw' re-echoes whenever *Arms and the Man* is performed.

His admiration for William Morris helped to convert into socialism his freelance radicalism and to divert into practical

[1] 'Mrs Graham is an ardent Socialist, and is to be seen sometimes on the platform at Kelmscott House, Hammersmith, and other socialist meeting-places.' (*People's Press*, 26 April 1890, p. 3.) Her correspondents included not only William and May Morris but also Walter Crane, Annie Besant, Anna Parnell and G. B. Shaw (ASA).

[2] 13 May 1891, p. 5, quoting *Liberté*.

[3] 26 April 1890, p. 3. In parliament, the writer explained, 'Mr. Cunninghame Graham looks just as we have seen him on a hundred platforms pleading the cause of the Docker, the Gas-worker, the Railway Man, the Shop Assistant, or any other worker that needs his help, with that native eloquence and evident sincerity that has won the hearts of the "unskilled labourers." Though he is himself a member of the capitalist—or rather the landowning—classes he has done more for the workers than most of the "Labour Members", one or two of whom have turned out downright Reactionaries under the capitalist influence of the House of Commons.'

[4] *Hansard*, vol. CCCXVI, col. 737 (22 June 1887).

[5] *Hansard*, vol CCCXXI, col. 437 (12 Sept. 1887); and vol. CCCXXXI, col. 733 (1 Dec. 1888).

political channels his aristocratic contempt for the bourgeoisie, his chivalrous sympathy with the underdog, and his aesthetic revulsion against the grime and squalor of industrial Victorian Britain. Morris's diary for 7 February 1887 records:

On the day that Parliament met, a young and new M.P., Cunninghame Graham by name, called on me by appointment to pump me on the subject of Socialism, and we had an agreeable talk. A brisk bright sort of man; the other day he made his maiden speech and produced quite an impression by its brilliancy and socialistic hints;[1]

though when he wrote to Bruce Glasier on 18 March, Morris had some second thoughts:

Cunninghame Graham is a very queer creature, and I can't easily make him out; he seems ambitious; and has some decent information. I am almost afraid that a man who writes such a preposterous illegible scrawl as he does must have a screw loose in him. We had a fine meeting last night to celebrate the Commune—crowded.[2]

Graham, however, might have answered, as Morris once did:

Political economy is not in my line, and much of it appears to me to be dreary rubbish..... It is enough political economy for me to know that the idle class is rich and the working class is poor, and that the rich are rich because they rob the poor;[3]

so that both men collaborated on Morris's spring campaign, when 'for the first time in the history of Britain a British M.P. presided at a Socialist meeting';[4] and Morris's admiration increased when later in the year Graham was arrested for his part in the Bloody Sunday demonstration—the 'Battle of Trafalgar Square' on which chapter XVII of *News from Nowhere* was to be based.

The strife of that Sunday (13 November 1887) was perhaps the most dramatic event in a period described by *The Times* as one of 'lawless agitation which under cover of zeal for the unemployed aimed at placing London under mob government'.[5] The immediate purpose of the demonstration was to assert the right of public assembly and free speech, in defiance of Sir Charles Warren's

[1] May Morris, *William Morris*..... (Russell and Russell, New York, 1966), II, 210–11.
[2] P. Henderson (ed.), *The Letters of William Morris to his Family and Friends* (Longmans, Green, London, 1950), p. 266.
[3] J. B. Glasier, *William Morris and the Early Days of the Socialist Movement* (Longmans, Green, London, 1921), p. 32.
[4] Report (probably by Glasier) quoted by May Morris, *William Morris*, II, p. 210.   [5] 13 Dec. 1887, p. 9.

order of 8 November which prohibited all meetings in Trafalgar Square. However, this order had been issued with the intention of preventing not only a repetition of those demonstrations by and on behalf of the vast army of unemployed workmen which had already resulted in mass arrests, but also a rally planned by the Metropolitan Radical Association to demand the release of William O'Brien and other imprisoned Irish patriots. On the afternoon of the 13th, thousands of demonstrators, some carrying banners of Morris's Socialist League and Hyndman's Social Democratic Federation, converged on the square, which had been cordoned by 1,600 constables. Scuffling and fighting followed—'I saw policemen.....repeatedly strike women and children', Graham wrote later;[1] Stuart Glennie saw 'perpetual charges of horse and foot police accompanying their bludgeoning of the people with oaths and curses'[2]—and at the height of the confusion Cunninghame Graham and John Burns were seen to charge the cordon. According to the police evidence, Graham

made a most determined rush at the police at the corner of the square and.....assaulted some of the constables in an attempt to get through the files. Mr Cunninghame Graham.....used his fists freely in his excitement. In the struggle the police used their *bâtons*, and Mr Graham received a blow on the forehead, inflicting a wound which bled freely. Mr Burns's arrest was effected without the interchange of blows.....
Later the two prisoners were taken to Bow-street and charged with 'riot and an assault on the police.'[3]

Meanwhile the turbulent crowds were dispersed by the Grenadier Guards, who had marched in from St George's Barracks with fixed bayonets and twenty rounds of ball cartridge in their pouches.

In a leading article on 14 November, *The Times* predictably made the following assertions and explanations:

It was no enthusiasm for free speech, no reasoned belief in the innocence of Mr O'Brien, no serious conviction of any kind, and no honest purpose that animated these howling roughs. It was simple love of disorder, hope of plunder, and the revolt of dull brutality against the rule of law.[4]

[1] *Commonweal*, IV, 354 (10 Nov. 1888).
[2] Quoted by May Morris in *The Collected Works of William Morris*, XX (Longmans, Green, London, 1913), xxxv.
[3] *The Times* (14 Nov. 1887), p. 6.
[4] P. 9. In the *Commonweal* William Morris published a contrasting interpretation: 'The police struck right and left like what they were, soldiers attacking an enemy.....London has been put under martial law, nominally for behoof of a party, but really on behoof of a class, and *war* (for it is no less, whatever the consequences may be) has been forced upon us. The mask is off now.....' (III, 369–70, 19 Nov. 1887.)

Graham had headed 'an insane rush', the writer continued; and the next day's leader added:

if.....he is convicted, the Government may think it worth while to consider.....whether his attitude towards law and order is compatible with his retention of the magistracy which he holds in three counties of Scotland.[1]

Eventually Graham and John Burns (who was later to hold office in the Liberal governments from 1905 to 1914) were acquitted of assaulting the police but found guilty of unlawful assembly: they were both sentenced to six weeks' imprisonment at Pentonville.[2]

After experiences which he later described in 'Sursum Corda',[3] Graham was released in February 1888; and in the same year he, in collaboration with Keir Hardie, helped to found the Scottish parliamentary Labour party. (This was twelve years before the founding of the Labour Representation Committee, the forerunner of the present Labour party.) Graham was elected president; Hardie became secretary. Their programme included nationalisation of transport, minerals and banking, graduated income tax, free education, and abolition of the House of Lords. As Hardie was not elected to parliament until 1892, it fell to Graham first to draw parliamentary attention to this programme.[4] Outside parliament, between 1888 and 1890 Graham found time to campaign vociferously on behalf of the Cradley Heath chainmakers,[5] to support Prince Kropotkin's campaigns among the London dockers,[6] to appear with Engels, Stepniak and Shaw at demonstrations for the eight-hour day,[7] to travel to Paris with Hardie and Morris to attend the Marxist Congress of the Second International,[8] and to write regular polemical articles for the *People's Press*, the trade-union journal of which he was one of the directors.[9]

At this period, for all the bitter and divisive theoretical disputes between the various British radical, Marxist, socialist and anarchist

[1] *The Times* (15 Nov. 1887), p. 9.   [2] *Ibid.* (19 Jan. 1888), p. 10.
[3] *SR*, LXXXIII, 681–3 (19 June 1897); later included in *Success* and other collections.
[4] See William Stewart, *J. Keir Hardie: A Biography* (Cassell, London, 1921), pp. 21–2, 44 (Graham's account of Hardie is given on pp. 51–3); Emrys Hughes, *Keir Hardie* (Allen and Unwin, London, 1956), pp. 35, 47–9; and Pelling, *Origins of the Labour Party*, pp. 69–71.
[5] *Pall Mall Gazette* (5 Dec. 1888), p. 3; *Hansard* vol. CCCXXXI, cols. 732–4 (1 Dec. 1888), and vol. CCCXXXIII, cols. 1054 ff. (5 March 1889).
[6] Woodcock and Avakumović, *The Anarchist Prince*, pp. 231–2.
[7] *People's Press* (10 May 1890), pp. 6–7.
[8] Stewart, *J. Keir Hardie*, p. 59; Pelling, *Origins of the Labour Party*, p. 86.
[9] For list of directors see *People's Press* (10 May 1890), p. 2.

groups, there was often an ample measure of co-operation between them in the practical field of labour unrest; New Unionism gave them a common incentive; and the distinction between the reformer and the revolutionary frequently became largely academic. Graham described himself, for example, both as a reformer, given that 'reform really means collective possession of the means of production',[1] and as a revolutionary—'if to be revolutionary was to wish to ameliorate the condition of the poor'.[2] In 1891 his expulsion from France, following a speech at Calais expressing sympathy with the strikers of Fourmies who had been fired on by the police, provoked a further rebuke from *The Times*—'Foreigners in France are expected to mind their own business, and not to head mobs or deliver inflammatory speeches'.[3] Notwithstanding *The Times*'s attempts to present him as a feckless hot-head, and notwithstanding the splenetic impatience of some of his polemics,[4] there were not many men who in the period 1886–92 did more than Graham did (by his support of Keir Hardie, by his share in the foundation of the Scottish Labour party, by his attempt to organise a conference in London to discuss labour representation,[5] by his propaganda up and down the country and in the *People's Press*, and above all by his persistent attacks in parliament on the inability of both Liberals and Conservatives to appreciate the miseries, needs and aspirations of the workers) to prepare the way for an independent parliamentary party which might represent the working class. The New Unionists lent him muscle, and he lent them an eloquent tongue.

And in those six years, while Graham in the House of Commons expounded Marx[6] and argued that 'we have as great white British slavery in Cheshire as they have in any portion of Africa or the East',[7] J. T. K. N. Korzeniowski, a fugitive Aeneas of a subjugated

---

[1] *People's Press* (31 May 1890), p. 5.
[2] *Hansard*, vol. cccxxiii, col. 128 (2 March 1888).
[3] *The Times* (12 May 1891), p. 5.
[4] For the trade-unionist readers of the *People's Press*, Graham's flourishes of anarchism, primitivism and revolution, his tribute to Stepniak's violence (10 May 1890, p. 6) and his wholesale denunciations ('Who's wrong? What's wrong? Is it employer or employed? Or both? My answer is, the system; the base, vile, commercial system that sees God in gold;'—16 Aug. 1890, p. 9) would have counted far less than his clear, persistent and practical advice to the New Unionists to stand on their own feet in congress and in parliament.
[5] Pelling, *Origins of the Labour Party*, p. 105.
[6] *Hansard*, vol. cccxxxiii, col. 1056 (5 March 1889).
[7] *Ibid.* col. 1064 (6 March 1889).

Poland, had sailed many seas, become a naturalised British subject, obtained his master's certificate, experienced the trials of the 'Otago' voyage and the horrors of the Congo, and had begun his literary life with the writing of 'The Black Mate' and *Almayer's Folly*; yet *Nostromo* was not to appear until he had come to know Graham's personality and past history.

In 1892 Graham's term in parliament ended; he contested the Camlachie division of Glasgow unsuccessfully as a Labour candidate. Thereafter his essays, tales and polemical articles appeared in an increasingly wide range of periodicals, including Keir Hardie's *Labour Leader* and H. M. Hyndman's *Justice* and the *Social-Democrat*; and when Frank Harris (who like Graham had been an outdoor speaker at S.D.F. meetings)[1] gained control of the *Saturday Review* in 1894, Graham joined the company of Shaw, Wells, Arthur Symons, and the other precocious contributors to that magazine: there he denounced the Jameson Raid and the Boer War, condemned the United States for its territorial ambitions in Central and South America, and defended the cause of Spain in the Spanish–American War.[2]

After 1900, as the Labour party gained parliamentary strength, Graham became increasingly critical of Labour M.P.s: he held that many of them were too transigent, too eager to compromise, too corruptible. 'I tell them.....that they would do more good if they came to the House in a body drunk and tumbling about on the floor.'[3] However, he continued to support Labour candidates during their election campaigns,[4] and he continued to appear at protest meetings with Hyndman and other socialist leaders. In 1909 he spoke in Trafalgar Square to denounce the Spanish authorities who had executed the anarchist Ferrer; and on 2 August 1914 he joined Hardie, Hyndman and Ben Tillett in a demonstration against Britain's impending entry into the war.[5] Within a few

---

[1] H. M. Hyndman, *The Record of an Adventurous Life* (Macmillan, London, 1911), p. 345.
[2] *SR*, LXXXI, 293–5 (21 March 1896), 340–2 (4 April 1896); LXXXIX, 138–9 (3 Feb. 1900), 203 (17 Feb. 1900), 267–8 (3 March 1900), 332–3 (17 March 1900), 491–2 (21 April 1900); XC, 822 (29 Dec. 1900); XCI, 80 (19 Jan. 1901); XCII, 398–9 (28 Sept. 1901), 430–1 (5 Oct. 1901), 740 (14 Dec. 1901), 808 (28 Dec. 1901); XCIII, 15 (4 Jan. 1902), 143 (1 Feb. 1902), 265 (1 March 1902), 300 (8 March 1902), 527 (26 April 1902).
[3] Wilfrid Scawen Blunt, *My Diaries*, pt. 2 (Secker, London, 1920), p. 197. Cf. *Glasgow Herald* (17 Oct. 1908), p. 13.
[4] *Ibid.* (3 Nov. 1906), p. 7; (27 Sept. 1912), p. 8.
[5] *The Times* (18 Oct. 1909), p. 8; and (3 Aug. 1914), p. 8.

months he tried to enlist in the army, in spite of being over-age,[1] and was eventually given the honorary rank of colonel and the task of buying horses in South America for the Western Front.[2]

In 1918 he stood as a Liberal at Stirling and Clackmannan, West Division, and came bottom of the poll to the Coalition Unionist and the Labour candidate. It was his last attempt to enter parliament; and a letter to Henry Arthur Jones in the following year expressed a general disillusionment with his early ideals:

As I gained this writing by the 28 years of the frontiers, so did I achieve 'Rhinitis' by the 6 years I was at the Gas Works (House of Commons). It was my sole reward.

I had hoped in Socialism to find a gradual demise of selfishness and the gradual establishment of a better feeling between man and man. You may remember that, then (28 years or more ago) the sweater was excessively aggressive, hours were long, and there was a brutal spirit of materialism about.....You will admit, I think, that my ambition was not a low ambition. That I was deceived, and that all the golden dreams of Morris have vanished in the nine bestial and inartistic years of the reign of King Edward, the War, and now in the increasing inartisticness of everything, the prostitution of the stage and literature, and now in the ever-increasing selfishness and lack of patriotism of the working classes, have not been my fault.

But he concluded:

Often with sea-boots on, or wet and miserable in a railway truck with the horses in the Argentine, or sweltering Colombia, or with the skipper on the bridge looking out for torpedoes, I have thought—where are the dreams of Morris? But on arriving at port, or at the camp, they have come back; they always do. Let us, I say, cherish them... *Vale*.[3]

It remains true that in the thirteen years before he wrote this letter, legislation for social security had alleviated many of the miseries that had once been Graham's concern. The Trade Boards Act to stop sweated labour, the enforcement of minimum wage rates, old age pension schemes, national health insurance—all these, one might have thought, could have given him grounds for optimism. Yet his socialism had been essentially romantic rather than practical; he was a man for protests rather than programmes; and he had worked with Kropotkin and Morris but never with Sidney and Beatrice Webb. For him the age of the council house and cheap medicine, the age in which the workers might become

[1] Graham to McIntyre (17 Aug. 1914), MS. 6519, NLS.
[2] *Glasgow Herald* (4 Nov. 1914), p. 6; *AFT*, p. 361.
[3] Doris Arthur Jones (ed.), *The Life and Letters of Henry Arthur Jones* (Gollancz, London, 1930), pp. 303–5; letter of 11 Dec. 1919.

morally bourgeois, would have offered a chilling contrast to the Elysian 'sweet June day' of *News from Nowhere*. And the letter to Henry Arthur Jones is the letter of an ageing man: Graham was then sixty-seven years old, and a widower; of his two brothers, Malise had died in 1885 and Charles in 1917. In the remaining years of his life he devoted his political energies increasingly to the cause of Scottish home rule. He became president of the National party of Scotland, and of its successor, the Scottish National party, whose supporters then included Hugh MacDiarmid, Compton Mackenzie and Eric Linklater; and he was still leader of the movement when he died on a visit to Argentina in 1936.

Scottish Nationalism enabled him to exercise his perennial talent for defending underdogs and apparently hopeless causes, while severing all his links with a Labour party which he now regarded as 'a party struggling for office and place like any of the other parties'.[1] His nationalism could not be dismissed as mere sentimentality: an economic case for Scottish autonomy could be (and was) based on the argument that Scottish taxes were subsidising the English rather than benefiting the Scots. Nor could it be considered a groping towards fascism: because Graham claimed that for him nationalism was 'the first step to the International goal which every thinking man and woman must place before their eyes';[2] his paradigms were 'Ireland, Finland, Poland, Estonia, Latvia';[3] and he cried '*Viva la Republica*' on hearing the news of King Alfonso's flight from Spain in 1931.[4] Yet it is difficult to

---

[1] Speech of 21 June 1930 quoted in *Scottish Newsletter* (issued by the Scottish National party) (May 1952), p. 3. Cf.: 'In the early days of the Labour and Socialist Movement all the Scottish pioneers.....were strong Scottish nationalists, and Scottish Home Rule was a constant plank in their platform, but the Labour Party went back on that during the inter-War period.' (Hugh MacDiarmid, *Twentieth Century*, CLXXIII, 77: Spring 1965.)

On 25 June 1934 Ramsay MacDonald wrote to Graham: 'You may depend upon it that I am as keen as ever for National Self-government for Scotland, although I cannot agree with the spirit of some of its advocates. Surely the present condition of the world is a proof that a narrow political nationalism contributes to nobody's good.....' (Letter quoted in *Scots Independent*, May 1936, p. 7.)

[2] R. E. Muirhead's MS. notes of a speech made by Graham at Stirling, 23 June 1931.

[3] Letter to Muirhead dated 27 June 1934, reproduced in *Scots Independent* (May 1936), p. 7.

[4] Letter to H. F. West, 23 April 1931 (MS., Dartmouth). Graham commented: 'In his place, I would have stuck it out, as first President of the Spanish Republic.'

avoid the conclusion that in the last years of his life (many years since he had once sat—by mistake—in Parnell's seat)[1] Graham's idealism was in its dotage, and that his awareness of injustice had finally parted company with his sense of proportion and priorities.

Perhaps, too, he then came closest to deserving the comparison with Don Quixote which in part was implicit in his nickname 'Don Roberto' and which was made explicit not only by Conrad but also by Epstein, Frederick Niven, Morley Roberts, Arthur Symons, Malcolm Muggeridge and other essayists and commentators.[2] There was obvious aptness in this: Graham's ancestry was partly Spanish, and when on horseback, lean, erect, with pointed beard, he resembled Quixote.[3] Graham was of course a Cervantophile and an admirer, as was Conrad, of Cervantes' hero. The comparison conveniently implied not only appreciation of Graham's idealism, independence and tenacity, but also criticism of the soundness of his judgement, the practicability of his schemes, and the relevance of his values. Conrad could admire in him the *frondeur*, the aristocrat who was 'not really a party man' and who protested against capitalism from partly chivalric and feudal premises. Before he met Graham, Conrad was engaged in the literary task of examining other chivalric survivals: was not Lingard 'a descendant of the immortal Hidalgo errant'?[4] Conrad himself had been called 'an incorrigible, hopeless Don Quixote'[5] for his first decision to go to sea; and in his later intervention in the cause of Polish independence, Conrad showed something of Graham's headlong enthusiasm.[6] Similarly, Graham's type of radicalism would not have seemed unfamiliar to Conrad, whose father was described in the following terms by Thaddeus Bobrowski:

Though he considered himself a sincere democrat and others even considered him 'extremist' and 'red' he had a hundredfold more traits of the gentry in him.....than I.....In point of fact, he had an exceedingly

[1] An incident in the House of Commons which had begun Graham's 'desultory friendship' with Parnell. See Graham's 'An Tighearna. A Memory of Parnell' in *Dana* (Dublin), VII, 193-9 (Nov. 1904); later included (as 'A Memory of Parnell') in *His People, Thirty Tales and Sketches*, and *Rodeo*.

[2] Epstein, *Let There Be Sculpture* (Joseph, London, 1940), p. 106. Niven, *Library Review*, III, 381 (Winter 1932). Roberts, *John O'London's Weekly*, XXX, 669 (3 Feb. 1934). Symons, *Notes on Joseph Conrad*, p. 33. Muggeridge, *Time and Tide*, XVII, 440 (28 March 1936).

[3] As in Lavery's portrait of Graham on 'Pampa'.

[4] *The Rescue* (Dent, 1924), p. 142.

[5] *A Personal Record* (Dent, 1923), p. 44.   [6] See *KRZ*, pp. 123-4, 127-33.

tender and soft heart—hence his great sympathy for the poor and oppressed; and this was why he and others thought he was a democrat. But these were only impulses of the heart and mind inherent in a member of a good family of the gentry; they were not truly democratic convictions.[1]

There were more reasons why Conrad 'hailed back lustily' on first hearing from Graham. Conrad, always acutely sensible of the exile's loneliness, was hungry for independent approbation to re-assure himself of the wisdom of becoming a professional writer; and in Graham he saw 'a friend at court'[2] who might (and did) try to obtain serialisation of his work in the *Saturday Review*. Politically, his contempt for the materialism and avarice that wear the masks of idealism and progress made his position ostensibly congruent with Graham's. Both men were horrified by the 'vilest scramble for loot' on the part of the imperial powers in Africa; both drew bitter parallels between the old and the new conquistadores; both had a cynical view of the United States' policies towards South and Central America; both were sceptical of the justice of British claims in the Boer War; and both were sympathetic with Spain in the Spanish–American War. Against the background of the jingoistic fervour of the 1890s it is easy to see why Conrad, whose native land had long been the prey of Russian and Prussian imperialism, frequently addresses Graham as though he were an ally in a lonely battle against widespread folly and imperception.

Yet Conrad could also observe: 'You are a dangerous man'. So far as they aided socialism, Graham's campaigns offered some threat to the continuity of moral and cultural traditions which for Conrad sustained Britain's reputation as a land of liberty—in contrast with the Prussian and Russian authoritarianism which Conrad had known in Poland. An England in which Graham's denunciations could be heard was what Conrad admired; an England in which all Graham's recommendations could be put into effect was what he dreaded. In his first reply, therefore, Conrad showed circumspection: 'I mean to hold my beliefs'; and in those first two letters it was not merely modesty which led Conrad to make a partial defence of Kipling.

In April and May 1897, Kipling's 'Slaves of the Lamp' had been serialised in *Cosmopolis*;[3] and it was immediately followed, in the issues for June and July, by the serialisation of Conrad's

---

[1] Baines, p. 8. [2] *EGL*, p. 119.
[3] VI, 1–19, 305–23.

'An Outpost of Progress'.[1] We know that Graham had read and enjoyed Conrad's tale in that magazine,[2] and probably it was the contrast between the two stories that first prompted him to write to Conrad. Graham naturally detested Kipling's political views, the semi-Darwinian mystique of Kipling's imperialism. S. P. Triana once wrote to Graham, with heavy irony:

I am really astonished at the little respect shown by the 'Catholic Tory' for Mr. Kipling who, whatever people may say is, as you & I inwardly believe, the quintessence of what a man should be. But we live in a sorry world where it is not enough to preach hooliganism & all sorts of violence & contempt for the weak, & to flatter the powerful to have one's merits acknowledged.[3]

And in another unpublished letter to Graham, Edward Garnett agreed:

Kipling is the enemy.....He is a creator; & he is the genius of all we detest.[4]

For Cunninghame Graham, 'the Imperial Mission' was a euphemism for 'the Stock Exchange Militant', and the White Man's Burden was the burden of a method of production which obliged the capitalist to seize, by force and cunning, raw materials, cheap labour, and markets for the unloading of his 'gin, bibles and shoddy goods'. 'Slaves of the Lamp' would have struck Graham as a particularly brazen endorsement of such baseness. In the first part of the tale, Stalky & Co. play a clever, savage and destructive trick on a carter and an unpopular teacher, setting the two unwittingly against each other so that the master's study is wrecked. In the second part we are shown how in adult life, while serving with the army in India, Stalky saves his men from ambush by using a similar ruse, as a result of which two tribes of Indians are tricked into attacking each other instead of the troops. The parallels go perhaps a little further than Kipling intended: the schoolboys have the

[1] VI, 609-20, and VII, 1-15.
[2] In *Mogreb* (1898), p. 53, Graham wrote as a footnote: '"Outpost of Progress", Cosmopolis, June, 1897. Story of an outpost of Progress told without heroics and without spread-eagleism, and true to life; therefore unpopular, if indeed, like most other artistic things it has not passed like a "sheep in the night".'
   In 1919 Conrad wrote: 'Sir Hugh Clifford.....is, if not the first, then one of the first two friends I made for myself by my work, the other being Mr. Cunninghame Graham, who, characteristically enough, had been captivated by my story, "The Outpost of Progress." These friendships which have endured to this day I count amongst my precious possessions.' (*A Personal Record*, p. vi.)
[3] Letter of 24 June 1904 (ASA).   [4] Letter of 26 January 1899 (ASA).

destructive ingenuity of conscienceless adults, while the same boys as soldiers are able to regard murder and wholesale slaughter as a schoolboy prank, a merry jape. The Empire exists; it is there to be guarded and extended by vigilance, ruthlessness and cunning. And thanks to men like Stalky—to the 'Cheltenham and Haileybury and Marlborough chaps'—England may look forward hopefully to the prospective 'big row' when the rival Great Powers come to blows. 'Just imagine Stalky let loose on the sunny side of Europe with a sufficiency of Sikhs and a reasonable prospect of loot.' (Kipling sanctions the gleeful tone.)

And it is precisely for the sake of a reasonable prospect of loot that Conrad's Kayerts and Carlier, other products of a perverse union of the virile and the puerile, find themselves in the Outpost of Progress, sustaining themselves with the whimsy that they are bringing light and civilisation to dark places; and it is for the sake of the loot that they gradually discard their principles and slogans. Natives are bartered for ivory, murder is condoned; and only after he has shot Carlier in the quarrel over a spoonful of sugar, and has hanged himself, does Kayerts make the gesture of 'putting out a swollen tongue at his Managing Director'. Conrad's multiple ironies of course transcended the merely political: he questioned not only the premises of imperialism but also the premises of 'civilised' moral conduct as a whole—how far are our ethical assumptions merely a tenuous social artefact? how far removed are the pith helmet and the savage's mask, the commodity and the fetish? The attack on Kayerts' and Carlier's credulous acceptance of the slogans about 'the sacredness of the civilising work' also implied a criticism of all rhetorical idealism, including even Graham's. Graham may not have seen this, but Conrad's letter of 5 August 1897 tactfully indicated as much. In any case, as his partial defence of Kipling's 'squint' may suggest, Conrad had respect for some of Kipling's attitudes as well as for his technical abilities. *The Nigger of the 'Narcissus'*, for example, was to resemble *Captains Courageous* not merely in the authority, sympathy and virtuosity with which the ship and her crew were presented, but also in the evident importance placed on the life of men at sea as an exemplar of initiation through trial-by-ordeal into a community whose moral sanctions arose chiefly from the discipline of co-operative labour in a challenging environment. (Nor is *The Nigger* free from an endorsement of the authority that asserts itself by means of peremptory physical violence.) It appears that Conrad later wrote a defence of Kipling for *The Outlook*,[1] and Kipling sent him a cordial letter of praise after reading *The Mirror of the Sea*.[2]

It is not difficult for us to understand why, in Graham's view, Kipling remained the 'prophet Kipling.....[who] has done much harm, leading away God's bestial people'.[3] The M.P. whose speech is mocked in 'At the End of the Passage' expresses opinions ('the [men of the] Civil Service in India.....force the unhappy peasant to pay with the sweat of his brow for all the luxuries in which they are lapped')[4] much like those that Graham had expressed in parliament at that time. Graham, who was to write sympathetically to and about the fallen Oscar Wilde,[5] reacted against the Kipling who commended a 'calamity of steel and bloodshed' as a healthy purge for decadence and as a solution to the unemployment problem ('One View of the Question').[6] And when the white soldiers in 'On the City Wall'[7] enthusiastically rout the Indian mob by methodically smashing bare toes with boots and rifle-butts, we can see why Graham regarded Kipling as the prophet of a brutal Yahweh. Kindred prophets spoke in the very issues of *Cosmopolis* which contained 'An Outpost of Progress'. In the June issue, for example, Sir Richard Temple's article 'The Reign of Queen Victoria' is a eulogy of the growth of British economic power, military strength, and territory; and 'The Globe and the Island',

---

[1] *EGL*, p. 122; *LL*, I, 227–8.

[2] Published in Jean-Aubry's *Twenty Letters to Joseph Conrad* (First Edition Club, London, 1926). Conrad commented: 'The Age of Miracles is setting in!' (*LL*, II, 3 n.)

[3] Letter to Garnett, 25 February 1899. A sense of rivalry to Kipling must have affected many of Graham's exotic narratives. Cf. Graham to Garnett, 24 January 1899: 'I fear that Mrs Ady (Julia Cartwright) in a review of "Mogreb" says that I "have much of Kipling in my literary *equipment*".....I know that "Julia C" thought she was doing me a great favour, (as she was, for even *with* a notebook I never could remember any of the parts of a steam engine), but...Do not think I am jealous, of his well earned bays (I think), but somehow the man revolts me, ask Conrad & tremble.'
   In 1900 Shaw said of Graham: 'His tales of adventure have the true Cervantes touch of the man who has been there—so refreshingly different from the scenes imagined by bloody-minded clerks who escape from their servitude into literature to tell us how men and cities are conceived in the counting house and the volunteer corps.' (*Three Plays for Puritans*, pp. 302–3.)

[4] *Life's Handicap* [1891] (Macmillan, London, 1907), p. 186.

[5] R. Hart-Davis (ed.), *The Letters of Oscar Wilde* (Hart-Davis, London, 1962), p. 706; and Graham's review of *De Profundis*, *SR*, XCIX, 266–7 (4 March 1905).

[6] *Many Inventions* (Macmillan, London, 1893).

[7] *Soldiers Three* (Macmillan, London, 1895).

22

by the regular political commentator, Henry Norman, praises British gunboat diplomacy in Africa. Kayerts and Carlier, before their demoralisation and mutual destruction, read a newspaper report on 'Our Colonial Expansion' which echoes the sentiments of Norman:

It spoke much of the rights and duties of civilisation, of the sacredness of the civilising work, and extolled the merits of those who went about bringing light, and faith, and commerce to the dark places of the earth.[1]

The July number of *Cosmopolis*, in which Kayerts shoots the un-armed Carlier and hangs himself from a cross, contains a commentary on the Jubilee celebrations in which Norman remarks:

Britain is Imperialistic now. The 'Little Englander' has wisely decided to efface himself. The political party which should talk of reducing the navy or snubbing the Colonies would have a short shrift. We are Imperialists first, and Liberals or Tories afterwards. I said this, for my own part, years ago, when the sentiment was not quite so popular. Now it has happily become a commonplace. The Jubilee is its culminating expression, and foreign observers should not fail to take note of this underlying significance.....[2]

'Foreign observers should not fail to take note.....': which reminds us that imperialistic fervour became most extreme not in the period of the Empire's greatest expansion, but rather towards the end of the century when this expansion was challenged and largely checked by the growing rivalry of Germany, Belgium and France in the search for markets and raw materials, when the birth-rate in Britain was beginning to decline, and when even her naval supremacy was questioned by Germany and the United States. And with one sentence of 'An Outpost of Progress' Conrad could strike at the centre of the whole debate:

The courage, the composure, the confidence; the emotions and principles; every great and every insignificant thought belongs not to the individual but to the crowd: to the crowd that believes blindly in the irresistible force of its institutions and of its morals, in the power of its police and of its opinions.[3]

The issue of *Blackwood's Magazine* for March 1899 contained an article called 'An Unwritten Chapter of History: the Struggle for Borgu', of which the practical efficiency of the following remarks is typical:

The little bush-fighting that was done against Lapai and elsewhere proved the superiority of the hard bullet over that used in the Sniders. The soft

[1] P. 616.   [2] P. 81.   [3] Pp. 611–12.

23

bullet is apt to break up when volleys are fired into bush where natives are hiding; but the Lee–Metford projectiles went through the cover so completely that the hidden party always ran before our men could get close.....[1]

and this article accompanies the episode of 'The Heart of Darkness' in which the 'pilgrims' empty their futile rifles into the bush, and in which Kurtz scrawls 'Exterminate all the brutes!'

Several years before Kurtz dies after having glimpsed 'the horror' of Africa, or of his own turpitude, or of sheer meaninglessness, Hummil (in Kipling's 'At the End of the Passage') had died in his Indian outpost after looking into an equally sanity-engulfing abyss. Conrad was by no means the first writer to describe the insidious destruction which a vast, exotic, alien wilderness offers to the psychology and moral fibre of the modern European: for Kipling the measure of the stoic heroism of the administrators' lives ('"Go back to work.....We can't do any more good here, and work'll keep out wits together"') is their ability to suspect a nightmarish absurdity in their labours amidst an impervious land where, outside the card-players' hut,

There was neither sky, sun, nor horizon,—nothing but a brown purple haze of heat. It was as though the earth were dying of apoplexy.[2]

In letter 1, when Conrad discusses Graham's view of Kipling he hedges a political issue by widening the area quickly to the discussion of a matter of technique and to a philosophical speculation; and those slightly evasive lines make a fitting precursor to the larger discussion which extends over many of the letters, in the course of which Conrad offers as tactful and amicable an opposition as possible to Graham's socialistic views. Conrad does not in these ensuing letters refer to the 'liberty, which can only be found under the English flag', nor does he deny the social evils which arouse Graham's indignation, but rather he invokes those aspects of the human condition which no amount of reforming activity might ameliorate. Conrad argues that reform is ultimately futile, because human nature is selfish and brutal (letters 5, 8, 17, 18 and 31); because there are no absolute moral criteria, so that one has at best a choice of illusions (an idea introduced in letter 1 and continued in letters 7, 9 and 31); and because humanity is in any case destined to perish of cold, amid a mechanistic and soulless universe (letters 4, 5, 7 and 18); so that even consciousness itself

[1] CLXV, 619.   [2] *Life's Handicap*, p. 183.

24

may be regarded as an evil, because its survey of our condition removes the illusion of freedom to improve our state (letters 4 and 9).

This summary of Conrad's arguments inevitably gives them the appearance of a logic which is more sequential and theoretical than the one they possess. Their particular frame of reference includes Conrad's temperamental pessimism, implanted by his Polish upbringing and nurtured by his immediate domestic worries; his degree of deference to the person addressed; and the literary element of his letter-writing, manifested for example in his ability to let an image catch his imagination and in his tendency to let the rhythm of a paragraph gather momentum so that an 'argument' flows into a characteristic pattern of Conradian rhetoric. Their general frame of reference is also a familiar one. In the late nineteenth century, the popularisation of the second law of thermodynamics, the influence of Lyell and Darwin, the prestige of physics, and the claims of positivism, had all made contributions to the current of scepticism concerning the bases of morality and ultimately concerning the value of consciousness itself. At times we may be reminded perhaps of Hardy's view of Nature as the inhuman 'automaton'; at others, of the anguish at man's moral isolation which sounds in many of the journals and letters of major figures of the period. Possibly the most direct literary contribution to Conrad's pessimism was made by Schopenhauer: Galsworthy tells us that Conrad knew Schopenhauer's work;[1] and certainly when Conrad came to write *Victory* he allowed to Heyst and his father a number of pessimistic aphorisms which bring to mind those in *Parerga* and *The World as Will and Idea*, while Conrad's explanation that Heyst had lost the practical abilities 'that come without reflection'[2] may recall Schopenhauer's claim that 'every man who wants to achieve something.....must *follow the rules without knowing them*'.[3] So we may construct our dissertations; Conrad had the sense to scrawl '*Assez*', because he was writing to a man who intuitively understood—'you of whom alone almost amongst my readers I always thought that *He* will understand'.[4] Conrad was thus attempting to curb the potentially subversive tendencies of Graham's romantic existentialism by re-

[1] *Castles in Spain* (Heinemann, London, 1927), p. 91.
[2] 'Author's Note', p. x (Dent, 1923).
[3] *Studies in Pessimism*, tr. T. Saunders (Swan Sonnenschein, London, 1891), p. 70.   [4] Letter 76.

minding him of the existential premises they held in common. In these letters, Conrad says by implication

I know you: you're a Hamlet choosing to be a Quixote; a man wearing masks in the hope that they will both mould and protect your features; an actor wearing a variety of guises in order to create and then to guard the thew within; and you indeed are a virtuoso of sustaining illusions, for you prove your virtuosity by flattering those who would drown.

When Stein in *Lord Jim* expresses his own nature by commenting on Jim in a deliberately ambiguous speech about 'the destructive element' which (by yielding contradictory glosses) makes the aptly hollow centre to the whole novel, one of the glosses has a sanction in Carlyle's assertion:

Work is of a religious nature:—work is of a *brave* nature; which it is the aim of all religion to be. All work of man is as the swimmer's: a waste ocean threatens to devour him; if he front it not bravely, it will keep its word. By incessant wise defiance of it, lusty rebuke and buffet of it, behold how it loyally supports him, bears him as its conqueror along.[1]

Given the ethical and psychological problems of a period in which even Bertrand Russell at the age of fifteen could write 'I do wish I believed in the life eternal, for it makes me quite miserable to think that man is merely a kind of machine endowed, unhappily for himself, with consciousness',[2] there was perhaps 'wise defiance' even in Graham's streak of apparent folly—as though he believed, with the narrator of *Notes from Underground*, that by means of spectacular, wilful and paradoxical conduct he could prove to himself 'that men still are men, and not the keys of a piano, which the laws of nature threaten to control so completely'. Jocelyn Baines says of Graham that he 'championed causes because he was roused to do so, not because he expected them to triumph (if he had he probably would not have bothered)';[3] and perhaps to the words 'he was roused to do so' we should add 'or was impelled to do so'. If in Morocco and South America he found disappointment after exhilaration, in Scotland he found, reaching from the bleak landscape and tenements into his book-lined study, a blight of spirit. In March 1899 he wrote to Edward Garnett from Glasgow:

My view of life is almost the same as yours. It is a joke, a black joke of course, but we must laugh at our own efforts.

[1] 'Labour' in *Past and Present* (Chapman and Hall, London, 1872), p. 171.
[2] Notes made on 9 April 1888, quoted in *My Philosophical Development* (Allen and Unwin, London, 1959), p. 30.   [3] Baines, p. 198.

Escape, too clever. Not I, it is far cleverer than any one, & the wheel will go right over my chest (completely over), as over yours & all. But it is a joke all the same. Allah Ackbar.

And in the following letter:

Significance in things, Ha, Ha, why even atoms themselves are all in a jumble.

Fornication, my masters, murder, adultery, cheating, lies, & the offertory, those are the leading motives of life, & ever will be.....A dingy farce played by fools & harlots, on a poor stage, with an incompetent stage manager, & the only laugh in it, being at one's own antics & folly for continuing to act.[1]

In a lecture which was published in the *Fortnightly Review*[2] three years before Graham first wrote to Conrad, Turgenev claimed that in Hamlet and Don Quixote 'two opposite types of human nature are incarnate—the ends as it were of the axle on which it turns';[3] and sometimes in the following correspondence it looks as though Conrad is playing Hamlet—Turgenev's Hamlet—before 'his friend the Don Quixote'.[4] But each of the correspondents bore in himself 'the ends.....of the axle';[5] and both men proved in their lives' work that however readily and at times self-indulgently they might in private hymn futility, Turgenev's dichotomy was, after all, a false disjunction.

With the exception of his strictures on the lack of focus of the ironies in 'Bloody Niggers' (letter 18), Conrad affords consistently high praise to Graham's work: praise which today may often seem excessive, in view of the relative obscurity into which Graham's books have fallen. 'The element of friendship comes in',[6] and it is true that for Conrad generosity was the better part of judgement: as Edward Garnett and Richard Curle remind us,[7] Conrad was naturally inclined to bestow over-generous praise on any work by his acquaintances. Graham himself wrote to Garnett in 1899:

I do not suppose he [Conrad] is much of a critic, but one never knows, in respect to a man of his genius, what he may or may not be.[8]

[1] Letters of 1 and 3 March. (MS., University of Texas.)
[2] N.S. LVI, 191–205 (July–Dec. 1894). [3] *Ibid.* p. 191.
[4] J. H. Retinger says that Conrad called Graham 'his friend the Don Quixote' (*Conrad and his Contemporaries*, Roy, New York, 1943, p. 96).
[5] Conrad told Waliszewski: 'Homo duplex has in my case more than one meaning.' (Najder, *Conrad's Polish Background*, p. 240.)
[6] Letter 33.
[7] EGL, p. xxv; Curle, *The Last Twelve Years of Joseph Conrad* (Sampson Low, Marston, London, 1928), p. 16. [8] 24 April 1899.

Nevertheless Conrad's enthusiasm for much of Graham's work seems entirely unforced (consider the explosion of glee in letter 27); and if his enthusiasm was facilitated by friendship, it was not compelled by charity. In his lifetime Graham enjoyed great prestige as a writer, and throughout his career his works were generally if not customarily reviewed in tones ranging from the respectful to the jubilant. He never wrote a best-seller, and he cultivated the hauteur of indifference to popular favour: many of his critics connived by presenting him as an esoteric—doubtless to Graham's gratification as he pasted into his scrap-books the items sent him by his press-clipping agency. And while few of his later critics were as sanguine as Ford Madox Ford, who claimed in 1931 that Graham was 'all in all, the most brilliant writer of that or of our present day',[1] his work impressed writers as diverse as Shaw, Frank Harris, Edward Garnett, Lawrence of Arabia, John Galsworthy and Arthur Symons[2]—Symons felt that Graham offered in his tales 'a more exciting interest than perhaps any writer of the day, with the one exception of Conrad, of whom his writings sometimes reminds [sic] me'. He enjoyed a steady reputation as a writer's writer with a distinctive ironic style, as a creator of vivid 'impressions and atmospheres', and as a provocative, discomfiting moralist. In view of his output and his literary husbandry (for it would not be unusual for one of his tales to appear twice in magazines and two or three times in collections) he could conceivably have lived by his pen alone, had he needed to do so. In his lifetime, Graham saw the publication of seventeen collections of the tales, from *Father Archangel* (1896) to *Mirages* (1936), in addition to four booklets containing single items; apart from well over 200 periodical contributions.[3] Besides these, his works include the early political pamphlets (*Economic Evolution*, 1891, and *The*

---

[1] *Return to Yesterday*, p. 39.
[2] Shaw, *Three Plays for Puritans*, p. 301. Harris, *Contemporary Portraits (3rd Series)* (Harris, New York, 1920), pp. 54–5; *Frank Harris on Bernard Shaw* (Gollancz, London, 1931), p. 129; and *My Life and Loves* (Allen, London, 1964), p. 704. Garnett, Introduction to *Thirty Tales and Sketches* (Duckworth, London, 1929); and essay in *London Mercury*, XXXIV, 125–9 (June 1936). Lawrence, *The Letters of T. E. Lawrence*, ed. D. Garnett (Cape, London, 1938), p. 750. Galsworthy, *Forsytes, Pendyces and Others* (Heinemann, London, 1935), pp. 273–4. Symons, *Notes on Joseph Conrad*, p. 32.
[3] See *The Bibliotheck* (Glasgow), IV, 186–99 (1965), which reproduces part of the bibliography of my thesis on Conrad and Graham. Previous bibliographies include: Leslie Chaundy's *A Bibliography of the First Editions of the Works of Robert Bontine Cunninghame Graham* (Dulau, London, 1924); H. F. West's

Imperial Kailyard, 1896), a guide book (*Notes on the District of Menteith*, 1895), two travel books (*Mogreb-el-Acksa*, 1898, and *Cartagena and the Banks of the Sinú*, 1920), seven histories of the Spanish Conquest (from *A Vanished Arcadia*, 1901, to *The Horses of the Conquest*, 1930), biographies of Antonio Conselheiro, Robert Graham, José Antonio Páez and Francisco Solano López, a translation from Gustavo Barroso (*Mapirunga*, 1924), and numerous prefaces—I have seen forty-five—to works by other writers. Most of his books ran to more than one edition; at least nine appeared in Spanish editions; not counting the reissue of *Thirteen Stories* by Penguin Books in 1942, there have been five posthumous collections of items, most notably Paul Bloomfield's *The Essential R. B. Cunninghame Graham*, 1952; and he has been represented in over twenty anthologies.

Perhaps he over-produced: Frank Harris called him 'an amateur of genius',[1] and an impetuous amateurism colours his political and his literary careers. Many of his tales display the faults of apparent haste: the occasionally slipshod grammar, haphazard constructions, and uncorrected proof-errors; and we will be reminded that D. H. Lawrence, when reviewing *Pedro de Valdivia* in 1927,[2] detected 'the absent-mindedness of mere egoism'—'The Conquistadores . . . . . never felt themselves *too good* for their job, as some of the inky conquerors did even then, and do still'. Graham himself remarked, late in life:

> But still I might have finished all those sentences; not broken off to moralize right in the middle of the tale; split less infinitives, and remembered those rules of grammar that I have disregarded, as freely as a democratic leader tramps on the rights of the poor taxables who put him into power.[3]

As in that last simile, Graham persistently thrusts his personality at the reader in so many asides, footnotes and digressions; and consequently, although the judgements may sometimes have satiric originality, and although such testy opinionativeness is often more engaging than magniloquent rhetorical moralizing, his better tales

The Herbert Faulkner West Collection of R. B. Cunninghame Graham (privately printed, 1938); and Hugh MacDiarmid's *Cunninghame Graham: A Centenary Study* (Caledonian Press, Glasgow, 1952).
[1] *Contemporary Portraits (3rd Series)*, p. 55; *Bernard Shaw*, p. 129.
[2] Review in *Calendar of Modern Letters* (April 1927), republished in *Phoenix* (Heinemann, London, 1936), pp. 355–60. Quotations from pp. 355 and 357.
[3] *Rodeo* (Heinemann, London, 1936), p. xvi.

are frequently those which, like 'Animula Vagula' in *Redeemed*, employ the oblique narrative form, so that the comments are assimilated to the personality of the fictional teller of the tale-within-the-tale. The very word 'sketches', which is the apt generic term for most of his tales, indicates his main limitations. He could sketch a character, a scene or an incident with deftness and at times with power and originality; but he was never a novelist, and scarcely a fiction-writer in the most significant sense, and his work peregrinates between reportage and invention. In November 1898 he wrote to Garnett:

You are hard on the poor "Impressionists"......Does a man's character ever really progress, except in books? If not, then the Impressionist is right who gives only an impression of what he sees once. To this extent, I allow one thing, i e, that different lights alter the *impression* of a hill.....[1]

Men, however, are more vulnerable than hills; and basically, perhaps, he feared time's ravages too much: he records with clarity a moment, an hour, an afternoon, or a journey of several days, but the predominant time-scale is the product of two moments only— the moment of experience then, and the moment of sighing recall now. The radicalism of his temperament and his occasional stylistic felicities never conceal his pervasive and almost narcissistic con- servatism: for he is attempting persistently to conserve against time's corrosion of memory the experiences of his own past, the sights, smells, conversations and chance encounters. It is as though he feared historic time too much to parody it by means of the fictional time-scale which would permit the development of a 'plot' or would show the inter-actions of fictional character on fictional character. And with this limitation in temporal and imaginative scope goes necessarily a limitation in imagery: he offers similes rather than metaphors, and pointers rather than symbols. He is an idiosyncratic writer, but the idiosyncrasies become predictable;[2] and after 1899 in any case he showed little development as an essayist and short-story writer. The elegiac obituary study, the nostalgic traveller's anecdote, the remembered glimpse of life in a Spanish settlement, the brief character-sketch of a soldier, a Spaniard, a Scot or a whore—these subjects recur, and so does the mood of pawky wistfulness and almost glib melancholy:

[1] 26 November 1898.
[2] In his prefaces (notably that to *Progress*, 1905), notwithstanding the praises of Tschiffely and indeed of Conrad, his tetchy scorn often results in sheer silliness.

I checked my horse, and began moralizing on all kinds of things; upon tenacity of purpose, the futility of life, and the inexorable fate which mocks mankind, making all effort useless, whilst still urging us to strive.[1]

Because of these limitations in technical resource and because of the dangers of this persona of the stoical, sceptical traveller, the reader's feeling when he concludes one of those tales which do not lapse into clichés of phrasing and attitude is sometimes akin to the relief felt after negotiation of a flimsy footbridge. This lack of ease was perhaps felt by Leonard Woolf when he wrote:

Mr. Graham.....is a competent writer, and he has a certain charm of personality which he often gets into his writing, but his sentences, and still more his paragraphs, never develop that fusion of thought, word, and rhythm which transmutes good writing into great prose.[2]

On the other hand, considering the thin but wiry texture, the artful artlessness, and the eye for telling detail that Graham employs on those occasions when he is writing at his best, and considering that 'when he makes his worst hash we can still taste the slice of life that went into the pot' (according to Paul Bloomfield,[3] who enjoyed Graham's 'ingredient of healthy roughage'), it is perhaps to be doubted whether this criterion of 'great prose', in Leonard Woolf's sense, is a helpful one. The 'realism' of the early works of both Conrad and Graham provoked some hostile criticism which seems largely to have stemmed from the view that certain subjects were, when treated without a conventionally 'romantic' approach or without explicit and obvious moralistic import, unworthy of literary presentation.[4] Conrad added an 'Author's Note' to *The Nigger of the 'Narcissus'* which seems mainly intended to answer such critics by asserting that an impressionistic or 'realistic' treatment of apparently mundane

[1] 'A Hegira' in *Thirteen Stories* (Heinemann, London, 1900), p. 74.
[2] *Nation and Athenaeum*, XXXV, 51 (12 April 1924).
[3] *The Essential R. B. Cunninghame Graham* (Cape, London, 1952), p. 17.
[4] For example, in reviews of *The Nigger of the 'Narcissus'* the *Illustrated London News* claimed that Conrad belonged to 'the school of fiction-brutality' and that his undoubted talents ('in his realism he almost equals Zola') were devoted to the depiction of 'worthless personages' (CXII, 50 and 172, 8 Jan. and 5 Feb. 1898). In an otherwise favourable review of Graham's *The Ipané*, the *Spectator*'s critic said: 'Some of his descriptions are perhaps a little too realistic; one.....is almost revolting, and might well have been spared..... Readers who object to a spade being called a spade had better look elsewhere for their entertainment.' (LXXXII, 887, 24 June 1899.) By 1917, however, Graham was being referred to as 'the Goya of letters': see *Bookman*, XLVI, 502 (Dec. 1917).

material can be of moral value both in concept and effect. In his unpublished M.A. thesis,[1] Edgar Wright has illustrated the parallels in idea and phrasing between Conrad's defence of *The Nigger* and Maupassant's essay, 'Le Roman'. Conrad claimed to be 'saturé de Maupassant',[2] and his avowals of admiration lend support to the view of Wright and Jocelyn Baines[3] that in the French writer Conrad found not merely the model for the technique of 'The Idiots', but also a more general support for a conception of the artist's responsibility which seemed to reconcile and surpass the 'temporary formulas' and the criteria used by both sides in the current debate about 'Art for Art itself'. Graham himself immensely admired Maupassant—he regarded Maupassant's short tales as superior to Conrad's;[4] like Conrad, he eventually wrote an appreciative introduction to a selection of Maupassant's tales; and in a letter to the *Daily Chronicle* (24 April 1898, p. 3), Graham had concluded a commentary on *Mrs. Warren's Profession* by comparing it with 'Yvette', saying:

> Mrs. Warren, being an Englishwoman, was probably sentimental, for sentimentality seems inborn in our race, and cuts us off in a measure both from passion and sentiment. The 'Marquise', on the other hand, was a Latin, and most likely asked no more from life than life could give.....
> Mr. Shaw writes powerfully, but with an evident eye to his reader, and loses no opportunity of both preaching and moralising; whereas Maupassant wrote as an artist, and let his readers draw their own conclusions.

Like Maupassant, Graham in his tales made persistent portrayals of the cruel insouciance of bourgeois and peasant, and used character-studies of prostitutes as the focus of comment on social hypocrisies; at his best he attempted to treat such material with the air of deliberately unsentimental and ironic detachment of which Maupassant had been the master; and from this source he seems

---

[1] 'Joseph Conrad: his expressed views about technique.....' (London University, 1955), chap. 3.

[2] *LFR*, p. 52.

[3] Baines, pp. 146–8.

[4] Graham alleged: 'Many great writers of short stories, as Edgar Poe, Turgenev, and even Conrad, though perfect in their art, have but a constricted choice of themes on which, in one form or another, they ring the changes; but Maupassant ranges at will.....' (Preface to *Tales from Maupassant*, Nash, London, 1926, p. 5). When reading Maupassant, Conrad had felt 'le plus profond désespoir' of envious admiration (*MPL*, p. 132), while Graham felt like exclaiming '"What is the good of writing after such a man. He has said it already in a way that I can never compass"', just as you may, after a passage of..... Conrad or Hudson.' (Preface, p. 4.)

also to have learnt a certain adroitness in the technique of building a slowly-accumulating description of a scene, after which a brief exchange of dialogue or a closely observed rendering of a figure in the foreground casts a retrospective and transforming light on the preceding events. In this emulation, some writers thought that Graham had been at least partly successful. Galsworthy claimed that 'A Hegira' and 'A Hatchment' approached 'the perfection' of Maupassant (adding that Graham 'is a realist with a steel-keen eye, and a power of colouring an exact picture hardly excelled..... He is a gallant foe.....of smugness, and fatty transcription');[1] a reviewer in the *Speaker*[2] made a similar judgement of the tales in *Progress*; the critic in the *Nation*,[3] when praising the volume *Charity*, pointed out the resemblance between 'Christie Christison' and 'Le Port'; and a reviewer of *Mogreb-el-Acksa* remarked that

the keenness of observation, the particular aspect inevitably seized upon, the biting—almost vitriolic—clearness of presentment, irresistibly remind one of Diaz and Maupassant.[4]

Such remarks, surprisingly favourable though they may seem today, suggest that the example of Graham's prose may have helped slightly to strengthen in Conrad's work the virtues of precise, original and ironic observation, and to lessen the tendency towards histrionic romanticism, lush and magniloquent rhetoric, and the associated imprecision. Certainly Graham shares with Conrad a keen interest in the moral and visual absurdities caused by the juxtaposition of the trappings of civilisation with the primitive, and of European customs with native ones: he has an eye for the incongruous image which may betray the logic of colonialism, for the grand piano which stands warping in the African sunshine,[5] for the tramp who when Queen Victoria's funeral procession has passed searches for food among 'the scum of sandwich papers, which, like the foam of some great ocean, clung to the railings',[6] for the missionary on a tramp steamer who stands with 'his elastic-sided boots fast glued to the dirty deck by the half-dried-up

---

[1] *Forsytes, Pendyces and Others*, pp. 273–6.
[2] XI, 492 (18 Feb. 1905).
[3] X, 1065–6 (30 March 1912).
[4] *Daily Chronicle* (14 Jan. 1899), p. 3.
[5] In 'At the River', *SR*, CVI, 140–2 (1 Aug. 1908); later included in *Faith*.
[6] In 'Might, Majesty and Dominion', *SR*, XCI, 168–9 (9 Feb. 1901); later in *Success*.

blood of the discarded fish',[1] and for that Berber chieftain, the Caid of Kintafi, who in his remote citadel in the Atlas Mountains treasures uncomprehendingly a Pandora's Box of common cardboard:

Just about forty years of age, thick-set, and dark complexioned, close black beard trimmed to a double point, rather small eyes, like those of all his race, he gave no indication of the cruelty for which he was renowned; not noble in appearance as are many of the Sheikhs of Arab blood, but still looking as one accustomed to command; hands strong and muscular, voice rather harsh but low, and trained in the best school of Arab manners, so as to be hardly audible. Just for a moment, and no more, I got a glimpse of the inside man as I caught his eye fixed on me, savage yet fish-like, but in an instant a sort of film seemed to pass over it, not that he dropped his gaze, but seemed deliberately to veil it, as if he had reserved it for a more fitting opportunity. By race and language he was a Berber, but speaking Arabic tolerably fluently, and adapting all his habits and dress to those in fashion among Arab Sheikhs. His clothes white and of the finest wool, and clean as is a sheet of paper before a writer marks it black with lies. The 'talebs' never stopped opening and writing letters, now and then handing one to the Caid who glanced it over and said 'Guaha' (good), and gave it back to have the seal affixed with one of the three large silver seals which stood upon a little table about six inches high. The sealing-wax was European, and kept in a box of common cardboard, which had been mended in several places with little silver bands to keep the sides together, as we should mend a lacquered box from Persia or Japan..... The room contained.....a Belgian single-barrelled nickel-plated breech-loading gun hung on a nail, and the before-named double-barrelled English gun (from the Haymarket of the mysterious Londres or Windres, in the isle of Mists), and a large pair of double field glasses; some bags of hide, two porous water bottles, a bundle of reed pens, and two or three pieces of bread, the staff of life, which fills so large a place in Moorish thoughts and life, and which an Arab of the old school breaks, but never touches with a knife. Two negro boys with dirty handkerchiefs, and boughs of walnut, stood on the right and left-hand of the Caid, and flapped away the flies. (*Mogreb-el-Acksa*, 1898, pp. 232–4.)

Probably the first response of the present-day reader to this passage will be one of impatience with the casual under-punctuation, the cataloguing tendency, and the occasional jarring aural effects ('life.....life.....knife'), and he may hunger for the energy, insight and exuberance of D. H. Lawrence's descriptive work. His second response may be to judge the passage in its literary context, the tradition of Victorian travel-writing, and to

[1] 'In a German Tramp', *SR*, LXXXIX, 41–4 (13 Jan. 1900); later in *Thirteen Stories*.

notice that if Kinglake's *Eothen* is more assured, confident, almost complacent in approach, Graham's lines, while certainly more hasty, offer some wry compensations for the absence of belletristic facility; and the personality behind the words is more reflectively critical than Burton's in *A Pilgrimage to Meccah and Medinah*.[1] There is nothing lush or theatrical here; and for all the accidentality of the constructions, the passage is raised slightly above the level of mere 'authentic reportage' by the way in which Graham just fufils the ironic expectations aroused by the simile 'clean as is a sheet of paper before a writer marks it black with lies'. The Caid has both absurdity and dignity, and the cardboard box (which Burton would not have noticed) offers mute criticism of the Berber and of the European. The patronising element of the parenthesis about 'the mysterious Londres or Windres' is curbed by the reference to 'the staff of life.....which an Arab of the old school breaks, but never touches with a knife', which, though marred by the tone of a tourist brochure, bears an ironic comment on the lethal presence of the English and Belgian precision weapons; and finally Graham narrows the perspective again from the historic to the immediate with the tableau of tawdry majesty in the last sentence—a sentence which might have brought faint echoes of Conrad to the ear of an Arthur Symons.

Jocelyn Baines suggests that Graham's work and presence may have encouraged Conrad to increase the autobiographical element in his tales and to introduce Marlow as a narrator in order to lend authenticity to the events.[2] While this may have been the case, Graham was scarcely an innovator in oblique narrative techniques, and Conrad's judgements in the correspondence (which in any case are rarely analytic) display far less interest in the structural devices and autobiographical elements of Graham's writings than in the ironic temperament and acuteness of perception shown there—'the ever-ready responsiveness', 'the "sens profond de la vie" characterised by irony that is gentle and by a fierce sympathy', and the ability to hew 'dans le vif'.[3] One further extract from *Mogreb-el-Acksa*, pp. 132–3, a passage which today may well seem antiquated and sentimental in its stoic melancholy, may remind us of what, for Conrad, was probably the true ground

---

[1] 'Burton's *Mecca* is nowhere near it', said Conrad of *Mogreb*—albeit in a letter to Mrs Bontine (*LL*, I, 258).
[2] Baines, p. 203.   [3] Letters 66, 58 and 16.

of his friendship and literary sympathy with Graham, as it was to be the ground of his friendship with the author of 'A Free Man's Worship':[1] the critical and humane compassion which draws its energy from despair.

So in a pass between two walls of earth, with bands of shale crossing them transversely, and roots of long dead Arars sticking through the ground, I came upon the human comedy fairly played out by representative marionettes of every age and sex. First, father, a fine old Arab, gaunt, miserable, grey-headed, ragged, hollow-cheeked, without a turban, shoes, or waist-belt, and carrying a child which looked over his shoulder, with enormous black and starving eyes; the mother on foot, in rags and shoeless, and still holding between her teeth a ragged haik to veil her misery from the passer by, a baby at her back, and in her hand a branch torn from an olive-tree to switch off flies; then three ophthalmic children, with flies buzzing about their eyelids; lastly, the eldest son stolidly sitting in despair beside a fallen donkey carrying salt, and rubbed by girth, by crupper, and by pack ropes, and an epitome of the last stage of famine and of overwork. And as we came upon them, from a saint's tomb near by, a quavering call to prayers rang out, and the whole family fell to giving praise to Him who sendeth hunger, famine, witholds the rain, and shows His power upon the sons of men, infidel or believer, Turk, Christian, Moor, and Jew, with such impartiality that at times one thinks indeed that He is God.

When Conrad had written 'Fraternity means nothing unless the Cain–Abel business', he folded the letter and posted it to Cunninghame Graham; and in due course, from the man who 'could not pass a mirror without looking at himself',[2] he received a reply which, it appears, was fraternal enough.

[1] Conrad's remarkable friendship with Russell is described in *The Autobiography of Bertrand Russell*, I (Allen and Unwin, London, 1967), pp. 207–10. In a letter dated 22 Dec. 1913 Conrad wrote: 'For the marvellous pages on the Worship of a free man the only return one can make is that of a deep admiring affection, which, if you were never to see me again and forgot my existence tomorrow, will be unalterably yours *usque ad finem*.' (*Ibid.* p. 225.)

[2] *AFT*, p. 419.

A note on the background to 'Nostromo'

In his major works prior to *Nostromo*, Conrad had been dealing with locations familiar to him: life on board ship or in regions like the Congo and the East Indies, of which he had had considerable first-hand experience. Yet for *Nostromo* he chose a region which was relatively unknown to him. He told Graham:

I just had a glimpse 25 years ago—a short glance. That is not enough pour bâtir un roman dessus. (Letter 47.)

This statement is partly confirmed by his letter to Curle (*LL*, II, 321–2) in which he says that his longest stay there was of '$2\frac{1}{2}$ to 3 days'.

His friendship with Graham may have been one of the main reasons for his interest in a relatively unfamiliar area: for in the five years preceding the writing of the book, Conrad had several times met and talked with Graham, whose many years as a traveller and rancher in Central and South America must inevitably have been one of the topics of conversation. Graham's extensive knowledge of South American affairs accounts for the note of deference in Conrad's letters when he refers to *Nostromo*: 'I hardly dare avow my audacity' (letter 45); 'When it's done I'll never dare look you in the face again' (letter 47); and 'I stipulate a profound and unbroken secrecy of your opinion as before everybody else. I feel a great humbug.' (Letter 52.) Consequently it was to Graham that Conrad sent perhaps his most detailed informal commentary on the completed work, together with his thanks for his friend's 'forgiveness' (letter 53).

Among Graham's papers at Ardoch is an unpublished letter from Edward Garnett, dated 23 June 1898, which contains the following passage:

Conrad told me you had once assisted at a battle in Paraguay. I look down the 'SR' columns to find that battle, but I see only Harris fighting with (& for!) Financial Companies. Will your Joss (or that familiar demon that makes you write) not conjure up for you & for us that battle? or won't you expand that sentence of yours about the 'six women to each man in Paraguay' into a moral sketch on Paraguayan manners, & refute Burton's saying that the only countries that had settled the social question were those that upheld polyandry.

Thus, less than five years before he began to write *Nostromo*, Conrad had apparently heard a first-hand account of a South American revolution, and the basis for 'a moral sketch on Paraguayan manners', from a friend whose arguments were already forcing Conrad into a fresh assessment of his political position. Certainly Graham claimed to have seen action, in his youth, with 'one or other of the revolutionary armies, in Entre Rios and in Uruguay' (*Portrait of a Dictator*, 1933, p. 132), and to have spent 'nearly a year in Paraguay but eighteen months after the conclusion of the war' (*ibid.* p. xi).

One of several tales in which Graham describes his experiences in post-revolutionary Uruguay and Paraguay is 'Cruz Alta', which Conrad judged to be 'tout simplement *magnifique*' (letter 41). In this tale, Graham tells how he had renewed his friendship with an Italian immigrant, Enrico Clerici, who kept a store overlooking the little port of Ytapua in Paraguay.

Enrico Clerici [was] an Italian, who had served with Garibaldi, and who, three years ago, I had met in the same place and given him a silver ring .....He kept a pulperia, and being a born fighter, his delight was, when a row occurred (which he styled 'una barulla de Jesu Cristo'), to clear the place by flinging empty bottles from the bar. A handsome, gentleman-like man.....withal well educated and no doubt by this time long dead..... (*Thirteen Stories*, 1900, pp. 60–1.)

It will be remembered that in May 1903 Conrad had intended *Nostromo* to be 'concerned mostly with Italians' (letter 45); and Edgar Wright has reasonably suggested that in Graham's reminiscences of Enrico Clerici may be found the genesis of Conrad's Giorgio Viola, the Garibaldino.[1]

[1] 'Joseph Conrad: his expressed views about technique.....', pp. 287–8. It is quite likely, as Jocelyn Baines and Richard Curle suggest (Baines, p. 295; Curle's *Joseph Conrad and his Characters*, Heinemann, London, 1957, p. 20), that Graham may have recommended to Conrad some of the South American source-books that he is known to have used during the writing of *Nostromo*. Indeed, the first important discovery in the field was made on this assumption. Edgar Wright read Graham's *Portrait of a Dictator* and found in it incidents and names (e.g. Barrios, Corbalan, Decoud, Gould and Fidanza) which have counterparts in *Nostromo*. Graham gave as his source for these names G. F. Masterman's *Seven Eventful Years in Paraguay* (1869). Wright then found sufficient parallels between Masterman's history and Conrad's novel to make it apparent that Conrad had referred to it. (See chapter 6 of Edgar's Wright's thesis.) A minor source-book which was known at some point to Graham as well as to Conrad was Ramon Páez's *Wild Scenes in South America* (1863), to which Graham makes complimentary reference in *José Antonio Páez* (1929), and which was among Conrad's books when they were auctioned in 1925, as well as being on the shelves of the London Library—

Graham's interest in South American affairs was accompanied by an equally perennial interest in and criticism of imperialistic adventures. Therefore when, at the time of the Spanish–American War, the United States began to emerge as a rival to the older imperialist powers, Graham was concerned to express in his *Saturday Review* articles the opinion that the United States' policies towards Spanish-American territories were as hypocritical as Britain's policies in Africa: in each case the basic motive, he suggested, was a simple desire for material profit and aggrandisement. The letters show that Conrad was a reader, at this period, of the *Saturday Review*, which contained not only Graham's warnings of the dangers and complexities of European and North American intervention in South American affairs, but also (at this time of Frank Harris's editorship) sceptical editorial comments on the United States' expansionist ambitions. (Conrad also read and approved the ironic comments on the Spanish–American War offered by the commentator in *Blackwood's Magazine*: see letter 21, n. 24.)

Of the relevant passages in his letters, the parts that were omitted from the Jean-Aubry texts show that Conrad shared much of Graham's antipathy to the policies of the United States, and they may also suggest some reasons why Conrad turned to the subject and setting of *Nostromo*. Thus in letter 15, when Conrad writes of the war, the unpublished lines (from 'The ruffianism' to 'spectacle.', and from 'The others' to 'sunshine.', with their reference to the 'silver dollar') may offer a reminder that Conrad was later to claim that

Nostromo has never been intended for the hero of the Tale of the Seaboard. Silver is the pivot of the moral and material events, affecting the lives of everybody in the tale. (*LL*, II, 296.)[1]

whose members included Conrad and Graham. (See *Review of English Studies*, N.S. XVI, 182–4, May 1965.)

On the basis of letter 6, lines 65–8, E. K. Hay speculates: 'Graham's suggestion that Brooke be thought of as a character in the Western Hemisphere may have planted a germ for the character of Charles Gould in *Nostromo*.' (*EKH*, p. 93.) In 1894 Graham had vainly prospected for gold in ancient Spanish mine-workings: see *AFT*, pp. 277–8.

[1] A few years before Nostromo made his melodramatically final visit to the silver, Graham had concluded an attack on western imperialism with these words: 'When was an empire ever builded secure and safely upon treachery and blood? Even our prototype, great Captain Kidd, though he amassed great treasure on the modern plan, was forced to hide it, and died (by cursed chance), upon the last safe trip he made to dig it up.' (*Justice*, 1 May 1898, p. 5.)

On 30 July 1898, in letter 21, Conrad added:

If one could set the States and Germany by the ears! That would be *real fine*. I am afraid however that the thieves shall agree in the Philippines. The pity of it!
Viva l'España! Anyhow.
Do you believe in a speedy peace. Write me all you know.....

And in December 1903, over eight months before the first draft of *Nostromo* was completed, Conrad's mention of a letter from Graham's friend, Pérez Triana, the Colombian ambassador, reminded him of the latest example of the United States' intervention in international affairs:

And à propos what do you think of the Yankee Conquistadores in Panama? Pretty, isn't it? (Letter 49.)

The best commentary on this remark is that provided by *The Cambridge Modern History*, XII (1910), chapter 21, section 2— a section written by Pérez Triana, Conrad's correspondent. In 1846 the United States had made a treaty guaranteeing the sovereignty of New Granada (later called Colombia) over the isthmus of Panama. In 1878, the Government of Colombia signed the contract for the construction of the Panama Canal. The potential wealth of the Canal attracted the United States: and in 1901 England consented to the abrogation of the Clayton–Bulwer treaty,

thus doing away with the one great obstacle to acquisition by the United States of political dominion over the isthmus of Panamá, though the sovereignty of Colombia over that territory still remained, and was guaranteed by the American Government.

On 3 November 1903, a revolution, which appeared to have been organised by the United States, took place in the Colombian province of Panama,

and the independence of the province as towards the republic of Colombia was proclaimed. American men-of-war had arrived on the Atlantic and on the Pacific ports of Panamá just a few days before. The Government of Colombia was informed by the American Government that no landing of Colombian troops would be allowed. The independence of Panamá was recognised by the Government of the United States within three days of the rebellion.....The high-handed policy of the United States with reference to Colombia sent a thrill of painful surprise throughout Spanish America.....[1]

Conrad's awareness of this incident may have been partly responsible for the fact that his novel, which appears originally to

[1] *The Cambridge Modern History*, XII, 699.

have been conceived as a treatment of the relations of Nostromo with the Viola family, developed into a wider study with detailed comments on the implications of American and European commercial and political intervention in Spanish-American affairs. In the novel, counter-revolution results in the secession of Sulaco, the Occidental Province, from Costaguana: a secession which is in the interests of American capital in that it secures, for the time being and with Holroyd's approval, the wealth of the mine, Holroyd's investment; and as in the case of Panama, the victory of the secessionists is assured by the arrival of the U.S. navy:

An international naval demonstration. . . . . put an end to the Costaguana–Sulaco War. . . . . The United States cruiser, *Powhattan*, was the first to salute the Occidental flag. (P. 487.)

Conrad wrote: 'Costaguana is meant for a S. Am^{can} state in general' (letter 53); and, as in 'Heart of Darkness' he had deliberately extended the frame of reference by giving a cosmopolitan background to Kurtz and the Company (*LFR*, p. 64), so in *Nostromo* he had naturally sought to give the work a relevance beyond that of topical commentary on specific current historical events. Nevertheless, just as 'Heart of Darkness' seems to have had its genesis in Conrad's observation of particular events in the Belgian Congo in 1890, so *Nostromo* seems to have had its genesis in his awareness of particular current events in Central and Southern America. The numerous references in the book to Santa Marta may suggest that Conrad had Colombia chiefly in mind. Conrad was probably also aware of the Venezuelan revolution which in 1902 had resulted in an 'international naval demonstration' by Germany and Britain, and which was given prominent discussion in the *Saturday Review* (XCIV, 662, 726, 728, 757, 793); but I have indicated the possible relevance of Colombian affairs because it is only to the Panamanian secession that Conrad makes direct reference in the letters.

Conrad's remark about 'the Yankee Conquistadores in Panama' is also a reminder of the fact that shortly before and during the writing of *Nostromo*, Conrad had read, re-read and praised Graham's histories of the Spanish conquest of America, *A Vanished Arcadia* (1901) and *Hernando de Soto* (1903): and letters 42, 44 and 49 indicate that his imagination was attracted by the frequent ironic parallels drawn in those books between the Conquistadores and the present-day imperialists and commercial adventurers, and by Graham's emphasis on the vanity and ultimate futility of the

41

achievements of the former, the hypocrisy and self-deceptions of the latter, and on the damaging transformations effected by both among the people and lands that they conquered. At the conclusion of *A Vanished Arcadia*, Graham laments that in spite of the humane work of the Jesuits in Paraguay,

The self-created goddess Progress was justified by works, and all the land left barren, waiting the time when factories shall pollute its sky, and render miserable the European emigrants, who, flying from their slavery at home, shall have found it waiting for them in their new paradise beyond the seas. (P. 286.)

And Graham's emphasis on the melancholy futility, the ephemerality of achievement, of the Spaniards, and on the ways in which the quest for treasure had vitiated and corrupted their most pious motives, seems to have found a reflection in Conrad's emphasis at the conclusion of *Nostromo* on the fact that though the 'material interests' may be 'a colossal and lasting success', the hopes of establishing a permanent and valid moral order have proved largely illusory.

THE LETTERS

I

5th Aug 1897.
Stanford-le-Hope.
Essex.

R. B. Cunninghame Graham Esqr

Dear Sir.

You've given me a few moments of real, solid excitement. I scuttled about for the signature—then laid the letter down. I am a prudent man. Very soon it occurred to me that you would hardly go out of your way (in the month of August) to kick an utter stranger. So, I said to myself "These—no doubt—are half-pence. Let us see" and—behold! it was real gold, a ducat for a beggar—a treasure for the very poor! You'll ruin yourself; but (I am a white man) what does it matter to me as long as the profit is mine.

And I feel distinctly richer since this morning. I admire so much Your vision and your expression that your commendation has for me a very high value—the very highest! Believe that I appreciate fully the kind impulse that prompted you to write.

Mr Kipling has the wisdom of the passing generations—and holds it in perfect sincerity. Some of his work is of impeccable form and because of that little thing he shall sojourn in Hell only a very short while. He squints with the rest of his excellent sort. It is a beautiful squint; it is an useful squint. And—after all— perhaps he sees round the corner? And suppose Truth is just round the corner like the elusive and useless loafer it is? I can't tell. No one can tell. It is impossible to know. It is impossible to know anything tho' it is possible to believe a thing or two.

Pray do not regret your letter; I mean to hold my beliefs— not that I think it matters in the least. If I had your eye-sight, your knowledge and your pen it would matter. But I haven't. Nevertheless I shall persist in my beastly attitude. Straight vision is bad form—as you know. The proper thing is to look round the corner, because, if truth is not there—there is at any rate a something that distributes shekels—And what better can you want than the noble metals?

You did not expect such a "tuile sur la tête" as this in answer

45

to your letter. Well! it's only five pages at the most and life is long—and art is so short that no one sees the miserable thing. Most of my life has been spent between sky and water and now I live so alone that often I fancy myself clinging stupidly to a derelict
40 planet abandoned by its precious crew. Your voice is not a voice in the wilderness—it seems to come through the clean emptiness of space. If—under the circumstances—I hail back lustily I know You won't count it to me for a crime.

45 I am very sincerly delighted to learn that you can stand my prose. It is so hard to realise that I have any readers!—except the critics, who have been very kind and moral, and austere but excessively indulgent. To know that *You* could read me is good news indeed—for one writes only half the book; the other half is
50 with the reader.
Believe me, dear Sir, very faithfully   Yours
Jph. Conrad

PUBLICATION
First published in *LL*, I, 207–8.

TEXT
See appendix I.
24 'elusive': written upon 'illusive'.

COMMENTARY
15 'your commendation': Graham had probably contrasted 'An Outpost of Progress' favourably with Kipling's 'Slaves of the Lamp'. See Introduction, pp. 19–24.
14–16 It is unlikely that Conrad was at this time acquainted with the two books by Graham which had appeared previous to the date of this letter: *Notes on the District of Menteith* (1895) and *Father Archangel of Scotland* (1896). (See letter 11, line 16; letter 12, lines 6–7; and letter 17.) However, Graham's tales, essays and letters had appeared in *Nineteenth Century*, *Pall Mall Gazette*, *People's Press*, the *Speaker* and other journals. Conrad subscribed to the *Saturday Review* and had probably encountered Graham's work there (cf. letter 3, lines 49 and 80–4; letter 5, lines 7–8; and letter 15, lines 13–15).
36–7 'life is long.....': an ironic inversion of the familiar maxim used in December near the end of the 'Author's Note' to *The Nigger of the 'Narcissus'* (*New Review*, XVII, 631).
40–3 Cf. Henry James to Graham, 8 December 1908 (ASA):
'My productions affect me as mostly dropping into a bottomless

46

abyss whence no echo comes back to me—& I am the more gratified accordingly when I do catch an attesting sound. Then I like making an impression on a man who is constantly seeing, as I imagine, far & strange & thrilling things—beyond any the likes of my so little adventurous muse can figure; & who still, though he might be so blasé, remains accessible to my mild magic.'

2

9th Augst 1897.
Ivy Walls Farm.
Stanford-le-Hope
Essex.

Dear Sir. 5

I was delighted to see your handwriting which—by the bye— I had not the slightest difficulty in reading—this time.

Of course I would be most happy to come whenever you say the word; and I'll be happier still if your recklessness carries you as far as Stanford. I presume bohemianism has no terrors for you. It 10 isn't pretty at my age but it's one of those facts one must face— with concealed disgust. My wife (she's a good girl "et pas du tout gênante") shall cook something and—please God—we may find for you some place to sleep—not absolutely on the floor.

I am both touched and frightened by what you say about being 15 the prophet of my inarticulate and wandering shadow. I can not help thinking with alarm of the day when you shall find me out or rather find out that there is nothing there. How soon will you begin to regret Your magnificent imprudence?—and will you ever forgive me the triumph of Your friends when they assail you with 20 reproaches and a great clamour of "I told you so!"

You understood perfectly what I tried to say about Mr Kipling —but I did not succeed in saying *exactly* what I wanted to say. I wanted to say in effect that in the chaos of printed matter Kipling's "ebauches" appear by contrast finished and impeccable. I judge 25 the man *in* his time—and space. It is a small space—and as to his time I leave it to your tender mercy. I wouldn't in his defence spoil the small amount of steel that goes to the making of a needle. As to posterity it won't smile. Not it! Posterity shall be busy thieving, lying, selling its little soul for sixpence (from the noblest 30 motives) and shall remember no one except perhaps one or two

47

quite too atrocious mountebanks; and the half-dozen men lost in that "bagarre" are more likely to weep than to smile over those masterpieces of our time.

35 I am very unhappy just now not being able to squeeze three consecutive sentences out of myself. The world however seems to be rolling on without a check—which is of course very offensive to me. I want to ask you a favour. There is a thing of mine coming out in the *New Review*. Being, as you inform me, my "Prophète en
40 titre" I am afraid you must consider it your sacred duty to read everything over my signature. Now in this special case *please don't*. In Nov^{er} I shall send you the book—if you allow me—and then you shall see the whole. I am conceited about that thing and very much in love with it, and I want it to appear before you at its best. The
45 instalment plan ruins it. I wouldn't make that fuss if I didn't care for your opinion.

Believe me very faithfully Yours

Jph. Conrad

I shall be here from now till the end of time—I fancy. So whenever
50 you are in town and have absolutely nothing better to do drop me a line. I am always ready to drop my work.

PUBLICATION

LL, I, 208–9.
45–6 'care for': Aubry reads 'value'.

TEXT

36 'out': an insertion.
42 'me': an insertion.

COMMENTARY

6–7 Graham's handwriting was notoriously illegible.
38 'a thing of mine': *The Nigger of the 'Narcissus'*, published in the *New Review*, XVII, 125–50, 241–64, 361–81, 485–510, and 605–28 (Aug.–Dec. 1897).
42 'In Nov^{er}': Heinemann issued *The Nigger*, bearing the date '1898' on the flyleaf, on 2 December 1897 (*TJW*, p. 14).

3

My dear Sir

I am horribly ashamed of myself. I ought to have written last week to thank you for the Stevenson. My inadequate excuse is I've been strangely seedy—nothing very tangible, but for nearly a week I have thought not at all and eaten very little—and didn't see the use of doing anything. This may seem to you an impertinent excuse but I assure you it is a very sad and fiendish—well, indisposition, and too real for words. I throw myself on your mercy. I shook myself at the sight of your letter and now what between shame and pleasure I am able to sit there like a galvanised corpse to write this flat and miserable apology.

The 'xmas at sea' is *all* what you said. I was glad of the book and Still more of your thought. I was glad to know I haven't been seen —and forgotten. Only—par-ce-que c'est Vous! There are people from whom I would beg on my knees the favour of an eternal oblivion. Would I get it? Croyez-Vous qu'on se retrouve—la bàs? To me 'la bàs' appears sometimes as a big hole—a kind of male-factors' cavern—very crowded (think how long mankind has been in the habit of dying!) with perspiring Shades—a moral perspira-tion of squeezed spirits—exhaling the unspeakable meanness, the baseness, the lies the rapacity, the cowardice of souls that on earth have been objects of barter and valued themselves at about two-and-six. But this is morbid—and I sat down intending to produce a good impression! I take it all back and declare my belief in lilies, gold harps—and brimstone, like my Podmore in the "Narcissus".

And à-propos of Podmore—I am afraid the 'Nigger' will bore you. C'est vécu—et c'est bête. There are twenty years of life, six months of scribbling in that book—and not a shadow of a story. As the critic in to-day's Dly Mail puts it tersely: "the tale is no tale at all". The man complains of lack of heroism! and is, I fancy, shocked at the bad language. I confess reluctantly there is a swear here and there. I grovel in the waste-paper basket, I beat my breast. May I hope you at least! won't withdraw your esteem from a repentant sinner?

No man can escape his fate! You shall come here and suffer hard-
40 ships, boredom and despair. It is written! It is written! You—as a
matter of fact—have written it yourself (at my instigation—very
rash of you) and I shall be inexorable like destiny and shall look
upon your sufferings with the idiotic serenity of a benevolent
Creator (I don't know that the ben: Crea: is serene;—but if he is
45 (as they say) then he *must* be idiotic.) looking at the precious mess
he has made of his only job. This letter reminds me of something
I used to know years ago: Algebra—I think. Brackets within
brackets and imbecility raised to the nth power.

I heard of the H & S play through G.B.S in the S R. More
50 Algebra. Do you understand? I allude in this luminous way to
Admiral Guinea. I haven't seen a play for years; but I have read
this one. And that's all I can say about it. I have no notion of a play.
No play grips me on the stage or off. Each of them seems to me an
amazing freak of folly. They are all unbelievable and as dis-
55 illusioning as a bang on the head. I greatly desire to write a play
myself. It is my dark and secret ambition. And yet I can't conceive
how a sane man can sit down deliberately to write a play and not
go mad before he has done. The actors appear to me like a lot of
wrongheaded lunatics pretending to be sane. Their malice is stitched
60 with white threads. They are disguised and ugly. To look at them
breeds in my melancholy soul thoughts of murder and suicide—
such is my anger and my loathing of their transparent pretences.
There is a taint of subtle corruption in their blank voices, in their
blinking eyes, in the grimacing faces, in the false light in the false
65 passion, in the words that have been learned by heart. But I love
a marionette show. Marionettes are beautiful—especially those of
the old kind with wires, thick as my little finger, coming out of
the top of the head. Their impassibility in love in crime, in mirth,
in sorrow,—is heroic, superhuman, fascinating. Their rigid vio-
70 lence when they fall upon one another to embrace or to fight is
simply a joy to behold. I never listen to the text mouthed somewhere out of sight by invisible men who are here to day and rotten
to morrow. I love the marionettes that are without life, that come
so near to being immortal!
75 Here's the end of paper. It is to morrow already and high time
for me to go to bed—to dream, perchance to sleep. You must forgive the writer, the letter, the mistakes of spelling, the obscurity of
the grammar—the imbecility of the nth power. Forgive! Forgiveness

has been invented to prevent massacres. Yours ever Jph Conrad. P.S. I haven't had yet *St Thérèse*. Expect it next week. I have 80
looked lately again at the Best scenery article—and am confirmed in my opinion that your Wife has said what is really fundamental, essentially true in the matter—and said it charmingly. Sorry to hear of Hudson's illness. A lovable man—a most lovable man.

PUBLICATION

LL, I, 212–14.
24 'baseness': Aubry reads 'bareness'.

TEXT

13 'am able to': inserted.
16 'Still': inserted.
24 'the lies the rapacity': *sic*.
37 'at least!': inserted.
46 'has': inserted.

COMMENTARY

1 The date. The reference in line 33 suggests that this letter was written on the 7th of December and not the 6th.
6 'the Stevenson': R. L. Stevenson's *Ballads* (Chatto and Windus, London, 1895) contains the poem 'Christmas at Sea', to which Conrad refers in line 15. In his own copy of this edition Graham drew his 'Bar 103' cattlebrand (⚬) as a mark of approbation beside the first stanza of 'Christmas at Sea'; and John Lavery refers to his fondness for this poem (see *The Life of a Painter*, Cassell, London, 1940, p. 122).
13 'galvanised corpse': This idea recurs in different guises throughout the grim whimsicalities of the letter: in the picture of the 'perspiring Shades', in the condemnation of actors, and in the description of the marionettes. ('We are conscious automata', T. H. Huxley had once remarked.) Madame de S—, of *Under Western Eyes*, is 'like a galvanized corpse out of some Hoffman's [*sic*] Tale' (Dent, London, 1923, p. 215).
20–6 Dostoevsky's 'Bobok' (1873) provides a literary precedent for this smelly and overcrowded Hell of mean spirits.
33–5 The anonymous reviewer in the *Daily Mail*, no. 500, p. 3 (7 Dec. 1897) had described the book as 'a disappointment', and had added:
'The tale is no tale, but merely an account of the uneventful voyage of the Narcissus from Bombay to the Thames . . . . . There is no plot, no villainy, no heroism, and, apart from a storm and the death and burial, no incident. The only female in the book is the ship herself, which Mr. Conrad describes lovingly and with an intimate knowledge of seamanship unrivalled even by Dana or Clark Russell.
   The one surpassingly good quality of this masculine narrative is the distinctness of Mr. Conrad's characterisation of old Single-ton . . . . . and the rest of them. Their talk and their swearing, especially the latter, is absolutely natural. One only regrets that they

4-2

never do anything else than their mere commonplace duties, and that they are not connected with a story.'

Conrad was already aware of W. Clark Russell's marine melodramas: cf. his comments on *The Rescue*:

'You see I must justify—give a motive—to my yacht people.....I must do that—or have a Clark Russell puppet show which would be worse than starvation.' (Conrad to Garnett, 5 Aug. 1896, *EGL*, pp. 42–3.)

39–42 Conrad had already met and dined with Graham, on 26 November. See *EGL*, pp. 105–6:

'Graham writes to ask me to dine with him to-night. I shall do so for I am interested in the man...The chiel writes to the papers—you know.'

42–6 For all the playfulness of this paragraph, the tinge of Schopenhauerian pessimism seems to anticipate that of Heyst and his father (cf. *Victory*, Dent, 1923, pp. 219–20).

49–51 *Admiral Guinea*, by W. E. Henley and R. L. Stevenson, had opened at the Avenue Theatre on 29 November 1897. The play was reviewed by Shaw under the title 'A Breath from the Spanish Main' in *SR*, LXXXIV, 619–21 (4 Dec. 1897).

55–6 Conrad's first play, *One Day More* (based on 'To-morrow'), was performed in 1905; and by the time of his dramatisation of *The Secret Agent* in 1922, his antipathy to actors had diminished: see *LL*, II, 282.

65–74 Cf. the meditation on the theme 'Serai-je un Polichinelle?' in *MPL*, pp. 128–9.

80 '*St Thérèse*': Gabriela Cunninghame Graham's *Santa Teresa: Being Some Account of Her Life and Times* (2 vols. Black, London, 1894).

81 'the Best scenery article': Gabriela Cunninghame Graham's essay 'The Best Scenery I Know' had been published in *SR*, LXXXIV, 256–7 (4 Sept. 1897). The article, which was not republished elsewhere, was one of a series to which Arthur Symons and Max Beerbohm were also contributors.

84 'Hudson's illness': W. H. Hudson had previously written to Graham: 'I.....am at present in bad health, and trying to medicine my ills with nature's greenness' (*WHH*, p. 40).

4

14 Dec. 1897
Stanford-le-Hope.
Essex.

My dear Sir.

5   Your good letter cheered me immensely but with my usual brutal ingratitude I've let the days pass without saying so. It was a friendly thought to send me the *Glasgow Herald*'s cutting. It

came in the nick of time and send me to bed at peace with my fellow men.

I've been thinking over the letter you have written me about the *Nigger*. I am glad you like the book. Sincerely glad. It is clear gain to me. I don't know what the respectable (hats off) part of the population will think of it. Probably nothing. They never think. It isn't respectable. But I can quite see that, without thinking, they may feel an instinctive disgust. So be it. In my mind I picture the book as a stone falling in the water. It's gone and not a trace shall remain. But the words of commendation you and a few other men have said shall be treasured by me as a proof that the book has not been written in vain—as the clearest of my reward.

So You may rest assured that the time you have given to reading the tale and to writing to me has not been thrown away—since, I presume, You do not believe that doing good to a human being is throwing away effort and one's own life. And You have done me good. Whatever may be the worth of my gratitude You have it all; and such is the power of men to show feelings that "helas! Vous ne vous en apercevrez même pas!"

But as I said I've been meditating over your letter. You say: "Singleton with an education". Well—yes. Everything is possible, and most things come to pass (when you don't want them). However I think Singleton with an education is impossible. But first of all—what education? If it is the knowledge how to live my man essentially possessed it. He was in perfect accord with his life. If by education you mean scientific knowledge then the question arises—what knowledge, how much of it—in what direction? Is it to stop at plane trigonometry or at conic sections? Or is he to study Platonism or Pyrrhonism or the philosophy of the gentle Emerson? Or do you mean the kind of knowledge which would enable him to scheme, and lie, and intrigue his way to the forefront of a crowd no better than himself? Would you seriously, of malice prepense cultivate in that unconscious man the power to think. Then he would become conscious—and much smaller—and very unhappy. Now he is simple and great like an elemental force. Nothing can touch him but the curse of decay—the eternal decree that will extinguish the sun, the stars one by one, and in another instant shall spread a frozen darkness over the whole universe. Nothing else can touch him—he does not think.

Would you seriously wish to tell such a man: "Know thyself".

Understand that thou art nothing, less than a shadow, more insignificant than a drop of water in the ocean, more fleeting than
50 the illusion of a dream. Would you?

But I hear the postman. Au revoir till next week. I won't now delay my thanks for your good and friendly letters. Yours Ever Jph Conrad.

PUBLICATION

LL, I, 214–15.
48 'thou art': Aubry reads 'you are'.
52 'delay my thanks': 'delay. Many thanks'.

TEXT

8 'send': *sic.*
19 'clearest': may possibly be 'dearest'.
21 'has': Conrad's alteration of 'have'.
33 'scientific': an insertion.
48 'thou': written upon 'you'.
52 'letters': may be 'letter'.

COMMENTARY

7 'the *Glasgow Herald*'s cutting': Like the *Daily Mail*'s critic (quoted in note 33–5 to letter 3), the *Glasgow Herald*'s anonymous reviewer compared Conrad with Clark Russell; but otherwise this review makes a strong contrast with the previous one, as the following extract shows:

'Accustomed as we are to the admirable word pictures of Mr Clark Russell, new marine story-tellers subject themselves to no mean comparisons, but Mr Conrad's book bears the test triumphantly. Nor does he seek any adventitious aid by the introduction in mid-ocean of beautiful but athletic young ladies.....Mr Conrad is all for plain, unvarnished realism, but realism which only the hand of a master could make attractive.'

After praising the treatment of the crew and comparing the book with 'The Ancient Mariner', the reviewer adds:

'On the voyage a storm is encountered. It takes very many pages to describe, but the reader follows the description breathlessly, and feels as if a storm had never been described before. We have nothing but the highest praise for this distinguished contribution to modern literature.....' (*Glasgow Herald*, 9 Dec. 1897, p. 10.)

27–50 The most important comment to be made on this passage is neither 'Thinking is the great enemy of perfection' ('Author's Note' to *Victory*) nor '"young Faust, regretting already the simple life"' ('The Life Beyond' in *Notes on Life and Letters*) but rather the maxim 'Never trust the teller, trust the tale'.

Conrad gives here a polemical account of one version of that 'antirational primitivism' (the view that a limitation of the individual's consciousness or reflective and ratiocinative abilities may best equip him for life) which operates in so many protean forms in literature of the last hundred years—though Singleton's ancestry is as old as Adam, older than Chuang Tzu, and older than Enkidu in the Gilgamesh epic.

If the instincts may be blindly destructive in Ricardo of *Victory*, and if the sophisticated intellect may produce a paralysing scepticism in Heyst as in Decoud, a *via media* is possible for Conradian seamen in whom instinct and intellect may sometimes be curbed and blended constructively by the school of tradition, necessity and authority (a special authority: they are on a ship, not in a factory, and in a merchant vessel, not a warship). When Singleton steers with care, he acts instinctively only in so far as his instincts have been chastened by training, and intellectually only within a narrow range of simple decisions which have become almost instinctive; and in a sense, judgements of his selfishness or altruism become irrelevant, because by doing what, for him, is natural, he preserves his shipmates and himself. A tempting integrity, to a man with Conrad's inner conflicts.

In Graham's work, the primitivism which is present in the earliest pamphlet, *Economic Evolution*, and which is at its tritest in tales like 'El Tango Argentino', is so much more a matter of simple contrasts that there would have been few surprises for the columnist (in *Vanity Fair*, 25 Aug. 1888, p. 145) who remarked of Graham 'He labours under a settled conviction that civilisation is a failure' (adding 'Despite his eccentricity, he is a high-minded and honourable gentleman and a first-rate fencer'). This may make it seem strange that Graham asked Conrad for a 'Singleton with an education' (rather as he was later to ask for 'Rajah Laut in London'). Some of Graham's late critical remarks on Conrad's works (in 'Inveni Portam', for example, or in the Preface to *Tales of Hearsay*) may lead us to suspect that he had missed the point here—the point emphasised at the end of *The Nigger of the 'Narcissus'* when the clerk approves of Donkin but scorns the 'disgusting' Singleton, and we realise that because of our imaginative voyage with the crew, because of the insights we have been given into the nature of co-operative labour and into the distinctions between constructive solidarity and sentimental pesudo-solidarity, it will be less easy for us in future to confuse 'intelligence', 'smartness' or 'sociability' with moral integrity. However, in asking for an 'educated' Singleton, Graham may well have been using critical shorthand for related questions like these: 'In so far as *The Nigger* is a conservative political allegory, doesn't it depend too much on the easy pessimistic distinction between an older "inarticulate and indispensable" generation of which Singleton is the representative, and the new "whining" generation of which Donkin is the extreme—Donkin who with glib cunning utters a cheap parody of socialism? If you, Conrad, have the intelligence to show with cruel irony the sun finally shining on the walls of the Mint, haven't you the intelligence not to give us the paean of praise to the "ship mother of fleets and nations"?'

47-50   Conrad had already told Singleton that, in chapter 4. ('Old! It
seemed to him he was broken at last.....He looked upon the immortal
sea with the awakened and groping perception of its heartless might.....')
Cf. Carlyle's attack on the maxim 'Know thyself' (*Past and Present*,
chapter 11).

5

20th Dec. 1897.
Stanford-le-Hope

My dear Sir.

Your letter reached me just as I was preparing to write to you.
5 What I said in my incoherent missive of last week was *not* for the
purpose of arguing really. I did not seek controversy with you—for
this reason: I think that we do agree. If I've read you aright (and
I have been reading You for some years now) You are a most hopeless idealist—your aspirations are irrealisable. You want from men
10 faith, honour, fidelity to truth in themselves and others. You want
them to have all this, to show it every day, to make out of these
words their rule of life. The respectable classes which suspect you
of such pernicious longings lock you up and would just as soon
have you shot—because your personality counts and you can not
15 deny that you are a dangerous man. What makes you dangerous is
your unwarrantable belief that your desire may be realized. This
is the only point of difference between us. I do not believe. And if
I desire the very same things no one cares. Consequently I am not
likely to be locked up or shot. Therein is another difference—this
20 time to your manifest advantage.

There is a—let us say—a machine. It evolved itself (I am
severely scientific) out of a chaos of scraps of iron and behold!—
it knits. I am horrified at the horrible work and stand appalled.
I feel it ought to embroider—but it goes on knitting. You come
25 and say: "this is all right; it's only a question of the right kind of
oil. Let us use this—for instance—celestial oil and the machine
shall embroider a most beautiful design in purple and gold." Will
it? Alas no. You cannot by any special lubrication make embroidery
with a knitting machine. And the most withering thought is that
30 the infamous thing has made itself; made itself without thought,
without conscience, without foresight, without eyes, without heart.
It is a tragic accident—and it has happened. You can't interfere
with it. The last drop of bitterness is in the suspicion that you

56

can't even smash it. In virtue of that truth one and immortal which lurks in the force that made it spring into existence it is what it is— 35 and it is indestructible!

It knits us in and it knits us out. It has knitted time space, pain, death, corruption, despair and all the illusions—and nothing matters. I'll admit however that to look at the remorseless process is sometimes amusing. 40

I've got Sta Teresa at last. I've just finished reading that wonderful introduction. Of course what I find in it is mostly new to me— new as impression. It seems as though I were reading of Spain for the first time. I am delighted and intensely interested. I feel myself in sympathy with the book. I shall breathe its atmosphere and 45 track its style for some time now—a charming prospect. As to the style I cant just yet "locate" its charm. For one thing I find it unexpectedly masculine—in the best sense. Don't you think so too?— And the Saga! Where haven't you been? I want more of the Saga. Why the devil did they divide it? I want the whole Saga and 50 nothing but the Saga. Ever Yours faithfully Jph. Conrad

P.S. As I may not write before the days of merriment and festivities I enclose herewith my best wishes. May you get as much happiness as is going on this merry planet. May You, without disappointment, see the accomplishment of *all* your desires! J.C. 55

PUBLICATION
LL, I, 215–16.
Lines 52–5 were omitted by Aubry.

TEXT
'*not*' (line 5) and 'them' (line 11) are insertions.
37 'time space': *sic.*
47 'cant': *sic.*

COMMENTARY
7–9 ff. In a review (1904) of Anatole France's *Crainquebille*, Conrad wrote:
    'He knows that our best hopes are irrealisable; that it is the almost incredible misfortune of mankind, but also its highest privilege, to aspire towards the impossible; that men have never failed to defeat their highest aims by the very strength of their humanity which can conceive the most gigantic tasks but leaves them disarmed before their irremediable littleness.....He wishes us to believe and to hope, preserving in our activity the consoling illusion of power and intelligent purpose.' (*Notes*, pp. 33–4.)

'M. Anatole France is something of a Socialist..... He may be able to discard his philosophy; to forget that the evils are many and the remedies are few, that there is no universal panacea, that fatality is invincible, that there is an implacable menace of death in the triumph of the humanitarian idea. He may forget all that because love is stronger than truth.' (*Ibid*. pp. 37–8.)

12–14 Conrad evidently knew about Graham's imprisonment at Pentonville in 1888 for his part in the battle of Trafalgar Square.

21–40 Cf.:

'The ethical view of the universe involves us at last in so many cruel and absurd contradictions, where the last vestiges of faith, hope, charity, and even of reason itself, seem ready to perish, that I have come to suspect that the aim of creation cannot be ethical at all. I would fondly believe that its object is purely spectacular.....' (*A Personal Record*, Dent, 1923, p. 92.)

'Come, don't you think the earth is *mad*, to go on producing these eternal birth pangs, these shameless swarms of stupid life mechanically, like an automatic mother in parturition, after one single impregnation by the Almighty?' (Garnett to Graham, 31 Jan. 1899, ASA.)

'The world of course, is a whore.....' (Graham to Garnett, 5 Feb. 1899. MS., University of Texas Library.)

41–2 Graham had written a preface to his wife's biography of Santa Teresa; the Introduction was by the authoress. See letter 9, lines 11–38.

49 'the Saga': Graham's Icelandic tale, 'Snaekoll's Saga', was first published in *SR*, LXXXIV, 708–9 (18 Dec. 1897) and 740–1 (25 Dec. 1897).

6

Stanford le Hope.
7th Jan 98.

Cher ami.

Business first. If a damned stack fetched away in a gale it would
5 have to stay down I fancy. But if it got only loose then chains, wire rope, any blamed thing you could lay hands on would serve to secure it. Never saw a stack quit its post, tho' I saw a cold green sea go right down into one.

Yes. A *fore*-stay-sail and a main stay-sail (if carried) could be set
10 to steady the roll of a steamship, providing the gale was not too heavy. Fore stay-sail alone—hardly; tho' it's quite conceivable. In a serious affair they would be useless and in any case would speedily vanish; the necessity of steaming head to sea causing a tremendous strain on the canvass.

15

And in exchange will You tell me whether that life-boat that cap-
sized (of which you wrote) was a steam-lifeboat? And what does
your brother think of steam-lifeboats? I hate machinery but
candidly must own that it seems to me that in most cases steam's
the thing for that work. A year of happy life for every good word 20
spoken of the *Nigger*—to You! Had you the pluck to read it again?
Eh! Man! Ye are perfectly fearless! What mad thing will you do
next?

Read the *Badge*. It won't hurt you—or only very little. Crane-
ibn-Crane el Yankee is all right. The man sees the outside of 25
many things and the inside of some.

I am making preparations to receive The Impenitent Thief
which all the honours due to his distinguished position. I always
thought a lot of that man. He was no philistine anyhow—and no
Jew, since he had no eye for the shent-per-shent business the other 30
fellow spotted at once. I hope your essay is sympathetic.

Do send everything you write—it does a fellow good. Or at any
rate let us know where the things are so that I may scuffle around
to get them.

As to the Saga it confirms me in my conviction that you have a 35
fiendish gift of showing the futility—the ghastly, jocular futility
of life. Et c'est très fin—très fin. C'est finement vu et c'est exprimé
avec finesse—presque a mots couverts, avec de l'esprit dans chaque
phrase. Excuse this polyglot epistle to the faithful.

Ever Yours   40

J. Conrad

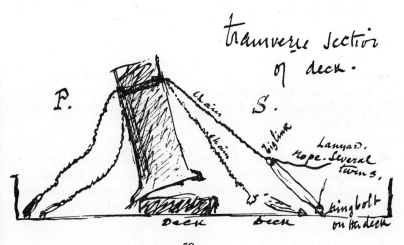

P.S. Re-reading your letter—

That's how a stack would go perhaps. And this would give you an idea how to secure it again. Here both lanyards to S have been
45 carried away—say, by a roll. the thing is then to catch the ends of chains hook quick a spare tackle into the big link and the ring on deck and set taut. Should chains go same principle of action must be followed or should only one of each pair of chains go then could secure in a hurry thus with a rope (5 inch line)

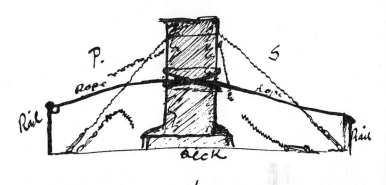

50 the steam-pipe would check the fall of a funnel and it would go over slowly and land on one of the ship's boats—probably—and smash it no doubt. Or if pitched forward it would damage the bridge—and the man on it too very likely. But the most dramatic circumstance would be the hellish mess of soot blowing about or
55 washing over the deck. Does the plot hinge on the funnel? You must have a *plot*! If you haven't, every fool reviewer will kick you because there can't be literature without plot. I am in a state of wild excitement about the stack. Let's know quick what happened in the tramp. A Scotch tramp is a very good tramp. The Engineers
60 tell anecdotes, the mates are grim and over all floats the flavour of an accent that gives a special value to every word pronounced on her deck. You must know I've a soft spot for Scotchmen. Be easy on the tramp.

65 Ah! Amigo! I've thought of Rajah Laut in London and if not in the W-H then next thing to it. But I haven't the heart. I haven't! Not yet. I am now busy about his youth—a gorgeous romance— gorgeous as to feeling I mean. Battles and loves and so on.

PUBLICATION

LL, I, 220–1. Aubry omitted lines 42–9, 50–63, and the two diagrams. The first diagram and lines 42–8 (to 'followed') and 65–8 have been reproduced as a facsimile illustration in *EKH*, p. 93.
20 'every good word': Aubry reads 'every word'.
32 'Do send': 'So send.'

TEXT

28 'which': *sic.*
44–8 (from 'Here' to 'followed'): These lines were squeezed in by Conrad as an afterthought, and lines 48–63 (from 'or should') were added after the passage here arranged as lines 65–8.
48 'pair of': inserted.

COMMENTARY

4 ff. 'a damned stack.....': Evidently Graham was then writing 'S.S. *Atlas*' (which appeared a few months later in *SR*, LXXXV, 652–3 and 676–7, 14 and 21 May 1898), and had asked Conrad to confirm the accuracy of the detail in the following description of the 'sea change' that the old Scottish tramp-steamer had suffered during a gale:
  'no boats, bulwarks all washed away upon the weather side, doors torn off the hinges, the "fetched loose" smoke stack, coated white with salt, and stayed up in a clumsy fashion with some chains.....' (P. 653.)
  The tale was based on two Atlantic crossings that Graham had made on the S.S. *Alps* in the autumn of 1872 and the winter of 1872–3: on the return journey the Scottish crew had become so drunken on New Year's Day that the passengers had had to turn to and man the ship (see Graham's letters to his mother, quoted in *AFT*, pp. 76–9).
9 'A *fore*-stay-sail': cf.:
  'fitfully came the strains of "Renzo" as the crew set the fore topmast staysail.....' (P. 652.)
18 'your brother': Since retiring from the navy, Charles Cunninghame Graham (1853–1917) had become deputy chief-inspector of lifeboats for the Royal National Lifeboat Institution, and won praise from the Institute's committee for his zealous rescue-work with the Harwich lifeboat in 1897 (*R.N.L.I.* Records).
18–20 Cf. Conrad's later arguments in favour of motor-engined lifeboats (*Notes*, pp. 244–6).
24–6 A reviewer in the *Daily Telegraph* (8 Dec. 1897, p. 4) had suggested that the technique of *The Nigger of the 'Narcissus'* had been modelled on that of Stephen Crane's *The Red Badge of Courage* (Heinemann, London, 1895), which had been widely acclaimed in England; and Conrad himself said later:
  'I.....had been dealing with the same subject ["the psychology of the mass"] on a much smaller scale and in more specialized conditions—the crew of a merchant ship, brought to the test of what I may venture to call the moral problem of conduct.'

This remark, and the description of his friendship with Crane, are to be found in Conrad's Introduction to Thomas Beer's *Stephen Crane: A Study in American Letters* (Heinemann, London, 1924; quotation, p. 3). Conrad appears to have met Crane for the first time in October 1897 (*ibid.* p. 2; *EGL*, p. 102). His affectionate admiration for Crane's 'untutored genius' was a guarded one; he described Graham's sketches as examples of 'much more of course than mere Crane-like impressionism' (letter 37, lines 16–17: cf. *EGL*, p. 107).

Crane had expressed his enthusiasm for *The Nigger*, and had invited the Conrads to visit him at Oxted, in a letter dated 11 November 1897 (see G. Jean-Aubry: *Twenty Letters to Joseph Conrad*, First Edition Club, London, 1926); and evidently he admired Graham's work (letter 12, lines 7–9).

27–31 Graham's essay, 'The Impenitent Thief', was first published in the *Social-Democrat* (London), II, 6–8 (Jan. 1898), and was first issued in book form in *Success* (Duckworth, London, 1902). It is discussed further in letters 8 and 9.

Like Conrad, Graham was highly sympathetic with the logical malefactor of Luke xxiii. 39. Seven months previously, on 11 June 1897, Conrad had told Garnett:

'Generally I feel like the impenitent thief on the cross (he is one of my heroes)—defiant and bitter.' (*EGL*, pp. 84–5.)

And to Marguerite Poradowska he had once written:

'The doctrine (or theory) of expiation through suffering.....a product of superior but savage minds, is quite simply an infamous abomination when preached by civilized people. It is a doctrine which, on the one hand, leads straight to the Inquisition and, on the other, discloses the possibilities of bargaining with the Eternal..... Each act of life is final.....' (*MPL*, p. 36.)

'That impenitent thief' was how Conrad (in the 'Author's Note' to *Nostromo*) described the Nicolo of H. E. Hamblen's *On Many Seas*: the rogue who, as John Halverson and Ian Watt have shown in *Review of English Studies*, N.S. x, 45–52 (Feb. 1959), was the original model for Nostromo himself.

30 'shent-per-shent': The *Labour Leader* for 27 March 1897 (IX, 101) had published a political cartoon in which a Jew with the label 'European Finance' exclaims 'Oh, dear! der goes anuder slump ob mein bootiful Turkish "shent per shent"'. As Graham wrote for the *Labour Leader* and was occasionally reported in it, he or Garnett may have sent Conrad this issue. It is certain that by June 1898 Conrad had received a copy or copies of the *Labour Leader* from Garnett: see letter 17.

35–9 Graham's tale, 'Snaekoll's Saga', was first published in *SR* (see letter 5, note 49), and was later included in *The Ipané*.

Before setting out on an exploratory journey across the Vatna from which he never returns, the hero of the tale, Thorgrimur, makes a speech which might later have interested Stein of *Lord Jim*:

'I go to try what I have dreamed of all my life; whether I shall succeed no man can tell, but still I shall succeed so far in that I have had the opportunity to follow out my dream. I hold that dreams are the reality of life and that which men call practical, that which down there in Reykjavik the folk call business, is but a dream.' (*Ipané*, Fisher Unwin, London, 1899, p. 221.)

53–5 Graham's idea of a tale whose centrepiece is the description of a tramp-steamer in a storm has so evidently captured Conrad's imagination that one might rashly conjecture that this letter contains the germ of *Typhoon*. Certainly this hint of 'the most dramatic circumstance' is used in the novel:

'The smoke struggled with difficulty out of the funnel, and instead of streaming away spread itself out like an infernal sort of cloud, smelling of sulphur and raining soot all over the decks.' (*Typhoon*, Heinemann, 1903, p. 23.)

This conjecture is partly supported by the fact that Graham's own copy of the book bears the following flyleaf-inscription in Conrad's hand:

'To / R. B. Cunninghame Graham / this copy of the book / that was his in / the writing / from / Joseph Conrad. / 22 April / 1903.'(ASA.)

55–7 Apparently the *Daily Mail*'s criticism of *The Nigger* ('The tale is no tale.....There is no plot') was still rankling in Conrad's mind. (See letter 3, note 33–5.)

65 'Rajah Laut': i.e. 'Tom Lingard, he whom the Malays.....recognised as "the Rajah-Laut"—the King of the Sea' (*Almayer's Folly*, Fisher Unwin, London, 1895, p. 12). Lingard's adventures had been based partly on those of James Brooke, Rajah of Sarawak; and Graham's enquiry had perhaps been occasioned by the fact that in writing 'S.S. *Atlas*' he had remembered an encounter with a chief engineer, 'a Greenock Ananias.....who had "gone out in '47, second engineer aboard the craft what took out Rajah Brook [*sic*]"' (p. 652).

65–6 In *The Rescue* (on which, as *The Rescuer*, Conrad had been working intermittently since 1896) Lingard is confronted by intruders from the Western Hemisphere.

7

10 pm. 14 Jan. 98.

Stanford le Hope

Essex

Cher ami.

A really friendly letter and my conscience smote me at every 5 word read when I thought of your work upon which I intrude with my miserable affairs.

Semm! Pronounce the Name—and write to F. Harris. This *is* a service and a most important one. I would rather owe it to you than

₁₀ to any one else—in fact don't *see* myself owing it to any one else. Frankly (you may have guessed) I was pretty nearly in my last ditch before I thought of attacking Harris. I talked to you in my letter as if I were ready to face fire and water and an Editor, but my heart was in my boots. Yours is a helping hand. And if You ₁₅ don't think you are thus sacrificing an old friend to a new one— Well then Say the Name—and write.

And since you offer to do me this good turn I had better tell you that it would be rather important for me to have the publication ₂₀ begin as soon as possible—say in two—three months. By that time there would be a good lot of copy to go on with while I twisted the remainder out of my bowels. (It's wonderful how this fool-business of writing is serious to one) The book is by no means near its termination. About 30000 out of 90000 words are ready. Won't ₂₅ it be too cheeky approaching H. with such a small beginning? I would be very glad, very, to see him—in any case. But you know I am shy of my bad English. At any rate prepare him for a "b—y furriner" who will talk gibberish to him at the rate of 10 knots an hour. If not forewarned the phenomenon might discourage him to ₃₀ the point of kicking me downstairs. This is submitted to your wisdom which embraces the world and the men in it from Patagonia to Iceland. Our ears are open.

Was the fire serious? And has Your wife got over the emotion? You ₃₅ know when I sprung that affair of mine on you I had no idea of the accumulation of troubles in Gartmore. But all the same it was dam' unkind of you to lead me on gently to make an ass of myself about smoke stacks and stay-sails and then fire off at me a lot of sailor talk about going down the leach of a topsail. What don't you know! ₄₀ From the outside of a sail to the inside of a prison! When I think of you I feel as tho' I had lived all my life in a dark hole without ever seeing or knowing anything.

Nothing would be more delightful to me than to read a review of the *N* by you. I never dreamed you would care to do this thing. ₄₅ I do not know who, when and how it is to be reviewed. But is the *N* worthy of your pen and especially of your thought! Is it too late. Do you really mean it?—There will be a *Vol* of short stories app^g in March. One of them *The Outpost*. Now if you are really anxious to give me a good slating...

"Put the tongue out" why not? One ought to really. And the 50
machine will run on all the same. The question is, whether the
fatigue of the muscular exertion is worth the transient pleasure of
indulged scorn. On the other hand one may ask whether scorn,
love, or hate are justified in the face of such shadowy illusions. The
machine is thinner than air and as evanescent as a flash of lightning. 55
The attitude of cold unconcern is the only reasonable one. Of
course reason is hateful—but why? Because it demonstrates (to
those who have the courage) that we, living, are out of life—utterly
out of it. The mysteries of a universe made of drops of fire and
clods of mud do not concern us in the least. The fate of a humanity 60
condemned ultimately to perish from cold is not worth troubling
about. If you take it to heart it becomes an unendurable tragedy.
If you believe in improvement you must weep, for the attained
perfection must end in cold, darkness and silence. In a dispassionate view the ardour for reform, improvement for virtue, 65
for knowledge, and even for beauty is only a vain sticking up for
appearances as though one were anxious about the cut of one's
clothes in a community of blind men. Life knows us not and we
do not know life—we don't know even our own thoughts. Half the
words we use have no meaning whatever and of the other half each 70
man understands each word after the fashion of his own folly and
conceit. Faith is a myth and beliefs shift like mists on the shore;
thoughts vanish; words, once pronounced, die; and the memory of
yesterday is as shadowy as the hope of to-morrow—only the string
of my platitudes seems to have no end. As our peasants say: "Pray, 75
brother, forgive me for the love of God". And we don't know what
forgiveness is, nor what is love, nor where God is. Assez.

Yesterday I've finished the Life. Ça m'a laissé une profonde
impression de tristesse comme si j'avais vécu toutes les pages du
livre. I can say no more just now. 80

Ever Yours

15th/1/98   Jph Conrad.

PS. This letter missed this morning's post because an infant of
male persuasion arrived and made such a row that I could not hear
the Postman's whistle. It's a fine commentary upon this letter! 85
But salvation lies in being illogical. Still I feel remorse.

PUBLICATION
LL, I, 221-3.

TEXT

13 and 67   'were': in each case an alteration of 'was'.
63   'attained': an insertion.
65   'improvement for virtue': *sic*.

COMMENTARY

8   'Semm!': Semm, or Shem, means 'Name' and 'Renown'.

8–30   Frank Harris was from September 1894 to November 1898 the editor of the *SR*, to which Graham was a prolific contributor and to which Conrad was a subscriber. On 6 January 1898 Conrad had written to Garnett:

> 'I can speak plainly to C.G. about the *Sat. R.* idea. I don't know whether he is on very good terms with F.H. tho'. Fact to note: *all* the fiction (it may be called) the *S.R.* publishes is furnished by C.G. alone.' (*EGL*, p. 118.)

Garnett had suggested that Graham should persuade Frank Harris to publish Conrad's work, including, evidently, *The Rescue*, in *SR*. Certainly Harris had a high opinion of Graham and his work: see, for example, *Frank Harris on Bernard Shaw* (1931), pp. 126, 129. On 15 January 1898 Conrad told Garnett:

> 'I had a warm letter from Graham. He offers to write Harris— thinks the idea splendid—and so on. I have in him a friend at court indeed. I replied telling him to go ahead.' (*EGL*, p. 119.)

However, nothing came of the idea, in spite of Graham's efforts (see letter 9, lines 6–10, and letter 10, lines 3–5). It was in any case a faint hope, because during the period 1890–1900 no novels were serialised in *SR*.

30–2   Many of Graham's tales are set in South America, and 'Snaekoll's Saga' is set in Iceland.

35–6   Graham's estate at Gartmore in Perthshire was a growing liability, and was soon to be auctioned: see letter 22, note 5–23.

36–9   See letter 6.

40   'the inside of a prison': Graham's tale 'Sursum Corda' (*SR*, LXXXIII, 681–3, 19 June 1897) was based on his experience of Pentonville in 1888.

43–4   'a review of the *N* by you': cf. *EGL*, p. 119:

> 'Graham said incidentally he would have liked to review the *Nigger*. I told him he may be in time yet.'

Eventually, however, the book was reviewed in *SR* not by Graham but by Harold Frederic (*SR*, LXXXV, 211: 12 Feb. 1898).

47–8   'An Outpost of Progress' was included in *Tales of Unrest*, published by T. Fisher Unwin, London, in April 1898 (*ECB*).

50   'Put the tongue out': a reference to the last words of 'An Outpost': the words to which Graham refers in *Mogreb* when praising that tale.

54–6   In an article published three months later ('Alphonse Daudet' in *Outlook*, 9 April 1898), Conrad said of Daudet:

'He saw life around him with extreme clearnesss, and he felt it as it is—thinner than air and more elusive than a flash of lightning. He hastened to offer it his compassion, his indignation, his wonder, his sympathy, without giving a moment of thought to the momentous issues that are supposed to lurk in the logic of such sentiments.' (*Notes*, p. 23.)

60–2   'Inevitably they [Daudet's characters] *marchent à la mort*—and they are very near the truth of our common destiny: their fate is poignant, it is intensely interesting, and of not the slightest consequence.' (*Ibid.* p. 24.)

64–8   In 'Books' (1905), Conrad wrote:

'It must not be supposed that I claim for the artist in fiction the freedom of moral Nihilism. I would require from him many acts of faith of which the first would be the cherishing of an undying hope; and hope, it will not be contested, implies all the piety of effort and renunciation.' (*Notes*, p. 8.)

68–75   In May 1897 Garnett had sent Conrad a copy of Peter's *Marius the Epicurean*, in which Marius reflects:

'Conceded that. . . . . all that is real in our experience [is] but a series of fleeting impressions:. . . . . given, that we are never to get beyond the walls of this closely shut cell of one's own personality; that the ideas we are somehow impelled to form of an outer world, and of other minds akin to our own, are, it may be, but a day-dream, and the thought of any world beyond, a day-dream perhaps idler still. . . . .' (Macmillan, London, 1892; I, 158.)

75–7   In 'Salvagia', first published in *SR*, LXXXII, 279–80 (12 Sept. 1896), and later republished in *The Ipané*, Graham wrote:

'Almost the most horrible doctrine ever enunciated by theologians is, in my opinion, the attribution of our misfortunes to Providence . . . . .Withal, nothing consoles humanity for their misfortunes like the presence of this unseen power, which might do so much good, but which serenely contemplates so many evils.' (*Ipané*, pp. 188–9.) Ford Madox Ford claims (in *Return to Yesterday*, p. 102) that during the London dockers' strike

'Graham who was on the platform quieted things down by saying that it was wrong of Mr. Tillett to throw imprecations at the Almighty. God was a man of the very best intentions who died young.'

78   'the Life': Gabriela Cunninghame Graham's *Santa Teresa*: see letter 9.

83   'an infant': Borys Conrad.

8

Cher Ami

I've got a bad wrist; that's why I did not write sooner. I gave it complete rest. Much better now.

5 The Impenitent Thief has been read more than once. I've read it several times alone and I've read it aloud to my wife. Every word has found a home. You with your ideals of sincerity, courage and truth are strangely out of place in this epoch of material preoccupations. What does it bring? What's the profit? What do we

10 get by it? These questions are at the root of every moral, intellectual or political movement. Into the noblest cause men manage to put something of their baseness; and sometimes when I think of You here, quietly You seem to me tragic with your courage, with your beliefs and your hopes. Every cause is tainted: and you reject this

15 one, espouse that other one as if one were evil and the other good while the same evil you hate is in both, but disguised in different words. I am more in sympathy with you than words can express yet if I had a grain of belief left in me I would believe you misguided. You are misguided by the desire of the impossible—and I envy you.

20 Alas! What you want to reform are not institutions—it is human nature. Your faith will never move that mountain. Not that I think mankind intrinsically bad. It is only silly and cowardly. Now *You* know that in cowardice is every evil—especially that cruelty so characteristic of our civilisation. But without it mankind would

25 vanish. No great matter truly. But will you persuade humanity to throw away sword and shield? Can you persuade even me— Who write these words in the fulness of an irresistible conviction? No. I belong to the wretched gang. We all belong to it. We are born initiated, and succeeding generations clutch the inheritance

30 of fear and brutality without a thought, without a doubt without compunction—in the name of God.

These are the thoughts suggested by the man who wrote an essay on the Impenitent Thief. Forgive their disconnected impertinence. You'll have to forgive me many things if you continue to know

35 me on the basis of sincerity and friendship.

I wanted to say a word or so about the technique of the essay but I can't. A la prochaine—donc.

Ever Yours Jph Conrad

PUBLICATION

LL, I, 229–30.
1 'Sunday.': Aubry reads 'Sunday Feb. 1898.'

TEXT

The handwriting of this letter testifies to the 'bad wrist' mentioned in line 3.
6 'several times': inserted.

COMMENTARY

1 The date. For the following reasons this letter may be ascribed to Sunday 23 January 1898.

(*a*) Lines 3–5 of letter 9 answer an enquiry about the 'bad wrist' mentioned in letter 8, line 3.

(*b*) Letter 8 gives a detailed criticism of 'The Impenitent Thief', which had just appeared in the *Social-Democrat* for January. Lines 39–49 of letter 9 add a coda to this criticism. In letter 9 (dated 31 Jan.) there are references to letter 8 (cf. 9, lines 44–5, and 8, lines 6–7: 'Every word has found a home').

Therefore letter 8, as it shortly precedes letter 9, must have been written in January. Furthermore it must follow that dated 14 Jan., in which there is no mention of gout or of the tale.

(*c*) The only Sundays between 14 and 31 January were on the 16th, 23rd and 30th of the month. Sunday 16 January may be eliminated because in the mere two days that would then have elapsed since the previous letter, there would not have been time for Conrad to suffer an attack of gout in the wrist and then to give his wrist the complete rest which he offers as an apology for not having written sooner. Sunday 30 January may also be eliminated because there would not then have been time for Graham to have received the letter and to have replied to it before the 31st.

5 Graham's essay. 'The Impenitent Thief', which Conrad had anticipated in letter 6, lines 27–31, was first published in the *Social-Democrat*, II, 6–8 (Jan. 1898).

7–31 Conrad was perhaps as much concerned to criticise the militant context provided by H. M. Hyndman's magazine as he was to criticise the essay itself, in which Graham had said:

'Perhaps, impenitent Gestas (or Dimas) was the most human of the three, a thief, and not ashamed of having exercised his trade. How much more dignified than some cold-hearted scoundrel who as solicitor, banker, or confidential agent swindles for years, and in the dock recants, calls on his God to pardon him, either because he is a cur at heart, or else because he knows the sodden public always compassionates a coward, feeling, perhaps, a fellow-feeling, and being therefore kind.' (P. 7.)

In 'Anatole France', Conrad wrote:

'He.....perceives that political institutions, whether contrived by the wisdom of the few or the ignorance of the many, are incapable of securing the happiness of mankind.'

'"We are all Socialists now." And in the sense in which it may be said that we all in Europe are Christians that is true enough..... Only, unlike religion, the cohesive strength of Socialism lies not in its dogmas but in its ideal. It is perhaps a too materialistic ideal..... M. Anatole France, a good prince and a good Republican, will succeed no doubt in being a good Socialist. He will disregard the stupidity of the dogma and the unlovely form of the ideal. His art will find its own beauty in the imaginative presentation of wrongs, of errors, and miseries that call aloud for redress.' (*Notes*, pp. 33, 37–8.)

9

31 Jan 98.

Cher et excellent ami.

In the wrist there was gout or some other devil which rendered it quite powerless, besides it being horribly painful. It's all
5 over now.

It is good of you to push my fortunes. You are the only man —in this or any other country—who took any effective interest in them. Still I think that F. Harris should not be pressed. You have given him two broadsides and if the man will not surrender,
10 well then let him run.

Now the first sensation of oppression has worn off a little what remains with one after reading the Life of Sta Theresa is the impression of a wonderful richness; a world peopled thickly—with the breath of mysticism over all—the landscapes, the walls, the
15 men, the woman. Of course I am quite incompetent to criticise such a work; but I can appreciate it. It is vast and suggestive; it is a distinct acquisition to the reader—or at least to me; it makes one *see* and reflect. It is absorbing like a dream and as difficult to keep hold of. And it is—to me—profoundly saddening. It is indeed old
20 life re-vived. And old life is like new life after all—an uninterrupted agony of effort. Yes. Egoism is good, and altruism is good, and fidelity to nature would be the best of all, and systems could be built, and rules could be made—if we could only get rid of consciousness. What makes mankind tragic is not that they are
25 the victims of nature, it is that they are conscious of it. To be part of the animal kingdom under the conditions of this earth is very well—but as soon as you know of your slavery the pain, the anger, the strife—the tragedy begins. We can't return to nature, since

70

we can't change our place in it. Our refuge is in stupidity, in drunkeness of all kinds, in lies, in beliefs, in murder, thieving, reforming—in negation, in contempt—each man according to the promptings of his particular devil. There is no morality, no knowledge and no hope; there is only the consciousness of ourselves which drives us about a world that whether seen in a convex or a concave mirror is always but a vain and fleeting appearance. "Ôte-toi de là que je m'y mette" is no more of a sound rule than would be the reverse doctrine. It is however much easier to practice.

What made you suspect that I wanted vous faire une querelle d'Allemand about the technique of the Impenitent Thief? I leave that to Wells, who is in the secret of the universe—or at least of the planet Mars. It struck me when reading your essay that the style was not the Cunninghame Graham I've known hitherto. As to the matter, however, there was not the slightest doubt—and, as I have said, every word has found a home. As to the form: c'est plus d'un seul jet if I may say so. It grips in a different way. The pictures and the figures are drawn without lifting pencil from paper. I like it very well. It's just the thing for that essay whether You did it of set purpose or by caprice or, perhaps, unconsciously?

I am glad your brother likes the *Nigger*. Symons reviewing *Trionfo della Morte* (trans:) in the last *Sat. Rev.* went out of his way to damn Kipling and me with the same generous praise. He says that *Captains Courageous* and the *Nigger* have no idea behind them. I don't know. Do you think the remark is just? Now straight!

I haven't written to your brother. I am not going to inflict myself upon the whole family. I shall devote all my spare time and what's left of my energy to worrying you alone of the whole of your House. And why not? Haven't you rushed upon your fate? I am like the old man of the sea. You can't get rid of me by the apparently innocent suggestion of writing to your brother. Seriously speaking I was afraid of trespassing—and then each man is so busy with his own futility that the handwriting of a stranger cannot be very welcome to him. Is he a naval officer? I *am* glad he likes the nigger. Please tell him so—if you ever do write to him.

"The Rescue: A Romance of Shallow Waters, spreads itself, more and more shallow, over innumerable pages. Symons (who lives on ideas) shall have an indigestion if he reads it. It would be for him like swallowing a stone; for there *I know* there are no ideas.

Only a few types and some obscure incidents upon a dismal coast
70 where Symons's humanity ends and raw mankind begins.

And so the end! The lamp is dim and the night is dark. Last
night a heavy gale was blowing and I lay awake thinking that I
would give ever so much (the most flattering criticism) for being at
sea, the soul of some patient faithful ship standing up to it under
75 lower topsails and no land anywhere within a thousand miles.
Wouldn't I jump at a command if some literary shipowner
suddenly offered it to me!

Thanks for your inquiries. My wife and the boy are very well.
I was very sorry to hear of your wife's indisposition. Nothing
80 serious I hope. If your horse has not eaten you up entirely I trust
you will write before the end of the week.

Ever Yours   Jph Conrad.

PUBLICATION

LL, I, 225–7.

11–12 'worn off a little what remains': Aubry reads 'worn off, a little
that remains'.
19–20 'old life re-vived. And': 'old life. And'.
35 'fleeting': 'floating'.
61 'each man is': 'each is'.
65 '"The Rescue': '*The Rescuer*'.
67 'an indigestion': 'no indigestion'.

TEXT

12 'after': inserted above the cancelled words 'is the'.
22 'fidelity' is immediately preceded by the cancelled beginning of the
word 'nature'.
24 'not': inserted.
30 'drunkeness': *sic.*
34 'whether': written above the cancelled words 'may be'.
65 'Waters,': *sic.*

COMMENTARY

6–10 See letter 7, lines 8–30.
11–38 Mrs Cunninghame Graham's socialist views encouraged her to
use a double perspective in her treatment of Santa Teresa which
resembles the double perspective of her husband's treatment of the
Conquistadores. Thus, while she is able to treat with some scepticism
and criticism the sources of the saint's inspiration and the activities of the
Roman Catholic Church, her belief that devotion to a spiritual goal,
however illusory, is preferable to the modern devotion to 'material
interests' enables her to treat her subject with considerable sympathy—
a sympathy which, as in her husband's histories, too often seems to find
expression in an embarrassing rhetoric:

'[Posterity] shall laugh to bitter scorn the electro-plated calf—, constructed by greed amidst the groans of the sweated and the pauper,—before which we fall down in the dust and prostrate ourselves as meekly and as fervently as the friars of an older world prostrated themselves before the image of a saint.

The efforts of these men at least were directed to a noble and transcendental end.....They asserted the equality of man—a lofty socialism.' (*Santa Teresa*, 1894, I, 58-9.)

'We shall follow her daily life, composed of the rigid and patient discharge of all the theological virtues inspired by her illusions (would that we were all alike deluded! it would be a better world!) .....' (*Ibid.* p. 72.)

Conrad's perennial concern to analyse and counterpoint the respective illusions of idealist and materialist perhaps accounts for the evident interest with which he read and re-read this book. (Cf. letter 60, lines 46-9.)

39-40 'querelle d'Allemand': a groundless quarrel.

40 Conrad had discussed 'The Impenitent Thief' at length in letter 8.

40-2 Martians invade the earth in H. G. Wells's *The War of the Worlds*, which had just been published (Heinemann, London, January 1898, *ECB*) and which perhaps gave Conrad a hint for *The Inheritors*.

In 1896 Wells had once criticised the technique of *An Outcast of the Islands* (*SR*, LXXXI, 509-10, 16 May 1896), and this review had led to Conrad's rather unstable friendship with him. Wells also censured Graham's writing (see *SR*, LXXXV, 211-13, 12 Feb. 1898).

50-4 In *SR*, LXXXV, 145-6 (29 Jan. 1898), Arthur Symons had reviewed *The Triumph of Death*, Georgina Harding's translation of D'Annunzio's *Trionfo della Morte*, and had said:

'We have a surprising number of popular story-writers, some of them very entertaining, some of them with great ability of the narrative kind. Look only at the last year, and take only two books: Mr. Kipling's "Captains Courageous" and Mr. Conrad's "Nigger of the 'Narcissus'". In one of these what an admirable mastery of a single bit of objective reality, of the adventure of a trade, of what is external in the figures who are active about it! In the other there is an almost endless description of the whole movement, noise, order, and distraction of a ship and a ship's company during a storm, which brings to one's memory a sense of every discomfort one has ever endured upon the sea. But what more is there? Where is the idea of which such things as these should be but servants? Ah, there has been an oversight; everything else is there, but that, these brilliant writers have forgotten to put in. Now, d'Annunzio, whether you like his idea or not, never forgets to put it in. Also he never forgets that the aim of all art is beauty; beauty of whatever kind you like, but beauty.'

Conrad asked Garnett, as well as Graham, for an opinion of Symons's charge (*EGL*, p. 122); and apparently as a result of the review he wrote the unprinted article on Kipling (presumably answering Symons's objection) for the *Outlook* (see *LL*, I, 227–8).

Symons's later view of *The Nigger* was more sympathetic: see his *Notes on Joseph Conrad* (Myers, London, 1925), pp. 16, 26.

50 'your brother': Later in the year, Conrad wrote to Graham's mother, Mrs. Bontine:

> 'The commendation of your son, Charles, is very precious to me. He can appreciate the intention and also the *detail* of my work..... There is between us that subtle and strong bond of the sea.....' (*LL*, I, 250.)

55–63 Cf.:

> 'I would have written direct [to Charles Cunninghame Graham] had I not been held back by the thought he is a busy man,—and a sailor.....' (*LL*, I, 250.)

71–7 Graham took Conrad at his word, and used his influence with the Glasgow ship-owners in the hope of obtaining a post for Conrad. See letters 19, 20, 23, 26 and 30; *LL*, I, 251; and *EGL*, p. 135.

80 'If your horse has not eaten you': In 'Snaekoll's Saga' it is implied that the hero has been devoured by his horse.

10

4th Febr 98

Cher ami.

I was glad to get your good letter. From his point of view Runciman is right. It would stereotype the paper. And after all they
5 did take a line which at any rate is not philistinish.

Pawling is a good friend to me and I think that my acceptance by "Scribner's"—thanks to his efforts—is assured *if* I can wait till they have space. Barrie blocks the way. I shall scout around energetically to find a shop where they take in pawn the future
10 of writers.

———

I haven't said half what I wanted to say about Sta Theresa—and what I have said has been stupidly expressed. I am glad Mrs Cunninghame Graham is not angry. This is the sweetness of
15 women, for there is nothing more exasperating than an ignorant appreciation.

—How did you come to know such a delightful man as your friend of the barquentine? A coaster eh? I've served in a coaster. Also a barque^{ne}. "Skimmer of the Seas" what a pretty
20 name! But she is gone and took a whole lot of good fellows away

74

with her into the other world. Comme c'est vieux tout ça! In that craft I began to learn English from East Coast chaps each built as though to last for ever, and coloured like a Christmas card. Tan and pink—gold hair and blue eyes with that Northern straight-away-there look! Twenty two years ago! From Lowestoft to Newcastle 25 and back again. Good school for a seaman. As soon as I can sell my damaged soul for two and six I shall transport my damaged body there and look at the green sea, over the yellow sands. Eheu! Fugaces!

30

Excuse these tears.

And to think you were dining my wretched carcass at the Devonshire while you might have been on board the "Tourmaline" giving invaluable tips to her owner about Sidi Haschem. Sir—you 35 have sinned. But as your sinning was my profit you are forgiven. But why the devil have they been arrested. One should never be arrested. And where exactly? Tho' I can read you with ease (honor bright) the proper names stump me. Is it west coast of Morocco? or about cape Blanco? I am lost in conjectures. 40

On the 19th all our tribe man, woman and child shift camp to Oxted to dwell for ten days in the tents of the Beni-Crane. A risky experiment.

Ever Yours
Jph. Conrad.

PUBLICATION

Lines 18–26 (from 'A coaster eh?' to 'a seaman.') were quoted in *LL*, I, 49. The remainder of the letter is unpublished in book form but has been printed in *Notes and Queries*, CCX, 263–4 (July 1965).

TEXT

11   In the manuscript there are four strokes of the pen, which may be intended to underline 'future' and 'writers', or simply to emphasise the paragraph-division.
38   'honor': *sic.*

COMMENTARY

3–5   J. F. Runciman (1866–1916) was assistant editor and music critic of *SR* during Frank Harris's editorship. These lines refer to Graham's efforts to have the unfinished *The Rescue* serialised there. (See letter 7, lines 8–30, and letter 9, lines 6–10.)

6–8   Cf. *EGL*, p. 118 (letter dated 6 Jan. 1898):

> 'Scribners would have made offer [for *The Rescue*] if they had not been full for '98 and '99. And even then if the book had been *finished* they would have made an offer.'

Sydney S. Pawling, a partner of William Heinemann's, had tried to secure the serialisation of *The Rescue* in *Scribner's Magazine*.

8   'Barrie blocks the way': J. M. Barrie's novel, *Tommy and Grizel*, appeared monthly in *Scribner's Magazine* from January to November 1900.

12   'Sta Theresa': Mrs Cunninghame Graham's book had been discussed in letter 9, lines 11–38.

17–18   'your friend': probably an ironic reference to the gun-running barquentine-skipper, Honest Tom Bilson, the hero of Graham's tale, 'Bristol Fashion' (first published in *SR*, LXXXV, 167–8 and 198–9, 5 and 12 Feb. 1898).

19   'Skimmer of the Seas': i.e. 'Skimmer of the Sea', a three-masted coaster which sank in October 1881 while carrying a cargo of coals from Shields to Lowestoft (Lloyd's). Conrad had made six voyages on her during 1878 (Baines, p. 61). He later introduced her into the pages of 'To-morrow' (finished in January 1902):

> '.....he used to go about looking very sick for three days before he had to leave home on one of his trips to South Shields for coal. He had a standing charter from the gas-works. You would think he was off on a whaling cruise—three years and a tail. Ha, ha! Not a bit of it. Ten days on the outside. The *Skimmer of the Seas* was a smart craft. Fine name, wasn't it? Mother's uncle owned her...' (*Typhoon and Other Stories*, Heinemann, London, 1903, pp. 291–2.)

See Conrad's account of his 'school-room' (*Notes*, pp. 155–7).

28–9   'Eheu! Fugaces!': 'Alas, the fleeting [years glide by].....' (Horace: *Odes*, II, xiv, 1.)

33–5   Graham's club was the Devonshire. The dinner with Conrad probably took place on 26 November 1897 (*EGL*, p. 105); and in that month Spilsbury was preparing to embark: cf. 'In November I met him [Spilsbury] at a London club' (*Mogreb-el-Acksa*, p. 321).

34–40   The 'Tourmaline' Venture. The Globe Syndicate of London had secured a concession to trade with the tribes of the Sus, in southern Morocco. The concession was illegal, as the Moroccan government had forbidden European traders to enter that region. Nevertheless, in the summer of 1897 Major A. G. Spilsbury set out on behalf of the Syndicate, made contact with the tribes, and offered to supply them with arms with which they might rebel against the sultan.

On 5 December 1897 Spilsbury again left England, taking with him on his yacht 'Tourmaline' a cargo of guns and ammunition. Before the cargo could be landed on the west coast of Morocco, the sultan's man-of-war appeared and the expedition was routed. Four of the Globe's men were jailed for smuggling, and Spilsbury was tried at Gibraltar on 10 April 1899 for illegally importing arms, but was acquitted. (See A. G. Spilsbury's *The Tourmaline Expedition*, Dent,

London, 1906; Graham's *Mogreb-el-Acksa*, pp. 36–42, 217, 239–40, and 313–23; and *The Times*, 1 Feb. 1898, p. 3, 23 Feb. 1898, p. 5, and 30 March 1898, p. 7.)

Graham knew and admired Spilsbury personally, but naturally detested his cause and had attempted to dissuade him (*Mogreb*, p. 321). Spilsbury's first expedition had incidentally resulted in Graham's arrest. The sultan, forewarned of the Syndicate's activities, had told his subjects to arrest any Europeans in the Sus region: consequently, when Graham attempted to reach the city of Tarudant in the autumn of 1897, he was captured, held in captivity for a week, and turned back. (Graham's account of this provided the basis for Shaw's *Captain Brassbound's Conversion*.) After his return, Graham attacked the Syndicate in articles for *SR* (LXXXV, 739–40 and 810–12, 4 and 18 June 1898); and in *Mogreb-el-Acksa* his references to the venture add some poignancy to his defence of the relative integrity of the archaic way of life of the Moors.

In letter 13, lines 9–10, Conrad says of Spilsbury's expedition: 'I've done better in my time but then I didn't act for a syndicate.' The apparent association in Conrad's mind of the unsuccessful attempts at gun-running by Spilsbury and by himself (and incidentally by Lingard in *The Rescue*, which he was then writing) provokes the speculation that Conrad may have attempted to conceal the name of the vessel on which he had done his own early gun-running, by borrowing the name 'Tourmaline' and altering the vowels to 'Tremolino'. This would account for the fact that Conrad's biographers have been unable to trace an actual vessel called 'Tremolino'; and there is no record that Conrad used this name before 1898.

35   'Sidi Haschem': Sidi Hosein ben Haschem, a chieftain of the Susi tribes (Spilsbury, *Tourmaline Expedition*, p. 128).

41–3   The Conrad family spent a fortnight with Stephen Crane at Ravensbrook, near Oxted. (*JEC*, pp. 57–8; letter 12, lines 6–9.)

I I

16 Febr 98

Cher ami.

I did not write because I was beastly seedy—nerve trouble —a taste of hell. All right now.

Thanks for sending me the paper and the letter about it which ⁵ reached me in an incomplete state—4 pages missing. Yes it did me good to read about the good fellows. That was a good ship because of the men in her. Yes. You do appreciate that kind of thing and that's why I seem to understand you in whatever You say.

The *Bristol Fashion* business is excellently well put. You seem ¹⁰

77

to know a lot about every part of the world and, what's more, you *can* say what you know in a most individual way. The skipper of the barque is "pris sur le vif". I've known the type. And the tongue is put out all along in a fine, effective way. More power to
15 your pen!

You have *not* sent any kind of guide book!!

An extreme weariness oppresses me. It seems as though I had seen and felt everything since the beginning of the world. I *suspect* my brain to be yeast and my backbone to be cotton. And I *know* that
20 the quality of my work is of the kind to confirm my suspicions. I would yell for help to anybody—man or devil if I could persuade myself that anybody would care—and, caring, could help. Well. No more.

Ever Yours.
25 Conrad.

PUBLICATION

This letter is unpublished.

TEXT

11 'a lot': an insertion.

COMMENTARY

5–8   Possibly Graham had sent a cutting about the loss of 'Skimmer of the Sea' and her crew of 'good fellows', to which Conrad had referred in the previous letter.

10–15   In 'Bristol Fashion', which had just been published in *SR*, LXXXV, 167–8 and 198–9 (5 and 12 Feb. 1898), and was later included in *The Ipané*, Graham gives a character-sketch of 'Honest Tom Bilson', the brutal, hypocritical and sentimental skipper of the barque 'Wilberforce', who trades on the West African coast and who punishes three native deserters by selling them to cannibals. ('"Treat a bloody nigger well if he works well; and if he kicks, why then speak English to him," was the burden of his speech.')

Graham appears to have gathered the material for this tale during a voyage made in 1875 (*AFT*, pp. 97–8). Conrad would have 'known the type' from his own experiences on the Congo in 1890.

13–14   'the tongue is put out': cf. *Mogreb-el-Acksa*, pp. 52–3, and letter 7, line 50.

16   Probably a reference to Graham's *Notes on the District of Menteith for Tourists and Others* (Black, London, 1895). See letter 12, lines 6–7.

78

12

Cher ami.

I see you don't bear malice for my delays in correspondence so
I don't apologise.

The Guide book simply *magnificent* Everlastingly good! I've
read it last night having only then returned home. During my
visit to the Cranes we talked of you and your work every day.
Stephen is a great admirer of yours. The man after all knows
something. Harold Frederic also enthused with perfect sincerity.
My opinion of them has gone up a hundred points.

Your engineer is immense! Wish I had seen him. It is good of
you to think of me when such a subject comes in your way. I never
seem to meet any one of that kind—now. I am on the shelf—I am
dusty.

Yes. We Poles are poor specimens. The strain of national worry has
weakened the moral fibre—and no wonder when you think of it. It
is not a fault; it is a misfortune. Forgive my jeremiads. I don't
repine at the nature of my inheritance but now and then it is too
heavy not to let out a groan.

I've sold my american *serial* rights of the *Rescue* for £250 to
Maclure (of New York). I get another £50 on acc/t of book rights
in the States (15% royalty)

I think—upon the whole—this is not bad. Pawling arranged it all
for me—free of charge. The worst is the book is not finished yet
and must be delivered end July at the latest. Pawling told me
they (Heinemann) are going to publish your book—the Morocco
book I understand. I wait for it anxiously.

My short tales—"Tales of Unrest"—shall appear (from Unwin's
shop) on the 25th of this month.

Well! Till next time...

Ever Yours Jph. Conrad

PS It was Harold Frederic who wrote the criticism of the *Nigger*
in the Satur: R. He affirmed to me that Runciman had cut out the
best passages. I tried to persuade him I did not care a hang—
which is true.

PUBLICATION

LL, I, 230–1.

6 'book simply *magnificent*': Aubry reads 'book is simply *magnificent*.'.
23 'I get another £50 on acc/t of': Aubry reads 'I'll get another £50 on accept. of'.

TEXT

21 In the manuscript Conrad makes two strokes to indicate the abrupt change of subject.

COMMENTARY

6 'The Guide book': Probably Graham's *Notes on the District of Menteith for Tourists and Others* (Black, London, 1895).
7–8 The visit to Stephen and Cora Crane at Ravensbrook is described in *JEC*, pp. 57–8.
10 'Harold Frederic': the novelist, critic for *SR*, agent for the *New York Times*, and friend of Crane.
12–13 Conceivably Graham had given Conrad the hint for 'An Anarchist', the study of Paul the engineer.
23 'Maclure': Samuel S. McClure, the publisher. *The Rescue* was not, however, finished until 25 May 1919 (*LL*, II, 222), and was then published in the United States (after its serialisation in *Romance* magazine) by Doubleday, Page and Co.
25 'Pawling': Sydney S. Pawling of Heinemann's.
28–9 'the Morocco book': *Mogreb-el-Acksa*, published by Heinemann in December 1898.
30–1 *Tales of Unrest* was published by Charles Scribner's Sons, New York, on 26 March 1898 (Gordan, p. 225); and by T. Fisher Unwin, London, on 4 April 1898 (*TJW*, p. 15).
34–7 The *Saturday Review* for 12 February 1898 (LXXXV, 211) had included an anonymous review of *The Nigger of the 'Narcissus'*. The reviewer had suggested that Conrad's early work suffered in comparison with Stevenson's, and might be derivative from it. He praised the description of the storm, but concluded:

'We are far from assuming plagiarism, unconscious or otherwise, and if "The Ebb Tide" had never been written, it is conceivable that Donkin might have established himself as the type [of the vicious cockney] instead [of Stevenson's Huish]. As it is, he only reminds us of somebody else. It cannot be said that the "Nigger" himself attains even that limited success. He wearies the reader from the outset, as one feels he bored and fatigued the writer.

In a word, Mr. Conrad has not realised, as yet, the importance of what is called the "human interest". There is, however, such substantial promise in Mr. Conrad's steady progress up to the present, and there is so much really fine work in this latest book, that we look with some confidence to see him strengthen himself in this weak point.'

13

Cher ami.

Only a word. I had your letter last night and am overjoyed to
learn you like the stories. I wonder if they will bring me the needed
success. I don't think so—and with mixed feelings don't know 5
whether I am pleased or sorry.

I send back the letter. *If* what the sheik said is true then it is
hard to find an excuse for the Major. The whole business seems to
have been managed in a mysteriously silly manner. I've done
better in my time but then I didn't act for a syndicate. And by the 10
bye the Sheik in saying the word " *Yahudi*" was only half wrong.
Isn't the Globe Syd^cte managed by one Sassoon?

However my criticism is impertinent since I do not know *all* the
circumstances. But it looks like a wretched fizzle.

Let me know how you get on. I am still lame. Ever Yours Conrad. 15
My wife sends her kind regards

PUBLICATION

Not published in book form, but given in *Notes and Queries*, CCX, 264
(July 1965).

COMMENTARY

1   The date. This letter was probably written on Thursday, 7 April 1898.
   It must have been written after 4 February (when Conrad, in letter 10,
   had asked for further information about the 'Tourmaline' venture) but
   before 4 June (when Graham's account of the venture began to appear
   in *SR*); therefore the 'stories' mentioned in line 4 must be *Tales of
   Unrest*, which according to *TJW*, p. 15, was issued on 4 April (in
   London). In this case letter 13 shortly precedes letter 14, in which
   Conrad refers to Graham's comments on 'Karain' (in *Tales of Unrest*);
   and letter 14 appears to have been written a few days after Graham's
   visit on 8 April. The only Thursday between 4 and 8 April fell on the 7th.
7   'the letter': an account of the 'Tourmaline' venture sent by Graham's
   French-Algerian correspondent in Mogador, and quoted in *Mogreb*,
   pp. 322–3.
7–8   The sheik was M'barek-ou-Ahmed, who had been arrested for his
   part in Spilsbury's landing, and who had claimed that Spilsbury had
   deceived him in promising the support of British troops. (*Mogreb*, pp.
   322–3.)
8–10   See letter 10, note 34–40.
11   'the Sheik.....*"Yahudi"'*: As M'barek-ou-Ahmed had been led

6   81   WCL

to captivity he had said: 'Ce sont des trompeurs les chrétiens.....;
par Dieu, ce chrétien doit être un Juif!' (*Mogreb*, p. 323.)

12   C. E. Sassoon was one of the directors of the Globe Syndicate (see
A. G. Spilsbury's *The Tourmaline Expedition*, Dent, London, 1906,
p. 171).

14

Thursday.

Cher et excellent ami.

Yesterday I hobbled out and away to London. Not hearing from
you imagined all kinds of serious things. So I called at Chester
5 Square.

The bird was flown! I thought very good! but had a suspicion you
went away too early. Your letter confirms my surmise. I thought
it wasn't a common cold you had. If I was You (or rather if You
were me) I would take it easy for a couple of weeks. It would
10 pay better in the long run.

The cutting is valuable. Do you possess Lavery's portrait of
yourself? Of Lavery I know only the *Girl in White*, but I knew he
had done some oriental things.

Don't you take it into your head you are getting old. You are
15 simply run down and strong men feel it so much more than
weaklings like me—who have felt overtasked ever since the age
of 28. True! And yet I had another ten years of sea—and did my
work too. It isn't Your body—it's your brain that is tired. The
battery wants recharging. Time, with common caution, will do that
20 My wife was very much concerned about you. Women have a
curious insight sometimes. She said to me after you left. "I am
sorry Mr Cunninghame Graham came. He ought to have been at
home. I am sure he will be ill."—I said "Oh bosh! you don't
know anything; that kind of man is never ill." I consider You
25 played a mean trick on me with your affectation of influenza. My
position as an infallible man is badly shaken at home. I never had
it elsewhere.

I am glad you like *Karain*. I was afraid you would despise it.
There's something magazine'ish about it. Eh? It was written
30 for Blackwood.

There is twilight and soft clouds and daffodils—and a great
weariness. Spring! Excellentissime—Spring? We are anually

82

lured by false hopes. Spring! Che coglioneria! Another illusion for the undoing of mankind.

Enough!   35
—Do spare yourself if not for your own sake then for the sake of the horse.

Ever Yours

Jph. Conrad

PUBLICATION

LL, I, 233–4.
1   'Thursday.': Aubry reads 'Thursday. April, 1898.'
8   'I was': 'I were'.
12–13 'knew he had': 'know he has'.
30   'Blackwood': '*Blackwood's*'.
33   'Spring! Che coglioneria! Another': 'Spring! Another'.

TEXT

14   'getting': an insertion.
19–20 'that My': *sic.*
32   'anually': *sic.*

COMMENTARY

1   The date. For the following reasons this letter may be ascribed to spring, 1898, and probably to Thursday 14 April: (*a*) the reference to *Tales of Unrest* in lines 28–30; (*b*) the reference to spring in lines 31–4; (*c*) the date of Graham's visit: note 21–3; and (*d*) the reference to lameness in line 3: cf. letter 13, line 15.

4–5   Graham's mother, Mrs A. E. Bontine, lived at 39 Chester Square, London S.W.

11–13   John Lavery (1856–1941) was an old acquaintance of Graham's, and had travelled with him to Morocco. Graham had publicised Lavery's first main exhibition, held at Lawrie's in Glasgow in 1890; and Lavery painted several portraits of him, perhaps the best-known being 'R. B. Cunninghame Graham on Pampa'. (Their friendship is described in Lavery's *The Life of a Painter*, Cassell, London, 1940, pp. 88–95.)

'A Girl in White' had been exhibited at the Goupil Gallery, London, in June 1891.

21–3   According to Jessie Conrad (*JEC*, pp. 58–9), Graham visited Ivy Walls on Good Friday 1898 (8 April).

28–30   'Karain' first appeared in *Blackwood's Magazine*, CLXII, 630–56 (Nov. 1897), and was later published in *Tales of Unrest*, April 1898.

83

15

Cher et excellent ami.

I take it for granted you are not angry with me for my silence.
Wrist bad again, baby ill, wife frightened, damned worry about my
5 work and about other things, a fit of such stupidity that I could
not think out a single sentence—excuses enough in all conscience,
since I am not the master but the slave of the peripeties and
accidents (generally beastly) of existence.

And yet I wanted badly to write, principally to say: "Je ne
10 comprends pas du tout!" I had two letters from you. The first
announced an inclosure which was not there. The next (a week
ago by the gods!) alluded no doubt to the absent enclosure and said
you corrected proof (of a sea-phrase) by wire. It being Saturday
I jumped at my N° of the S.R. making sure to see there the story
15 of the Scotch tramp on a Christmas Eve. Nix! Exasperation
followed by resignation on reflecting that unless the world came to
a sudden end I would worm out of you the secret of these letters.
I want to know! Istaghfir Allah! O! Sheik Mohammed! I take
refuge with the One the Invincible.

20

By all means V i v a l ' E s p a ñ a !!!!
I would be the first to throw up my old hat at the news of the
slightest success. It is a miserable affair whichever way you look
at it. The ruffianism on one side, an unavoidable fate on the other,
25 the impotence on both sides, though from various causes, all this
makes a melancholy and ridiculous spectacle. Will the certain issue
of that struggle awaken the Latin race to the sense of its dangerous
position? Will it be any good if they did awaken? Napoleon the
Third had that sense and it was the redeeming trait of his rule.
30 But, perhaps, the race is doomed? It would be a pity. It would
narrow life, it would destroy a whole side of it which had its morality
and was always picturesque and at times inspiring. The others
may well shout Fiat lux! It will be only the reflected light of a
silver dollar and no sanctimonious pretence will make it resemble
35 the real sunshine. I am sorry, horribly sorry. Au diable! Après
tout cela doit m'être absolument égal. But it isn't for some obscure
reason or other. Which shows my folly. Because men are "fourbes
lâches, menteurs, voleurs, cruels" and why one should show a pre-

84

ference for one manner of displaying these qualities rather than for
another passes my comprehension in my meditative moments.   40

However I need not worry about the Latin race. My own life is
difficult enough. It arises from the fact that there is nothing handy
to steal and I never could invent an effective lie—a lie that would
sell, and last, and be admirable. This state of forced virtue spreads
a tinge of fearsome melancholy over my wasted days.—But I am   45
ever Yours Conrad.

PUBLICATION

LL, I, 235–6.
   Lines 24–6 (from 'The ruffianism' to 'spectacle.') and lines 32–5 (from
   'The others' to 'sunshine.') were omitted without indication by Aubry.

COMMENTARY

4–5   'damned worry about my work': particularly with the difficulties in
        finishing *The Rescue*: cf. *EGL*, pp. 126–8.
11–15 Graham's story, 'S.S. *Atlas*', in which the New Year celebrations
        on a Scottish tramp steamer are described, did not appear in *SR* until
        a fortnight later (LXXXV, 652–3 and 676–7, 14 and 21 May 1898):
        Conrad comments on it in letter 16.
18   'O! Sheik Mohammed!': During the Moroccan journey described
        in *Mogreb-el-Acksa*, Graham had disguised himself as 'Mohammed el
        Fasi', a sheik or sherif.
21–35 Conrad's opinions of the Spanish–American war echo those of
        Graham, who was a vociferous opponent of the United States in this
        conflict. See *SR*, LXXXVI, 707 (26 Nov. 1898); LXXXIX, 138–9 (3 Feb.
        1900), 203 (17 Feb. 1900), 267–8 (3 March 1900), 332–3 (17 March 1900);
        XCII, 398–9 (28 Sept. 1901), 430–1 (5 Oct. 1901).
28–9   Cf.:
        'The war of 1870, brought about by the third Napoleon's half-
        generous, half-selfish adoption of the principle of nationalities, was
        the first war characterised by a special intensity of hate.....'
        (*Notes*, p. 105.)

16

17 May 98

Excellentissime
   Heer's Garnett's letter. I've looked in of course because he told
me I may. I've heard all this said with greater warmth of appreciation, since you have been (in your work) a subject of long dis-   5
cussions between us.

By the Gods! *Atlas* is magnificently good. Vous taillez dans le vif là dedans! My envy of your power grows with every new thing I see. I am glad—very glad the sketches are going to be collected. One will be able to live with them then. Now one hunts for them in a waste of paper and printer's ink.

I wonder how things are with you. I trust Your Wife is better by now. I would like to know.

I am still miserably unwell, working against the grain while all the time I think it's no good no good. Quelle misére!

Ever Yours Conrad

PUBLICATION
This letter is unpublished.

TEXT
3 'Heer's': *sic.*

COMMENTARY
3–6, 9–11 This letter from Edward Garnett, which is also mentioned in *EGL*, p. 129, does not appear to be among the Ardoch manuscripts. Garnett had persuaded his employer, T. Fisher Unwin, to issue a series called 'The Over-Seas Library' (partly with the intention of challenging—while exploiting—Kipling's readership); and the first volume was to be *The Ipané*, a collection of items by Graham which had previously appeared separately in *SR*, *Badminton*, and other periodicals.

In the missing letter, Garnett evidently impressed on Graham the feasibility and value of gathering the previously scattered items for the 'Over-Seas' volume; and it was sufficiently flattering to cause Graham to begin his reply, dated 18 May, as follows:

'Dear Mr Garnett,
    In times gone by (I speak of the dark ages) when a lady in Spain or South America, tried to address a compliment, à brûle pourpoint, to any one (this I have heard has been observed by travellers), the unlucky recipient, was wont, to mutter something & look foolish. What more can I do. Thanks for all you say.
    I am glad you like my stuff, for I am, & have been a man of action all my life (& like Cervantes, at some distance off, "mas versado en desdichas que en versos"), & writing came to me with grey hair.'

In appendix 4 I give the surviving leaf of a Garnett letter which closely followed the missing one, as an example of Garnett's enthusiastic literary midwifery at this period.

7 The first part of 'S.S. *Atlas*', with its account of a stormy and squalid trans-Atlantic crossing, had appeared on 14 May in *SR*, LXXXV, 652–3. The tale was later included in *The Ipané*.

86

17

Cher et excellent ami

Thanks ever so much for the book.

I have read it once so far.

The more I read you the more I admire. This is a strong word but not a bit too strong for the sensation it is supposed to describe. In your Wife's sketches I came again with delight upon the hand that had called to life the incomparable saint and the mankind of that place and time.

I and Garnett have used up most of the adjectives we know in talking you over yesterday. He has sent me the *Bloody Niggers* and the Labour Leader. Très bien!!

You are the perfection of scorn—not vulgar scorn mind, not scorn that would fit any utterance No! Scorn that is clear in the thought and lurks in the phrase. The philosophy of unutterable scorn.

Ah! Amigo de mi corazon (is that right?) you may fling contempt and bitterness, and wit and hard wisdom, hard unpractical wisdom, at this world and the next—l'ignoble boule roulera toujours portant des êtres infimes et méchants dans un univers qui ne se comprends pas lui-même.

I put first (of yours) *Horses* then *Father Arch*—or bracket them. But I like every line of the others. Of your Wife's *The Will* is a perfect little thing and Yuste—Batuecas and Plasencia are pictures of a rare charm. They breathe like things of life seen in a dream.

Ever Yours Jph Conrad.

P.S. You are the most *undemocratic* of men. By what perversion of sentiment vous vous êtes fourré dans une galère qui n'arrivera nulle part? Du reste ça importe peu. The truth of your personality is visible, would be visible anywhere.

P.P.S. No. The *Vanishing Race* decidedly is first in my affection.

P.P.P.S. I have also received *Badminton* with the most interesting Bolas You are good to let me have all you publish. Continuez. Yahudi seems greatly impressed by you. Just like his cheek.

PUBLICATION

LL, I, 239–40.

28 'vous vous êtes': Aubry reads '*vous êtes-vous*'.

32–4 These lines were omitted by Aubry.

COMMENTARY

3 'the book': *Father Archangel of Scotland, and Other Essays*, by G. and R. B. Cunninghame Graham (Black, London, 1896). Letter 16, lines 9–11, had probably indicated to Graham that Conrad was unaware of this early collection of sketches.

8 'the incomparable saint': Santa Teresa.

11 'the *Bloody Niggers*': Graham's essay 'Bloody Niggers' had been published in the *Social-Democrat* (London), I, 104–9 (April 1897). It was selected by Graham and Garnett for *The Ipané*, in which it re-appeared under the title 'Niggers'. Garnett said of it later:
'The immortal "Niggers".....and its fellow sketch "Success" stamp him, in W. H. Hudson's words, as "Singularísimo Escritor Inglés," the most singular of English writers, and they would confer immortality on him if he had written nothing more.' (Introduction to Graham's *Thirty Tales and Sketches*, 1929, p. v.)

12 'the Labour Leader': The most recent of Graham's occasional contributions to Keir Hardie's journal had been 'Castles in the Air' (10th year, p. 148; 30 April 1898).

22 '*Horses*': i.e. 'The Horses of the Pampas', first published in *Time: A Monthly Magazine* (London), N.S. I, 370–8 (1 April 1890); later in *Living Age* (Boston, Mass.), CLXXXV, 823–4 (28 June 1890); and afterwards in *Father Archangel of Scotland*.

22 '*Father Arch*': 'Father Archangel of Scotland', first published in the *Nineteenth Century* (London), XXXIV, 384–98 (Sept. 1893); and afterwards in the collection to which it gives the name.

23–5 *Father Archangel* contains four tales by Mrs Cunninghame Graham: 'A Will', 'Yuste', 'The Batuecas', and 'La Vera de Plasencia'.

31 'A Vanishing Race' was the ninth sketch in *Father Archangel*.

32–3 'The Bolas' was first published in *Badminton Magazine*, VI, 633–41 (June 1898), and was later included in *The Ipané*.

34 'Yahudi': apparently a sarcastic reference to T. Fisher Unwin: cf. letter 21, lines 14–19.

18

15 June 1898

Cher et excellent ami.

I need not tell you how delighted I am with your declaration of friendly purposes. Please tell the kind Author of Sta Theresa
5 that we both are waiting impatiently for the day when we shall have

the honour and the pleasure of seeing her in our camping place in the wilds of Essex.

This is the kindest and the most friendly thing that has been done to me for many years and I hope you will persevere in your charitable and rash intention.

Yes. B. N. is or are good—very good, very telling; in fact they tell one all about you. And the more one is told the more one wants to hear more. Mais—cher ami—ne Vous eparpillez pas trop. Vos pensées courent de par le monde comme des chevaliers errants, tandis qu'il faudrait les tenir en main, les assembler, en faire une phalange penetrante et solide—peut être victorieuse—qui sait?— Peut-être——

Et puis—pourquoi prêchez Vous au convertis? Mais je deviens stupide. Il n y a pas des convertis aux idées de l'honneur, de la justice, de la pitié, de la liberté. Il n y a que des gens qui sans savoir, sans comprendre, sans sentir s'extasient sur les mots, les repètent, les crient, s'imaginent y croire—sans croire a autre chose qu'au gain, a l'avantage personel, a la vanité satisfaite. Et les mots s'envolent; et il ne reste rien, entendez vous? Absolument rien, oh homme de foi! Rien. Un moment, un clin d'œil et il ne reste rien—qu'une goutte de boue, de boue froide, de boue morte lancée dans l'éspace noir, tournoyant autour d'un soleil éteint. Rien. Ni pensée, ni son, ni âme. Rien.

Jess sends her best regards. I am ever Yours Jph Conrad.

P.S. Mes devoirs a Madame Votre Femme et mes remerciments.

PUBLICATION
This letter is unpublished.

COMMENTARY
11 'B. N.': i.e. Graham's essay 'Bloody Niggers' (*Social-Democrat*, I, 104–9), which Conrad had received from Garnett a few days before (see letter 17, line 11).
Graham's celebrated and savage attack on British imperialism concluded:
'So many rapes and robberies, hangings and murders, blowings up in caves, pounding to jelly with our Maxim guns, such sympathy for Crete, such coyness to express our opinion on our doings in Matabeleland; our clergy all dumb dogs, our politicians dazed about Armenia; "land better liked than niggers", "stern justice meted out" —can England be a vast and seething mushroom bed of base hypocrisy, and our own God, Jahve Sabbaoth, an anthropomorphous fool?' (P. 109.)

The quotation may indicate the aptness of Conrad's censures. The passion of the article, and the range of reference, seem ill-controlled; the constructions suggest that it was written in haste; and the ironies soon lapse into outbursts of spleen. Nevertheless this piece, unlike most of his polemical essays, was republished several times (under the title 'Niggers', in *The Ipané*, *Thirty Tales and Sketches*, and *Rodeo*).

Graham seems to have noted Conrad's criticisms, because he made uncharacteristically large excisions and alterations to this article before it was republished: the digressions and topical references were curtailed. Garnett had also been initially critical of it: he told Graham that 'the core of it, the blasphemy against the Stupidities might damage all the other Sketches with those who do not understand—i e—with Everybody.

It is too good to retouch, but if you do, I should like to look at it again.' (Letter dated 23 June 1898.)

In another letter, Garnett approved the revised version:

'I sat down & read Niggers when it came, & was so ravished that the folly of criticism passed leagues away.....Formerly you *remained* on the spot, after an outburst, defying the Anglo-Saxon world, with your best card played. But *now* you have *struck* & vanished!' (9 August 1898.)

23–8   Cf. letter 7, lines 50–77. Conrad's linkage of a pessimistic view of human nature with the thermodynamist's view of a cooling, dying earth (which perhaps recalls section 11 of Wells's *The Time Machine*) has the characteristically defensive implication that *all* attempts at reform are ultimately futile. The 'public' Conrad could write, however,

'Many a man has heard or read and believes that the earth goes round the sun; one small blob of mud among several others, spinning ridiculously with a waggling motion like a top about to fall. This is the Copernican system.....But while watching a sunset he sheds his belief; he sees the sun as a small and useful object, the servant of his needs and the witness of his ascending effort,.....and then he holds the system of Ptolemy.' ('The Ascending Effort', 1910, in *Notes*, pp. 73–4.)

19

Saturday.

Très illustre Seigneur.

I write at once because to morrow is Sunday et dans le village arriéré where you sojourn now there is no postal delivery to morrow.

5   Pourquoi-pas? It is a jolly good idea for the play. Of that particular bit of history (and of every other) I have but the slightest, the haziest idea. In the way of writing I *do not* see Your limitations. Revez la dessus, and something very good may come out of it. You are as romantic as the rest of us. Nous sommes tous dans cette

galère. The thing is—the expression. Now as to that I have no ¹⁰
doubt. You'll find it for the simple reason it is in you. Il s'agit
de fouiller au plus profond and You will reach the vein. I am only
afraid You would make it too good—much too good for scenic
success. The gods are stupid. You'll not be conventional enough,
for them to understand you.   ¹⁵

These are brave oaths! Ils me mettent du cœur au ventre. I shall
write to you re Sir F. E when I hear. It occurs to me however that
it may not happen for a long time—may never happen! Quien
sabe? La plus belle fille du monde ne peut donner que ce qu'elle a.
You know this proverb? Therefore if before you return to your ²⁰
native wilds you come across the Donald creature just whisper
softly into his ear. I've served in so many Scotch ships (from the
Duke of Sutherland to the Highland Forest—the list is too long)
that I imagine myself to possess some sort of claim. A word from
Sir Donald would go a long way with any firm north of the Tweed. ²⁵
Let the big-wigs compete for the honour of employing the immortal author of—of—I forgot now.

I conclude from your letter I shan't see you here this time.
Tans pis. Let me know when you are passing through London on
your way to Morrocco. Veuillez presenter mes très respectueux ³⁰
devoirs a Madame Votre Femme. Ever Yours Jph. Conrad.

Boris is better. I find it difficult yet to forgive him for preventing
your visit here. On ne rattrappe l'occasion qui passe, qui est passée!

PUBLICATION

LL, I, 242–3.
1   'Saturday.': Aubry reads 'Saturday, July 1898.'
17   'It occurs': 'It seems'.
33   'On ne rattrappe l'occasion': 'On ne rattrape pas l'occasion'.

TEXT

27   'forgot': *sic.*
29   'Tans pis': *sic.*
30   'Morrocco': *sic.*

COMMENTARY

1   The date. This letter was probably written after 15 June and before
     15 July 1898, because of the reference in lines 32–3 (cf. letter 18,
     lines 4–7), the reference to Sir Francis Evans in line 17 (cf. letter 20,
     line 5), and the visit mentioned in note 3–4. Saturdays during this period
     fell on 18 and 25 June, and 1 and 8 July.

3–4   Aubry noted: 'Graham was then in Scotland'; but in view of lines 20–1 and 28–30 it looks more likely that Graham was then in London and was about to return to Scotland. 'Le village arriéré' could well be an ironic reference to London, for in London in 1898 there was no postal delivery on Sundays, whereas most provincial towns in England and a few in Scotland still had Sunday deliveries. Letterheads on Graham's letters to Garnett prove that he was in London in July but in Scotland in August; and on 15 July Conrad succeeded in visiting Graham at 28 Margaret Street, W. 1 (Graham to Garnett, 16 July 1898).

5–15   I have found no trace of a play written by Graham, though he did translate Rusiñol's *La Verge del Mar*. This play, in Graham's translation (*The Madonna of the Sea*), was produced at the Maddermarket Theatre, Norwich, from 31 January to 8 February 1958.

16   'These are brave oaths!': cf.:

   'Cunng-m Graham is very unhappy.....He got into his head to get me the command of a steamer or ship and swears he will do it.' (*EGL*, p. 135.)

   'Conrad cannot get a ship. Let us make an Argo & sail to Colchis (Hell).' (Graham to Garnett, 3 Aug. 1898.)

17   'Sir F. E': Sir Francis Evans of the Union Line. Cf. letter 20, lines 5–17.

21   'the Donald creature': Sir Donald Currie of the Castle Line. Cf. letter 23, lines 3–7.

22–3   'The Duke of Sutherland' was a wool clipper, plying between London and Sydney, on which Conrad served from 12 October 1878 to 19 October 1879 (Register of the crew).

23   'The Highland Forest' was a sailing ship on which Conrad served as first mate from 16 February 1887 to 1 July 1887 (Register of the crew).

29–30   Graham set out for Morocco on 8 September (Graham to Garnett, 27 Aug. 1898).

20

19 July 1898

Cher ami.

Thanks for Cyrano. I haven't yet read it but shall do so before the sun rises again.

5   I've seen Sir Francis Evans this morning. He was full of business with twenty people waiting for an interview, but he received me at once and was kindness itself. The upshot of it is this: It is of course impossible to place me in the Union Line—I said I did not even dream of such a thing but explained that I thought he
10   might have some tramp or good collier. The Company he said owns no tramps or colliers but he might hear of something of the

kind and in such a case would let me know."—He has my card
but my address is not on it. Perhaps you would drop him a line
pour l'entretenir dans la bonne voie and mention where I live.—
He said he would be "extremely pleased to do anything for a 15
friend of Mr Cunninghame Graham". Thereupon I salaamed
myself out and another man rushed in.

Something may come of it. In any case many thanks. Since you
have begun that trouble yourself I feel less compunction in asking
you to keep it up when an opportunity offers. Now some shadow 20
of possibility to go to sea has been thus presented to me I am almost
frantic with the longing to get away. Absurd!
I return Don Jaime's letter. It *is* amusing. The glimpse into the
"cuisine" of criticism is very entertaining. I would expect anything
from a man like Traill. C'est une vieille ganache. He wrote once a 25
book about Flaubert for which he deserves to be disembowelled and
flung to die on a garbage-heap. Who's Watt? And why is he
inimical to the Ingenious Hidalgo, as presented by Don Jaime?
Moi je suis naïf et je ne comprends pas. Enough of this twaddle.
Ever Yours Conrad. 30
Mes devoirs a Madame Votre Femme. Jess who sends her kind
regards is as anxious for the sea as I am. She is very touched by
Your references to Borys, in your letters, and full of gratitude for
your efforts on my behalf.

PUBLICATION

LL, I, 241–2.

COMMENTARY

3–4 A translation (by G. Thomas and M. F. Guillenard) of Rostand's
   Cyrano de Bergerac had been published by Heinemann, London, in
   July 1898 (*ECB*).
5–22 See letter 19, lines 16–27.
23 'Don Jaime': i.e. James Fitzmaurice Kelly (1857–1923), the author,
   translator, Spanish scholar and critic. His work received favourable
   publicity from Graham in several periodicals. Thus in *SR*, LXXXIII,
   445–6 (24 April 1897) Graham praised his edition of Shelton's translation of *Don Quixote*, and elsewhere he praised de Rojas' *La Celestina*,
   introduced by Kelly (*SR*, LXXXIV, 116–17 and 144–5, 31 July and
   7 Aug. 1897), another edition by Kelly of *Don Quixote* (*Daily Chronicle*,
   6 Sept. 1898, p. 3, and 17 Oct. 1899, p. 3), and Kelly's *A History of
   Spanish Literature* (*SR*, LXXXVI, 417–18, 24 Sept. 1898).
25 'Traill': H. D. Traill (1842–1900), journalist, critic and biographer;

and incidentally the author of a ballad called 'A Degraded Artisan' (reprinted from *SR* in Traill's *Saturday Songs*, Allen, London, 1890, pp. 108–10) which had satirised Graham's claim that 'the English Workmen are degraded by the pipe, the Bible, beer, and admiration for the upper classes'.

25–7 I have been unable to trace any book on Flaubert by H. D. Traill. Perhaps Conrad here confuses Traill with J. C. Tarver, author of *Gustave Flaubert as seen in his Works and Correspondence* (Constable, London, 1895): cf. Conrad's reference to 'the "Flaubert" Tarver' in *EGL*, p. 228.

27 'Who's Watt?': Henry E. Watts (1826–1904), Kelly's rival in the field of Hispanic and particularly Cervantic studies.

27–9 On 26 February 1898 *Literature* (London), then edited by Traill, had published a letter by H. E. Watts in which a detailed attack was made on Kelly's projected new edition of *Don Quixote*: among other points, Watts claimed that Kelly's nationality alone made it unlikely that he could 'purify' the text of a Spanish work (II, 237–8). Graham, in his eventual favourable review of his friend's edition, criticised at length each of Watts's arguments (see *Daily Chronicle*, 6 Sept. 1898, p. 3). Clearly Graham had just told Conrad of this developing controversy.

21

Saturday
30th July
98

Très cher ami.

5 This morning I had the Aurora from Smithers *N°2* of the 500 copies.

C'est, tout simplement, magnifique yet I do not exactly perceive what on earth they have been making a fuss about.

I am afraid Henley is a horrible bourgeois. Who drew the frontispiece? I can't imagine anybody whose name I know. Is it an
10 English drawing? It does not look like it. I notice variations in the text as I've read it in the typewritten copy. This seems the most finished piece of work you've ever done. Il y a une note, une resonnance là dedans, vibrant de ligne en ligne. C'est très fort. No one will see it. I had a note from Fisher Unwin written evidently for
15 the purpose to inform me that he had met "Our Mutual Friend (!) Mr Cunninghame Graham at Wilfrid's Blunt."

Quel toupet! As long as such a man exists I *will not* admit equality, fraternity—as to liberty vous et moi nous savons bien a quoi nous en tenir. I've read the little book three times this morning—and
20 behold! I am disgusted with what I write. No matter.

Blackwoods magazine for this month has an appreciation of FM. Kelly's edition of Don Quixote. Very fair. Nothing striking but distinct recognition.

I do like the attitude of the *Maga* on the Spanish business.

If one could set the States and Germany by the ears! That would be *real fine*. I am afraid however that the thieves shall agree in the Philipines. The pity of it!

Viva l'España! Anyhow.

Do you believe in a speedy peace. Write me all you know. I would like to see the thing over and done with tho' mind I think that Spain is perfectly invulnerable now and may keep the yanks capering around for an indefinite time.

When do you start for Morocco?

I've been seedy—in my head—in my idiotic cabeza. I feel lazy (always did) and sleepy. When I've written a page I feel it ought to be sold to the ten-cent paper man in New York. It's all it's good for.

C'est Zolaesque ce que je viens d'écrire Hein? But look at the circumlocutions. If you want to know how I exactly feel to my work put the above into plain Zola language and it will give you a faint idea then. ————————————

Assez. Toujours le votre

JConrad.

Mes devoirs a Madame Votre Femme.

PUBLICATION

LL, I, 243–4. Aubry omitted lines 14–19 (from 'I had' to 'tenir.') and lines 25–7 (from 'If one' to 'of it!'). The latter omitted passage has been published in *EKH*, p. 167.
39 'to my work': Aubry reads 'towards my work'.

TEXT

2 '30th': written upon '20th'.
13–14 (from 'C'est' to 'see it.'): Conrad has apparently emphasised these two sentences by means of a vertical stroke in each margin beside them.
16 'Wilfrid's Blunt': *sic*.

COMMENTARY

5 'the Aurora': Graham's *Aurora la Cujiñi: A Realistic Sketch in Seville*, published in a limited edition of 500 copies by Leonard Smithers, London, 1898. (August 1898, according to *ECB*.)

6–8   Cf. Edward Garnett's letter to Graham, dated 26 August 1898:
'Only an "impression" you will say [of *Aurora*]. Yes, but something
that transfers the intoxication *to us*: you infect us with the snaky
poison of that woman, the delicious madness. Admirably seen,
admirably felt, admirably described! amigo: for the strange emotion
works in us too, & that is why the great lords of literaryism, the
Henleys & Whatnots (so Conrad told me) looked askance on your
cunning pages: it was because *Aurora* is so successful that these Over-
lords looked round saying "Lord a mussy where *am* I?" This *must*
"be pernicious because I really *feel*!"
Oh what idiocy! Roughly speaking the Anglo-Saxon nature con-
demns all feeling not conducive to its dry salter's code of preserved
virtue!' (ASA.)
W. E. Henley (1849–1903) was the editor of the *New Review*.

8–10   The last paragraph of the tale seems to refer to this frontispiece,
a lithograph of a Spanish dancer.

10–12   Unlike much of Graham's work, this piece does give the impression of having been revised and corrected. The fact that Conrad
had read the typescript may account for this care, and is a reminder
of the intimacy in literary matters which the two men had reached
within twelve months of the beginning of their correspondence.

14–19   Conrad's sympathy with Garnett (who worked reluctantly for
Fisher Unwin and was eventually sacked by him) must have increased
his contempt for Unwin: cf. the contrast drawn in *The Inheritors*
(chapter 5) between the mercenary publisher Polehampton and his
conscientious reader Lea.
In a letter to Garnett, dated 8 July 1898, Graham wrote:
'Yes, I have seen Mr Unwin, thank you.
He knew me in "the glorious days when we (FU & I) stood shoulder
to shoulder together on public platforms to support the sacred
cause of Liberty".
I have had a Turkish Bath.
Do you think he can be right?.....
It appears that Mr F. Unwin has published once a most curious
book for Hudson, "The Chrystal Age". He regrets that it was a
"pecuniary" loss to him, & he pursed up his lips as he spoke.....'

16   'Wilfrid's Blunt': Wilfrid Scawen Blunt (1840–1922), the traveller,
diplomat, political agitator, diarist and poet, was an acquaintance and
correspondent of Graham's. On 23 July, Graham and Fisher Unwin
had been among his guests at the annual Arab stud sale at Crabbett Park.
Graham, but for his Scottish birth, would probably have joined
Blunt in Shaw's category of
'the free-thinking English gentlemen-republicans of the last half of
the   nineteenth   century.....Dilke,   Burton,   Auberon   Herbert,
Wilfrid   Scawen   Blunt,   Laurence   Oliphant: great   globe-trotters,
writers, *frondeurs*, brilliant and accomplished cosmopolitans so far
as their various abilities permitted, all more interested in the world
than in themselves, and in themselves than in official decorations;

96

consequently unpurchasable, their price being too high for any modern commercial Government to pay.' (G. B. Shaw, *Pen Portraits and Reviews*, Constable, London, 1949, p. 129.)

Graham's obituary essay on Blunt was published in *English Review*, xxxv, 486–92 (Dec. 1922).

17–18 'I *will not* admit equality, fraternity': cf. the ironic General of 'Gaspar Ruiz':

"'I've always believed in the equality of men; and as to their brotherhood, that, to my mind, is even more certain. Look at the fierce animosity they display in their differences. And what in the world do you know that is more bitterly fierce than brothers' quarrels?"' (*A Set of Six*, Dent, 1923, p. 26.)

18 'as to liberty.....': cf. the remarks on man's essential slavery in letter 9, lines 24–38.

21–3 Conrad is referring to the August number of *Blackwood's Magazine* (not the July number, as the date of this letter might suggest). In vol. CLXIV, pp. 274–82, an anonymous critic reviewed and praised the edition by J. Fitzmaurice Kelly and J. Ormsby of *Don Quixote* (Nutt, London, 1898), and criticised H. E. Watts for objecting to the project. Conrad brought this review to Graham's notice because he knew that Graham was already aware of Watts's attack on the work of his friend (see letter 20, note 27–9). Graham's own review of this edition (in the *Daily Chronicle*, 6 Sept. 1898, p. 3) was to express the same general opinions as the *Blackwood's Magazine* reviewer, who had claimed that 'in literature, as in science, there is no Chauvinism'.

24 Conrad is probably referring to the political article which followed the review of *Don Quixote*. In July, *Blackwood's Magazine* had published no comment on the Spanish–American war; but in August (CLXIV, 283–9: 'The Looker-on'), the political commentator made a dispassionate and partly ironic survey of it, his main points being:

(*a*) The Americans had glorified the war; yet it was a rather tawdry series of minor engagements.

(*b*) At the outset, most English papers had urged Spain to sacrifice one or two colonies 'as a cheap means of peace'. But

'now we have lately heard a great deal of the possibility, the not-unlikelihood, of a great European coalition to redistribute the colonial possessions of Great Britain.....*At what point* would the beautifully accurate reasoning addressed to Spain be our own guide to giving in?'

(*c*) The Americans had originally claimed that they were helping the rebels to attain independence, but now they claimed that the rebels were mere cut-throats: so that in Cuba and Manila

'there is a considerable likelihood that.....the Americans will have to deal not with a population grateful to its liberators, but with a malcontent people well practised in rebellion who think themselves tricked into a change of masters'.

(*d*) Therefore the war which had revealed the United States as a new imperialist power might well result in increased sympathy for Spain from other countries.

25–32   See letter 15, lines 21–35 and note. On 3 August Graham wrote to
        Garnett:
            'Eheu Hispania. The "Yank" has prevailed, but cannot wipe out
            Velasquez, the Celestina, & the "restos de antiguo esplendor".'
27   'The pity of it!': *Othello*, IV, i.
33   Graham was in Morocco in October (*LL*, I, 250–1).
34   'cabeza': (Sp.) 'head'.
38   In February, a critic of *The Nigger of the 'Narcissus'* had compared
        Conrad with Zola (*Illustrated London News*, CXII, 172, 5 Feb. 1898).
        Graham, too, was later compared with Zola: a reviewer of *Mogreb-
        el-Acksa* said that 'the coarse strength and absence of restraint are purely
        Zolaesque' (*Daily Chronicle*, 14 Jan. 1899, p. 3.)

22

Stanford-le-Hope
Essex
2ᵈ Augˢᵗ 1898

Très cher ami.

5   Indeed I do understand, and though I do not want to say much
I wish you to know that I feel the pain of your defeat with an
intimate comprehension. I know you well enough to be certain that
the fight was a good fight. It is a satisfaction but not a consolation
—not to me at least tho' it may be to you. When one responds
10 with such depth as one has to a friend's trouble it is difficult to
delude oneself as to the brutality of facts. The end is seen—
nothing else. He who strove has the memories of blows struck—of
hopes—of sensations. I have only the knowledge of the catastrophe
—as unexpected as a stab in the dark.

15   It is good of you to think of my miserable affairs.—When one
hears news of that kind the natural selfishness leaps out and the
first pain is the pain of perceiving how useless one is. And there
is humiliation in this finding out that all one's friendship goodwill,
affection that seemed so strong, so far reaching are powerless to
20 ward off the slightest pain or the greatest misfortune, are as
though they had not been!

I did not intend to disregard your wishes but indeed I understand too well to be altogether silent.

Ever Yours

Jph Conrad

Mes hommages très respectueux a Madame Votre Femme.
Jess sends her Kind regards.

PUBLICATION
This letter is unpublished.

COMMENTARY

5–23   Since his father's death in 1889, Graham had been struggling to
redeem the debt on the family estate of Gartmore in Perthshire.
   '"I, who am none of these things, was farmer, land agent, business
   man," he told me once, "and my wife kept the estate books."' (S. L.
   Bensusan: 'Don Roberto', *Quarterly Review*, April 1938, p. 298.)
At the beginning of August 1898 Graham felt obliged to give up the
struggle; and he wrote to Garnett on 17 August:
   'To a nature like mine, capitulation is the one hard thing to
   bear.....After 30 years of fighting & at 45, to get a kind word as
   from you & Conrad is a new experience, & it I think affects me, as
   if a man were to kiss a whore on the mouth & to say he loved her,
   apart from whoredom.'
On the 27th, however, he was able to tell Garnett:
   'There is again hope re Gartmore, for I have been able to find
   the money for a large bond (just shifted) & if I can hold on a bit,
   things will come right.'
This merely postponed the inevitable: on 17 August 1900 he told
Dr McIntyre:
   'No, not only is there *no* chance of things getting better, but,
   not only here but on every estate in Scotland they must get worse.
     It stands to reason, that with increased taxation & rates & in-
   creased standards of living (amongst farmers, which is right), &
   with labour scarce, dear, & bad, & the decreasing purchasing power
   of money, that it must be so.
     If I do not get out now, I shall never get out.' (MS. 6519, NLS.)
By the end of that year Gartmore was auctioned: it was bought by
Sir Charles Cayser. Graham retained the estate of Ardoch in Dunbartonshire.
   Graham's melancholy at leaving his ancestral home is expressed in
his sketch 'A Braw Day' (first published in the *English Review*, IX,
609–14, Nov. 1911; later included in *Charity*, 1912), in which, with
understandable self-indulgence, he adopts the consoling clichés offered
by Conrad in letter 22.
   'The fight had gone against them; but still they had the recollection
   of the struggle, for all except the baser sort of men fight not to win,
   but simply for the fight.' (*Charity*, p. 138.)

23

Excellent Ami.

Thanks for letter with communication from Sir Donald.

It is sound advice but does not meet the case. If I wanted to
5 do what he advises I would hunt up some of my old skippers. That
however I can't do. It would be giving up everything to begin
life for the third time and I am not young enough for that. Do not
worry about that affair. If I thought that in the midst of your
troubles my silly desire to get out to sea added to your occupations
10 my conscience wouldn't let me sleep.

Je suis triste a crever. I think of you preparing your capitulation
with fate et j'ai le cœur gros. Fourteen years! How much that
means in the past—and for the future too—since this fight must
have grown and taken root in your life.
15 Toujours a vous de cœur
Jph Conrad.

Jess sends her best regards. She understands enough to be very
sorry. Write only when you have time. Could I do anything in the
way of reading the proofs for you?

PUBLICATION

LL, I, 244.
3 'communication': Aubry reads 'commission'.

COMMENTARY

3 'Sir Donald': Sir Donald Currie: cf. letter 19, line 21.
11–14 A continuation of the commiseration in letter 22 with Graham's
decision to sell Gartmore.
19 'the proofs': probably of *Mogreb-el-Acksa*. In the event Conrad
corrected 'Higginson's Dream' but not *Mogreb*.

24

26th Aug 98.

Cher et bon.

I return the pages *To Wayfaring Men*.

I read them before I read your letter and I have been deeply
5 touched. I think I can understand the mood from which the thing

flowed. And if I can't understand your mood—which is probable—
I can understand my own emotion at the reading of these pages—a
silly thing for which you should disclaim resposibility because
your words are meant for better men.

Ah! The lone tree on the horizon and then bear a little—(a very
little) to the right. Haven't we all ridden with such directions to
find no house but many curs barking at our heels. Can't miss it?
Well perhaps we can't. And we don't ride with a stouter heart for
that. Indeed my friend there is a joy in being lost, but a sorrow
in being weary.

I don't know whether it is because I know too much—but there
seems to me to be a deeper note in this preface than in any of your
writings I've seen. But what business have you O! Man! coming
with your uncomprehended truth—a thing less than mist but
black—to make me sniff at—the stink of the lamp.

Ride on to the tree and to the right—for verily there is a devil
at the end of every road. Let us pray to the potbellied gods, to
gods with more legs than a centipede and more arms than a dozen
windmills, let us pray to them to guard us from the mischance of
arriving somewhere. As long as we don't pray to the gods made in
man's image we are sure of a most glorious perdition.

Don't know tho'. I wouldn't give two pence for all its glory—
and I would pray to a god made like a man in the City—and do
you know for what? For a little forgetfulness. Say half an hour.
Oh bliss. I would give him my soul for it and he would be cheated.
To be cheated is godlike. It is your devil who makes good bargains,
legends notwithstanding.

Meantime let us look at Soheil and reflect that it is a speck in the
eternal night even as we are. Only we don't shine. At least some
of us don't. We are as celestial as the other bodies—only we are
obscure. At least some of us are. But we all have our illusion of
being wayfarers. No more than Soheil, Amigo! The appointed
course must be run. Round to the left or round to the right what
matters if it is a circle. Ask Soheil. And if you get an answer I shall
with my own hands give you a piece of the moon.

Ever Yours

J. Conrad.

I've got your short note. Thanks for sending on my papers. Look
here! Shorter of the Ill. Lond. News who bought *Rescue* from
McClure suddenly decided to put it into the last quarter of the

News. Begins in Oct^{er}! I thought I had months before me and am caught. The worst is I had advances from McClure. So I must write or burst. It is too awful. Half the book is not written and I have only to 1st Nov^{er} to finish it! I could not take a command till December because I am in honour bound to furnish the story to time. Yet to get to sea would be salvation. I am really in a deplorable state, mentally. I feel utterly wretched. I haven't the courage to tackle my work.

PUBLICATION

LL, I, 244–6.
22 'potbellied': Aubry reads 'poor bellied'.
27 'tho'. I': 'tho' I'.
35 'don't. We': 'don't. But we'.

TEXT

4 'them': apparently written upon 'these'.
6 'your mood': an insertion.
8 After 'thing', the inserted word 'for' replaces the cancelled word 'with'.
8 'resposibility': *sic*.

COMMENTARY

3 'To Wayfaring Men' was to be the preface to Graham's *Mogreb-el-Acksa*, which was published in December 1898.
3–40 The body of this letter is an errant commentary on, and criticism of, Graham's preface.

'To Wayfaring Men' is addressed to 'you who, like myself, have crossed, or even now are crossing, desert or pampa in the night; riding towards Capella, if in the southern hemisphere (Sohail in Africa), keeping the wind a little blowing on your right cheek.....' (*Mogreb*, p. vii). Graham explains that his book contains little to interest those who look for 'theory of empires', but deals with such matter as 'lonely rides,.....simple folk who pray to Allah seven times a day, and act as if they never prayed at all;.....[and] men who never bother much to think, but chiefly act' (p. ix); and he concludes that in the account of his travels, so different from those made by men 'who thundered through the land, Bible and gun in hand,.....confident that the one way to win a "nigger's" heart "is to speak English to him," and doing so even at the rifle's mouth', travellers may recognise their own journey through life,

'making it as they do in general on horses hipshot, lean and saddle-galled, asking their way from those they meet, who answer them as wise as they, "Ride on to the lone tree on the horizon, then bear a little to the right, and if you keep the line, you cannot miss the houses, for the barking of the dogs will guide you, if it falls dark."

And then comes evening, and the travellers still kicking at their horses' sides, straining their eyes, keep pushing forward, stumbling and objurgating on the trail.' (Pp. x–xi.)

Conrad caps this sentimentally pessimistic view of life with the characteristic observations in line 36–40: Even the thought that we are wayfarers is but a consoling illusion, for it implies a measure of freedom; whereas, like the star Sohail (Canopus), all our progress is determined by causes which we cannot control.

39–40 The motto on the title-page of *Mogreb* is the Arab proverb 'Show me Sohail and I will show you the moon'.

44 'Shorter': Clement Shorter, editor of the *Illustrated London News*.

45 'McClure': Samuel S. McClure of McClure, Phillips & Co., New York.

44–9 Cf. *LL*, I, 247. *The Rescue* was not serialised until 1919 (in *Land and Water*: 30 Jan.–31 July).

25

27 Aug 1898

Cher et excellentissime.

I have been thinking of You every day and more than once a day.

Garnett just left. He showed me your preface to the Fisher Unwin's volume of Your sketches. We howled with satisfaction 5 over it. Vous étes tout a fait unique et inimitable.

He read *Aurora* here. He thinks it is simply great. On the other hand he abused you bitterly for spoiling the effects of *Victory*. As he said he had written to you about it I shan't repeat his criticism. Moreover I dissent. 10

Sometimes I feel deeply distressed. At times a little angry. But I think and think—et la terre tourne. How long O Lord! How long?

If this miserable planet had perception a soul, a heart, it would burst with indignation or fly to pieces from sheer pity.

I am making desperate efforts to write something. Why the 15 devil did I ever begin. Que tonteria!

I am writing coglionerie while I don't know how the Teufel I am going to live next month. The very sea breeze has an execrable taste. Assez.

Ever Yours 20
Jph. Conrad.

Mes devoirs très respectueux a Madame Votre Femme. Jess sends her kind regards.

Can't understand Rimbaud at all. You overrate my intelligence.
25 Je ne suis bon qu'a lire Cyrano and such like coglionerie. That's
what I am fit for only since I am no longer fit to carry sacks of
wheat in a hold. I wish you would come to shoot me.

PUBLICATION

LL, I, 246.

COMMENTARY

4–7 Edward Garnett wrote to Graham on 26 August, praising the
preface to the projected volume *The Ipané* (which begins thus: 'None
of the following sketches and stories have the least connection with one
another.....'), as well as the tale *Aurora la Cujiñi*.

> 'I find your Preface admirable. It is your touch spirit attitude, it is
> admirably to the point; it is the living *you* in a page.....
>
> At Conrad's the other day I read your *Aurora la Cujiñi*. *It is one of
> the finest things you have done,* & certainly the richest in colour. Only
> an "impression" you will say. Yes, but something that transfers the
> intoxication *to us*.....'

Conrad's opinion of this tale is given in letter 21, lines 6–20.

7–10 'Victory' was published in the volume *Thirteen Stories* by Heinemann in September 1900. Garnett's criticisms can be inferred from
Graham's reply, dated 28 July 1898:

> 'Querido Amigo y Critico.
>
> Yes, I think you are right, & I told you that I should spoil the thing.
>
> But, I do not agree that the Spaniard should have been introduced
> first.
>
> 1. He & his daughter were aliens in Paris & to introduce them first
> would have made passengers of them—result inartistic.
>
> 2. I wanted a heavy background, & I think if I had put them in first,
> that they would have "gone into" the background, as painters say.
> Again I am not a story teller, but an impressionist, & if I kept to the
> story & cut out my digressions & impressions nothing would be left.'

16 'Que tonteria!': (Sp.). 'What stupidity!'

17 'coglionerie': (Ital.) 'nonsense'.

24 'Rimbaud': cf. Blackburn, p. 46: 'I happen to know Rimbaud's
verses'—Conrad having just praised Charles Whibley's essay on
Rimbaud, 'A Vagabond Poet' (*Blackwood's Magazine*, CLXV, 402–12;
Feb. 1899).

25 'Cyrano': cf. letter 20, note 3–4.

26

Pent Farm.
Stanford near Hythe.
9th Nov 98

Très cher et excellent ami.

I only got your letter on Monday and the tray came this morning. 5
And for both thanks. We shout cries of welcome. Traveling is
victory.

As to returning bredouille well that's better than a crack on the
head—if not for yourself perhaps (note how habit of cynicism
clings to me) then for your friends. A virtuous man lives for his 10
friends. "Remember this!" as the edicts of the Emperor of China
conclude.

I was just thinking of sending a note to the Dev^{re} Club to meet
you when your letter arrived "announcing presents". Days had
slipped disregarded full to the brim with the botheration of moving. 15
Now I am here I like it. I can write a little a very little. A little is
better than nothing but it is so little that out of the present worries
I look with terror into the future still. Oh the weariness of it, the
weariness of it.

They did not send me the proofs of Higgon's Dream. There 20
is a misprint in French. When sending *Pulperia* I repproached
them. They sent me proofs of that but without the MS, so if
there is anything wrong it is not so much of my fault as it may
look.

I had a most enjoyable trip to Glasgow. I saw Neil Munro and 25
heaps of shipowners and that's all I can say. The fact is from
novel writing to skippering il y a trop de tirage. This confounded
literature has ruined me entirely. There is a time in the affairs of
men when the tide of folly taken at the flood sweeps them to
destruction. La mer monte cher ami; la mer monte and the pheno- 30
menon is not worth a thought

My letter is disjointed because I can't think to-night. I am
touched to think that when wandering through the brass-workers'
bazaar (in Fez—was it?) you thought: There's that Conrad. Well
yes—there he is—for a little while yet. I have been looking at the 35
thing all day. It has a fascination. I seem to see the face bending
over it the hands that touched it. A brown meagre hand, a hooked
profile, a skullcap on a shaven head, lean shanks ending in splay

slippers, thus I picture the man who hammered the brass according
40 to the design known to his remote forefathers.

Pressing both your hands
Ever Yours Conrad.

I didn't know the review was by your Wife. I liked it immensely.
I noted it. I hope her health is good. Mes hommages les plus
45 respectueux. I shall levy toll of one copy upon your book—comme
de juste.

PUBLICATION
LL, I, 253–4.

TEXT
6 'Traveling': *sic.*
21 'repproached': *sic.*

COMMENTARY
5–10   On 16 October Conrad, discussing the journey in Morocco that
Graham was making, had told Mrs Bontine:
> 'I can well understand your anxiety. Want of water and wild tribes
> are dangers, but the absolute magnitude of such perils depends in
> a great measure upon the man who affronts them. Robert is coura-
> geous and foresighted. He has also experience.' (*LL*, I, 250–1.)

On 20 November Graham wrote to Garnett:
> 'My journey failed.
> The tribes were fighting & all advance in the direction I wished
> to go, was impossible.'

14–16   Conrad had moved from Stanford-le-Hope in Essex to Pent Farm
in Kent around 26 October. (*LL*, I, 251.)

20–1   While Graham was abroad, his tale 'Higginson's Dream' had
appeared in *SR*, LXXXVI, 431–3 (1 Oct. 1898); it was later to be published
in *Thirteen Stories* (1900) and *Rodeo* (1936). Conrad told Mrs Bontine:
> 'It is much too good to remind me of any of my work, but I am im-
> mensely flattered to learn you discern some points of similitude. Of
> course I am in complete sympathy with the point of view.' (*LL*, I,
> 251.)

Graham's slight story makes the point that the presence of the white
merchant in the tropics 'exterminates the people whom he came to
benefit, to bless, to rescue from their savagery' (p. 431); so possibly
Mrs Bontine had with some temerity compared it with 'An Outpost of
Progress'. (Conrad began 'Heart of Darkness' the next month.) She,
of course, held that
> 'the African question.....is chiefly the doings of swindlers &
> murderers oppressing harmless natives.....' (Letter to Gabriela,
> 17 Aug. 1894, ASA.)

Graham had asked Conrad to correct the *SR* proofs in his absence (*LL*, I, 251).

21–4 'La Pulperia' had been published in *SR*, LXXXVI, 529–30 (22 Oct. 1898); and it was later included in *Thirteen Stories*, *Thirty Tales and Sketches*, *Rodeo* (under the title 'Pampa Store'), and *Los Pingos*.

25 'Munro': Work by Neil Munro (1864–1930), the poet and historical novelist, had appeared alongside Conrad's in *Blackwood's Magazine*. Conrad described his verses in *Blackwood's* as 'excellent', and said *à propos* of *John Splendid*, *A Highland Romance*, 'Munro *is* an artist— besides being an excellent fellow with a pretty weakness for my work' (Blackburn, pp. 46 and 35).

25–8 Conrad mentions this visit in *EGL*, pp. 135–7, and *LL*, I, 251. Neil Munro refers to it in his *The Brave Days* (Porpoise Press, Edinburgh, 1931), pp. 113–14, and in *GTK*, pp. 288–9.

As an explanation of Conrad's failure to gain employment with the ship-owners, A. F. Tschiffely claimed that Graham deliberately asked them

'on no account to give him employment, for, should they do so, he assured them that a great writer would be lost to the world.' (*AFT*, p. 331.)

Jocelyn Baines has dismissed this claim on the grounds that Tschiffely offered no source and that

'Cunninghame Graham was not even in Scotland at the time and anyhow it is most unlikely that he would have behaved so double-facedly to Conrad.' (Baines, p. 214 n.)

Tschiffely's assertion might still be defended in the following ways: First, Tschiffely based his book partly on conversations with Graham, and this oral source might be assumed; secondly, although Graham visited North Africa in the autumn, he was certainly (as his letters to Garnett show) in England and Scotland for much of the period July 1898– February 1899, during which negotiations with the ship-owners took place, and he could therefore have influenced those men both in person and by post, as Tschiffely suggests; and thirdly, *Mogreb-el-Acksa* shows that its author was capable elsewhere of melodramatic but well-intentioned deceptions. Nevertheless Baines's scepticism is fully justifiable. Tschiffely's approach is at times uncritically romantic; if Graham intended Conrad's applications to be futile, it is difficult to see why he should have encouraged them at all; and above all it seems quite unlikely that a ship-owner would agree to give an interview under such conditions.

However, Conrad's efforts were not entirely unproductive. While in Glasgow for interviews on this trip in September, Conrad was given hospitality by Graham's acquaintance and correspondent, Dr John McIntyre (1857–1928). McIntyre was a pioneer radiologist: in his house was one of the first X-ray machines, and as a party entertainment Conrad's hand was X-rayed and Neil Munro then stood at the machine so that Conrad and the doctor might admire his skeleton.

In the years 1896–8 Conrad had begun a correspondence with H. G.

Wells, whose *The Time Machine* he had read (*EGL*, p. 31); and he had written twice to Wells a few days before travelling north (*LL*, I, 248–50). Therefore it is not surprising that his encounter with McIntyre's astonishing machine should have provoked the excited speculations in the letter to Garnett that Conrad wrote immediately after returning from Glasgow:

'All day with the ship-owners and in the evening dinner, phonograph, X rays, talk about *the* secret of the Universe, and the non-existence of, so called, matter. The secret of the universe is in the existence of horizontal waves whose varied vibrations are at the bottom of all states of consciousness.....But, don't you see, there is nothing in the world to prevent the simultaneous existence of vertical waves.....Therefore it follows that two universes may exist in the same place and in the same time—and not only two universes but an infinity of different universes—if by universe we mean a set of states of consciousness. And, note,.....*all matter* being only that thing of inconceivable tenuity through which the various vibrations of waves.....are propagated, thus giving birth to our sensations—then emotions—then thought. Is that so?

These things I said to the Dr. while Neil Munro stood in front of a Röntgen machine.....

I returned to the bosom of my family at 1 pm. today and wrote to Hueffer at once to clinch the matter (there's no matter) of Pent Farm (which is only a vain and delusive appearance).' (*EGL*, pp. 136–7: letter of 29 Sept.)

The speculations in this letter appear to have provided the 'scientific' mechanism of *The Inheritors*, which Conrad and F. M. Hueffer were shortly to write (it was begun by November 1898, finished in 1900 and published in 1901: Baines, pp. 222, 238–9). I conjecture that when Conrad discussed with Hueffer the renting of Pent Farm he mentioned the encounter with the Röntgen machine, and that the two men, remembering the success of Wells's science-fiction (and the fact that *The Time Machine* begins with a discussion of 'the geometry of Four Dimensions'), decided to employ Conrad's surmises in the construction of *The Inheritors*. It will be remembered that in their novel, civilisation is undermined by the dispassionate 'Fourth Dimensionists' who have always co-existed with the humans but who inhabit a different plane, an alternative universe, a higher yet somehow intersecting level of consciousness: and the heroine first demonstrates her powers to the sceptical hero by momentarily making the solid world dissolve like a mirage before his eyes (Dent, 1923, pp. 6–8).

Conrad's share in the actual writing of *The Inheritors* may well have been small; but nevertheless he assured Richard Curle that 'it had been the cause of long and heated discussion lasting well into many nights' (R. Curle, ed.: *Notes by Joseph Conrad*....., privately printed, London, 1925, p. 21).

(This note first appeared in *Notes and Queries*, CCXII, 245–7, July 1967.)

28–30 A pessimistic inversion of Brutus's words (*Julius Caesar*, IV, iii).
32–40 Cf.:
> 'At intervals he [Graham] used to send useless and tawdry
> presents.....: a Moroccan dagger, a brass lamp.....' (*DG*, p. 68.)
43 'the review': presumably anonymous; untraced. Gabriela Cunninghame Graham contributed to various periodicals, including *The Yellow
Book, Chambers's Journal* and *SR*.
45 'your book': *Mogreb-el-Acksa*, which appeared on 1 December. See
letter 27.

27

⟨Station,
Sandling Junction,   PENT FARM,
S.E.R.   STANFORD, near HYTHE.⟩
                                                    1st Dec 1898

Cherissime et excellentissime.   5

Your photograph came yesterday (It's good!) and the book
arrived by this evening's post. I dropped everything—as you may
imagine and rushed at it paper knife in hand. It is with great
difficulty I interrupt my reading at the 100th page—and I interrupt
it only to write to you.   10

A man staying here has been reading over my shoulder; for we
share our best with the stranger within our tent. No thirsty men
drank water as we have been drinking in, swallowing, tasting,
blessing, enjoying gurgling, choking over, absorbing, your thought,
your phrases, your irony, the spirit of your vision and of Your   15
expression. The individuality of the book is amazing—even to me
who know you or pretend to. It is wealth tossed on the roadside,
it is a creative achievement, it is alive with conviction and truth.
Men, living men are tossed to these dogs—the readers, pictures are
flung out for the blind, wisdom—brilliant wisdom—showered   20
upon fools. You are magnificently generous. You seem to be plung-
ing your hand into an inexhaustible bag of treasure and fling
precious things at every paragraph. We have been shouting
slapping our legs, leaping up, stamping about. There was such an
enthusiasm in this solitude as will meet no other book.   25
I do not know really how to express the kind of intellectual
exultation your book has awakened in me; and will not stay to try;
I am in too great a hurry to get back to the book. My applause,
slaps on the back, salaams benedictions, cheers. Take what you

30 like best of these, what you think most expressive. Or take them all.
I *can't* be too demonstrative.

Ever Yours with yells
Conrad.

Why did you lug in J.C. into your pages. Oh Why? Why take
35 a sinner on your back when crossing a stream.

PUBLICATION
LL, I, 257–8.

TEXT
6   '(It's good!)': inserted.
8   'rushed': inserted.
18   'it is a': inserted.
27   'and will not': may be 'and I will not'.

COMMENTARY
6–31   Graham's *Mogreb-el-Acksa*, an account of his journey in Morocco
   in autumn 1897, had just been published by Heinemann. See Conrad's
   further comments in letters 28 and 30.
11   'A man': possibly F. M. Hueffer, who lived at Aldington, not far
   from Pent Farm, and who was about this time collaborating with Conrad
   on *The Inheritors* and *Seraphina*; or perhaps either H. G. Wells or
   Edwin Pugh, both of whom Conrad had towards the end of November
   invited to visit him (*LL*, I, 254, 256–7).
34–5   Graham pays tribute to 'An Outpost of Progress' in *Mogreb*,
   pp. 52–3.

28

⟨Station,
Sandling Junction,   PENT FARM,
   S.E.R.   STANFORD, near HYTHE.⟩
                              9th Dec 1898

5 My dearest Amigo.
   I wrote to your mother about your book. I found it easier to
speak to a third person—at first. I do not know what to tell you.
If I tell you that You have surpassed my greatest expectations you
may be offended—and this piece of paper is not big enough to
10 explain how great my expectations were. Anyway they are left behind. I am ashamed of my moderation and now I am looking at the
performance I ask myself what kind of friend was I not to foresee,

110

not to understand that the book would just be *that*—no less. Well it is there—for our joy, for our thought, for our triumph. I am speaking of those who understand and love you. The preface is a gem—I knew it, I remembered it—and yet it came with a fresh force. To be understood is not everything—one must be understood as one would like to be. This probably you won't have.

Yes—the book is Art. Art without a trace of Art's theories in its incomparably effective execution. It isn't anybody's art—it is C-Graham's art. The individuality of the work imposes itself on the reader—from the first. Then come other things, skill, pathos, humour, wit, indignation. Above all a continuous feeling of delight; the persuasion that there one has got hold of a good thing. This should work for material success. Yet who knows! No doubt it is too good.

You haven't been careful in correcting your proofs. Are you too grand seigneur for that infect labour? Surely I, twenty others, would be only too proud to do it for you. Tenez vous le pour dit. I own I was exasperated by the errors. Twice the wretched printers perverted your meaning. It is twice too often. They should die!

I write because I can't come. Can't is the truth. I am sorry to hear of your depression—but O friend who isn't—(I mean depressed). I am not able to say one cheering word. It seems to me I am des-integrating slowly. Cold shadows stand around. Never mind. I thought it was next Tuesday you were coming to town. Stupid of me. Now this letter'll be probably too late to catch you. I am very sorry to hear of your wife's indisposition. Remember me to her please. I trust she is better.

I daren't ask you to come down. I am too wretched, and its worse than the plague. Au revoir

Ever Yours

Jph. Conrad.

PUBLICATION

LL, I, 260–I.
10–11 'they are left behind. I': Aubry reads 'thus left behind, I'.
13–14 '—no less. Well it is there': omitted by Aubry.

TEXT

33–44 These lines present a textual problem. In the manuscript collection of the Baker Library, Dartmouth College, the leaf on which these lines are written is arranged as pp. 5–6 of the letter dated '9ᵗʰ Dec

1898'; and Aubry prints these lines as the continuation of that letter. This arrangement may be correct: among the Dartmouth MSS there is no letter with a surplus ending; nor is there one lacking an ending, which would be completed by lines 33–44. On the other hand, there is some evidence that these may form the ending of a different letter. For example, lines 4–31 are written in a small, neat, level hand; yet lines 33–44 are in a large, sprawling hand, with what appears to be a different nib, and the lines tend to slope slightly upwards from left to right; and the mood of the first part contrasts oddly with the sudden gloom of the second part. However, because letter 29 appears to comment on the gloom of these lines, and for the sake of clarity and of consistency with Dartmouth and *LL*, I give them in their present position.

35–6 'desintegrating': *sic.*

COMMENTARY

6–7 Conrad had written to Mrs Bontine, praising *Mogreb-el-Acksa*, on 4 December: there he said of it:

'It is a glorious performance. Much as we expected of him, I, and two men who were staying with me when my copy arrived, have been astonished by the completeness of the achievement. One said: "This is *the* book of travel of the century." It is true. Nothing approaching it had appeared since Burton's *Mecca*. And, as the other man pointed out, judging the work strictly as a book,—as a production of an unique temperament,—Burton's *Mecca* is nowhere near it. And it is true. The *Journey in Morocco* is a work of art. A book of travel written like this is no longer a book of travel,—it is a creative work. It is a contribution not towards mere knowledge but towards *truth*,— to truth hidden in men,—in things,—in life,—in nature,—to the truth only exceptional men can see, and not every exceptional man can present to the ordinary dim eyes of the crowd.

He is unapproachable in acuteness of vision,—of sympathy: he is alone in his power of expression: and through vision, sympathy and expression runs an informing current of thought as noble, unselfish and human as is only the gift of the best.' (*LL*, I, 258–9.)

15–17 The preface, 'To Wayfaring Men', was previously discussed by Conrad in letter 24.

28 'infect': (Fr.) 'foul'.

29

⟨Station,
Sandling Junction,
S.E.R.

PENT FARM,
STANFORD, near HYTHE.⟩
21. 12. 98.

5 Cherissime ami.

With a bad pen by a smoky lamp Hail to you! May all the infernal Gods look upon You with favour; and may all the men who are food for Hell shake their heads at your words and gestures. To be happy we should propitiate the gods of evil and fly in the faces of evil men.

I cannot sufficiently recover from the shock of missing your dear visit to relieve my feelings by strong swears. Not yet. When you come (and you will) I shall explain what infamous thing had me by the neck then. I have eaten shame and my face is black before you.

I toil on. So did the gentleman of the name of Sisiphus. (Did I spell it right?) This is the very marrow of my news.

Mes devoirs les plus respectueux a Madame Votre Femme et mes souhaits de la Nouvelle année. As to you O Friend! Time overtakes us. Time! Voilà l'ennemi. And must I even congratulate you upon a defeat because men lie to each other to conceal their dismay and their fear. Not I!

Ever Yours Conrad.

PUBLICATION

This letter is unpublished.

TEXT

7   'You': inserted.
12   'me': inserted.

COMMENTARY

11–13   Cf.: 'I have been in a wretched state of health—miserable rather than bad. . . . .' (Conrad to Aniela Zagorska, 18 Dec. 1898, *LL*, I, 261).
15–16   Cf.:
'. . . . . you may well believe it is not laziness that keeps me back. It is, alas, something—I don't know what—not so easy to overcome. With immense effort a thin trickle of MS is produced—and that, just now, must be kept in one channel only lest no one gets anything and I am completely undone.' (Conrad to William Blackwood, 13 Dec. 1898, Blackburn, p. 34.)
Conrad was apologising for his delay in producing material for *Blackwood's Magazine*: the 'one channel' was presumably *The Rescue*, with which he was unsuccessfully struggling.

30

〈Station,
Sandling Junction,   PENT FARM,
    S.E.R.   STANFORD, near HYTHE.〉
                                            2ᵈ Febr 99

5   Cher et excellent ami.

I haven't two ideas in my head and I want to talk to you all the same. Horrid state to be in.

Pawling says says your book is going off. The reviews are *good* tho' positively repulsive. Que voulez vous. They are good selling reviews.

10   We sang songs of praise before your greatness this morning with G. G is preparing your Unwin vol. for the press. May the best of lucks attend it.

A thing of mine began in B'wood's 1000ᵗʰ Nº to conclude in Febʸ. I am shy of sending it to you—but have no objection to you looking

15 at it if it should come in your way

Don't, don't ask about the Rescue. It will finished about end March unless it makes an end of me before.

I was in London one day, amongst publishers and other horrors. My heart is heavy but my spirits are a little better.

20   McIntyre is really "impayable"—and so are you. D'ye think the shipowners of "Glesga" are gone mad. They will never never give a ship to a "chiel" that can write prose—or who is even suspected of such criminal practices.

I am writing an idiotic letter.

25   If I could tell really what I feel for you for your work and for the spirit that abides in the acts and the thoughts of your passage amongst this jumble of shadows and—well—filth which is called the earth you would think it fulsome adulation. So I won't say anything and shall hug myself with both hands in the assurance

30 of your friendship.

This is stupidly put and a cynic would say it was stupidly felt. *Are* you a cynic?

Quelle bête de vie! Nom de nom quelle bête de vie! Sometimes I lose all sense of reality in a kind of nightmare effect produced

35 by existence. Then I try to think of you—to wake myself. And it does wake me. I don't know how you feel about yourself but to me you appear extremely real—even when I perceive you enveloped in the cloud of your irremediable illusions.

I had better stop before I say something that would end in bloodshed.

40

Now I haven't said anything and that's enough.

Ever desperately yours

Conrad.

PUBLICATION

LL, I, 266–7.

11 'G. G is preparing': Aubry reads 'E.G. preparing'.

TEXT

8 'says says': *sic.*
12 'lucks': *sic.*
16 'will finished': *sic.*
26 'your': inserted.
29 'both': inserted.

COMMENTARY

8–9 Sydney S. Pawling was a partner of William Heinemann, publisher of *Mogreb-el-Acksa*. Graham's book received very favourable reviews in the *Athenaeum* (CXIII, 108), *Daily Chronicle* (14 Jan. 1899, p. 3), *Literature* (IV, 57–8), *Spectator* (LXXXII, 562–3), and *The Times* (4 Feb. 1899, p. 4).

Later publications of *Mogreb* were by Duckworth (revised edn., 1921; cheap edn., 1928), by the Viking Press, New York (1930), and by the National Travel Club, New York (1930).

10–12 Edward Garnett was preparing Graham's collection of tales, *The Ipané*, for Fisher Unwin. In the *Academy*, Garnett described *Mogreb* as 'a delicious commentary on our Anglo-Saxon civilisation; a malicious and ironic comparison of British commercialised world [*sic*] with the feudal world of Morocco; a subtle, witty commentary that must rejoice all who are rejoiced by Candide.' (LVI, 153–4, 4 Feb. 1899.)

13–15 'Heart of Darkness' was serialised in *Blackwood's Magazine* from February to April 1899.

16–17 The unrevised MS of *The Rescue* was finished on 25 May 1919 (*LL*, II, 222).

20 'McIntyre': John McIntyre had entertained Conrad in Glasgow during the visit to the ship-owners in September 1898. See letter 26, note 25–8.

115 8-2

31

Cherissime ami.

I am simply in the seventh heaven, to find you like the *H of D*
so far. You bless me indeed. Mind you don't curse me by and bye
for the very same thing. There are two more instalments in which
the idea is so wrapped up in secondary notions that You—even
You!—may miss it. And also you must remember that I don't start
with an abstract notion. I start with definite images and as their
rendering is true some little effect is produced. So far the note
struck chimes in with your convictions—mais après? There is an
après. But I think that if you look a little into the episodes you will
find in them the right intention though I fear nothing that is
practically effective.

Somme toute c'est une bête d'histoire qui aurait pu être quelque
chose de très-bien si j'avais su l'écrire.

The thing in West. Gaz. is excellent, excellent. I am most
interested in your plans of work and travel. I don't know in which
most. Nous allons causer de tout cela.

As to the peace meeting. If you want me to come I want still
more to hear you. But—I am not a peace man, nor a democrat
(I don't know what the word means really) and if I come I shall go
into the body of the hall. I want to hear you—just as I want always
to read you. I can't be an accomplice after or before the fact to any
sort of fraternity that includes the westerners whom I so dislike.
The platform! I pensez-Vous? Il y aura des Russes. Impossible!
I can not admit the idea of fraternity not so much because I believe
it impracticable, but because its propaganda (the only thing really
tangible about it) tends to weaken the national sentiment the pre-
servation of which is my concern. When I was in Poland 5 years
ago and managed to get in contact with the youth of the university
in Warsaw I preached at them and abused them for their social
democratic tendencies. L'idée democratique est un très beau
phantôme, and to run after it may be fine sport, but I confess
I do not see what evils it is destined to remedy. It confers distinction on Messieurs Jaurès, Liebknecht & C° and your adhesion
confers distinction upon it. International fraternity may be an
object to strive for and, in sober truth, since it has Your support
I will try to think it serious, but that illusion imposes by its size

alone. Franchement what would you think of an attempt to promote fraternity amongst people living in the same street. I don't even mention two neighbouring streets. Two ends of the same street. There is already as much fraternity as there can be—and thats very little and that very little is no good. What does fraternity mean. Abnegation—self-sacrifice means something. Fraternity means nothing unless the Cain–Abel business. Thats your true fraternity. Assez.

L'homme est un animal méchant. Sa mechanceté doit être organisée. Le crime est une condition nécéssaire de l'existence organisée. La société est essentielment criminelle—ou elle n'existerait pas. C'est l'égoisme qui sauve tout—absolument tout—tout ce que nous ab- horrons tout ce que nous aimons. Et tout se tient. Voilà pourquoi je respecte les êxtremes anarchistes.—"Je souhaite l'extermination generale"—Très bien. C'est juste et ce qui est plus c'est clair. On fait des compromis avec des paroles. Ça n'en finit plus. C'est comme une forêt ou personne ne connait la route. On est perdu pendant que l'on crie—"Je suis sauvé!".

Non. Il faut un principe défini. Si l'idée nationale aporte la souffrance et son service donne la mort ça vaut toujours mieux que de servir les ombres d'une eloquence qui est morte, justement par ce qu'elle n'a pas de corps. Croyez moi si je Vous dis que ces questions là sont pour moi très sérieuses—beaucoup plus que pour Messieurs Jaurès, Liebknecht et Cie. Vous—vous pouvez tout faire. Vous êtes essentielment un frondeur. Cela Vous est permis. Ce sont les Nobles qui ont fait la Fronde du reste. Moi je regarde l'avenir du fond d'un passé très noir et je trouve que rien ne m'est permis hormis la fidélité a une cause absolument perdue, a une idée sans avénir.

Aussi souvent je n'y pense pas. Tout disparait. Il ne reste que la verité—une ombre sinistre et fuyante dont il est impossible de fixer l'image. Je ne regrette rien—je n'espère rien car je m'aperçoit que ni le regret ni l'espérance ne signifient rien a ma personalité. C'est un egoisme rationel et féroce que j'exerce envers moi même. Je me repose la dedans. Puis la pensée revient. La vie recommence, les regrets, les souvenirs et un desespoir plus sombre que la nuit.

Je ne sais pas pourquoi je Vous dis tout cela aujourd'hui. C'est que je ne veux pas que Vous me croyez indifferent. Je ne suis pas indifferent a ce qui Vous interesse. Seulement mon interet est

ailleurs, ma pensée suit une autre route, mon cœur desire autre
80 chose, mon áme souffre d'une autre espèce d'impuissance. Comprenez Vous? Vous qui devouez Votre enthousiasme et Vos talents
a la cause de l'humanité, Vous comprendrez sans doute pourquoi
je dois—j'ai besoin,—de garder ma pensée intacte comme dernier
hommage de fidelité a une cause qui est perdue. C'est tout ce que
85 je peux faire. J'ai jété ma vie a tous les vents du ciel mais j'ai
gardé ma pensée. C'est peu de chose—c'est tout—ce n'est rien—
c'est la vie même. Cette lettre est incoherente comme mon existence
mais la logique suprême y est pourtant—la logique qui mène a la
folie. Mais les soucis de tous les jours nous font oublier la cruelle
90 verité. C'est heureux.
    Toujours à Vous
        de cœur
            JphConrad.
    PS
95 Jessie sends her kind regards and thanks for message about the
story. It delights her. I shall talk with Garnett about your work.
He is a good fellow.
Eye and ear? Eh? Not so bad. Only if I *could* write like you—if
I *knew* all you know—if I *believed* all you believe! If, if if!

PUBLICATION

LL, I, 268–70.
Variants are listed in Appendix 1. The most important are these:
16 'in West. Gaz.': Aubry reads 'on West. Gar.'.
24 'westerners': 'westerness [?]'.
63–4 'vous pouvez tout faire.': omitted.
96 'It delights her.': 'It delights.'

TEXT

(See also Appendix 1.)
8 'their': an alteration of 'they'.
9 'rendering is': inserted above the cancelled word 'are'.
20 'a peace man': 'a' is an insertion.
62 'que pour': 'pour' is an insertion.
77 'me': an insertion.
89 'nous': an insertion.

COMMENTARY

An interesting discussion of this crucial letter is in *EKH*, pp. 17–28,
where a desperate attempt is made to mitigate the harshness of Conrad's

word 'méchanceté'. The letter should perhaps be read in conjunction with section III of 'Books' (in *Notes*) in which Conrad says:

'What one feels so hopelessly barren in declared pessimism is just its arrogance. It seems as if the discovery made by many men at various times that there is much evil in the world were a source of proud and unholy joy unto some of the modern writers.....

To be hopeful in an artistic sense it is not necessary to think that the world is good. It is enough to believe that there is no impossibility of its being made so.....I would wish him [the writer] to look with a large forgiveness at men's ideas and prejudices, which are by no means the outcome of malevolence.....' (Pp. 8–9.)

3–4 The first instalment of 'The Heart of Darkness' had just been published in *Blackwood's Magazine* (CLXV, 193–220, Feb. 1899).

4–9 Conrad, when discussing *Youth* on 31 May 1902, told Blackwood: 'in the light of the final incident, the whole story in all its.....descriptive detail shall fall into its place—acquire its value and its significance. This is my method based on deliberate conviction.....I beg to instance Karain—Lord Jim (where the method is fully developed)—the last pages of Heart of Darkness where the interview of the man and the girl locks in—as it were—the whole 30000 words of narrative description into one suggestive view of a whole phase of life.....' (Blackburn, p. 154.)
Cf.:

'To him [Marlow] the meaning of an episode was not inside like a kernel but outside, enveloping the tale.....' (*Blackwood's Magazine*, p. 195.)

9–10 One such note would be the ironic comparison of the Roman with the Anglo-Saxon imperialists:

'[Marlow:] "What saves us is efficiency—the devotion to efficiency. But these chaps [the Romans] were not much account, really. They were no colonists; their administration was merely a squeeze....."' (*Blackwood's Magazine*, p. 196.)

[Graham:] 'Material and bourgeois Rome, wolf-suckled, on its seven hills waxed and became the greatest power, conquering the world by phrases as its paltry "Civis Romanus", and by its "Pax Romana", and with the spade, and by its sheer dead weight of commonplace, filling the office in the old world that now is occupied so worthily by God's own Englishmen.' ('Bloody Niggers', *Social-Democrat*, I, 107, April 1897.)

16 'The thing in West. Gaz.': Graham's 'A Pakeha' (*Westminster Gazette*, 31 Jan. 1899, pp. 1–2): a sketch describing an encounter between Graham and a Mr Campbell, an old neighbour who reminisces in Scots dialect about his early years in New Zealand. Through Campbell's dry and callous recollections Graham makes the points that in New Zealand the whites took the natives' lands by legal robbery and took the native women as concubines while enforcing a brutal summary justice. Thus he offers yet another instance of despoliation in the name of colonisation.

19 ff. 'the peace meeting': This meeting was convened by the Social
Democratic Federation to take place at the St James's Hall, Piccadilly,
on the evening of 8 March 1899, under the chairmanship of H. M.
Hyndman. In addition to Graham, the speakers included Jean Jaurès and
Wilhelm Liebknecht (whom Conrad mentions), Pete Curran (organiser
of the Gasworkers' Union), Harry Quelch, Fred Brocklehurst and
Emile Vandervelde. The resolution proposed in the crowded hall was:
> 'This meeting of the citizens of London declares that the solidarity
> and fraternity of the workers of all civilized countries on the lines of
> international Socialism constitute the only hope of permanent peace
> among the peoples and adjures the industrial classes everywhere to
> drop all antagonism to their fellows of other nationalities and to com-
> bine in vigorous attack upon their worst enemies, the landlords and
> capitalists at home.' (*The Times*, 9 March 1899, p. 7.)

> 'Cunningham Graham's [*sic*] rising evoked a perfect storm of
> applause. He seconded the resolution in the speech of a man of action
> who scorned everything mean, ignoble and base. He had nothing but
> contempt for the huckster's soul which seemed to animate the policy
> of Britain at home and abroad. Our national hypocrisy was as well
> known as our smug sanctimony and our gin and gatlings. The workers
> themselves would have to settle the problem of international peace
> for themselves, as they, and they alone, held the key of the whole
> situation.' (*Labour Leader*, 18 March 1899, p. 84.)

20-2 Conrad did in fact attend the meeting. Graham told Garnett later:
> 'At the meeting I had the influenza & thought I should have died.
> Conrad & Hudson were both there, & I introduced them to one
> another (or, each other).
>
> Conrad was I think revolted a little, but Hudson stood the trial
> well. I am glad a competent judge said I was coherent, I did not
> feel so. Jehovah *is* a craftsman dentist.' (Letter of 27 March 1899.)

23-4: 'I can't' to 'dislike.' I take this to mean: 'By my presence I will
support the meeting in so far as it is an attack on the fraternal gathering
of heads of state proposed by Russia, because I know that that proposed
conference would be attended by those westerners (people living west of
Russia) whom I detest—viz., the representatives of Germany, "the
evil counsellor of Russia" where Poland is concerned; but at the same
time I will not appear on the platform at your meeting and thus
become an accomplice to the fraternity of a socialism which embraces
Germans like Liebknecht.'

25 'Il y aura des Russes': As Liebknecht's speech from the platform
made abundantly clear, the meeting was partly intended as a socialist
counterblast to the tsar's recent proposals (fiercely debated throughout
England: see *Westminster Gazette*, 31 Jan. 1899, p. 4) for a disarmament
conference to be attended by the European heads of state—the eventual
Hague Conference; so that Conrad here thinks of the Russian anarchists
and socialists (e.g. Stepniak, Kropotkin and Volkhovsky) who were
known to Graham, Garnett and Hueffer, and who would have particular
interest in the meeting.

Graham remembered Conrad's phrase twenty-five years later: see appendix 5.

25–32 In 'The Crime of Partition' (1919) Conrad wrote:
'The Polish State offers a singular instance of an extremely liberal administrative federalism which, in its Parliamentary life as well as its international politics, presented a complete unity of feeling and purpose.....
Even after Poland lost its independence this alliance and this union remained firm in spirit and fidelity. All the national movements towards liberation were initiated in the name of the whole mass of people inhabiting the limits of the old Republic, and all the Provinces took part in them with complete devotion. It is only in the last generation that efforts have been made to create a tendency towards separation, which would indeed serve no one but Poland's common enemies. And, strangely enough, it is the internationalists, men who professedly care nothing for race or country, who have set themselves this task of disruption, one can easily see for what sinister purpose.' (*Notes*, pp. 120–1.)

35 'Jaurès': Jean Jaurès: born 1859, assassinated by a French nationalist in 1914. He was a radical deputy from 1885 to 1886, a socialist deputy in 1893–8 and 1902–14, an outstanding socialist writer and orator, and founder in 1904 of *L'Humanité*.

35 'Liebknecht': Wilhelm Liebknecht (1826–1900), founder of the Social Democratic party, an associate of Karl Marx, a life-long revolutionary agitator, and a member of the Reichstag.

36–45 Cf. the remarks on 'brotherhood' in *Notes*, p. 105, and in 'Gaspar Ruiz' (*A Set of Six*, Dent, 1923), p. 26.

48–50 Cf. Anatole France, *Les Opinions de M. Jérôme Coignard* (Calmann Lévy, Paris, 1893), p. 23:
'l'homme est naturellement un très méchant animal, et.....les sociétés ne sont abominables que parce qu'il met son génie à les former.'

50–4 Cf. Conrad's remarks on the rôle of the Professor in *The Secret Agent*: letter 60, lines 31–6.

53 'les êxtremes anarchistes': Marcel Bourdin in 1894 accidentally blew himself up in Greenwich Park with a home-made bomb, and thus contributed to *The Secret Agent*; Johann Most, who arrived in England in 1878, later wrote a pamphlet for anarchists entitled *Revolutionäre Kriegswissenschaft* (a manual on the making and use of bombs), and perhaps contributed to Conrad's Professor; Sergei Stepniak and his *Career of a Nihilist* may have provided a few hints for *Under Western Eyes*; and here Conrad may have in mind Max Stirner's *Der Einzige und sein Eigentum* (*The Ego and His Own*), which enjoyed a popular revival during the 1890s.

55 'On fait des compromis avec des paroles': cf. letter 7, lines 69–72.

58–61 Cf.:
'The conscience of but very few men amongst us.....will brook the restraint of abstract ideas as against the fascination of a material

advantage.....The trouble of the civilised world is the want of a common conservative principle abstract enough to give the impulse, practical enough to form the rallying point of international action tending towards the restraint of particular ambitions. Peace tribunals instituted for the greater glory of war will not replace it. Whether such a principle exists—who can say?' (*Notes*, p. 111.)

74 ff. 'la pensée.....ma pensée.....ma pensée.....j'ai gardé ma pensée': perhaps Conrad knew of Hohenlohe's misquotation of La Fontaine's *Fables*, XI, 8. *The Times* for 21 January 1898, p. 3, had quoted a speech made by Prince Hohenlohe in the Prussian Chamber on 20 January. The prince claimed that the Prussian element in Poland had to be strengthened, and he warned Polish patriots that they must abandon all hopes of independence.

'In conclusion, he reminded the Poles of the advice of the French poet—"Quittez le long espoir et la vaste pensée." If the Poles did this and abandoned their impracticable hopes they would become and remain honest Prussians and their German neighbours would arrive at an understanding with them and would live with them in peace.....

Prince Hohenlohe's speech.....provoked a storm of hisses from the Poles and their Clerical allies.'

The cause of Polish independence was not always to be 'une cause absolument perdue'. Conrad's efforts, at the time of the first world war, to promote support for an independent Poland which might be a post-war 'anti-German element.....to create equilibrium against Prussian preponderance in Europe' have been documented in *KRZ*, pp. 111–42.

In *Success* (1902), pp. 3–4, Graham once wrote:

'Causes which hang in monumental mockery quite out of fashion, as that of Poland, still are more interesting than is the struggle between the English and the Germans, which shall sell gin and gunpowder to negroes on the Coast.'

In this letter, Conrad attacks socialism while defending Polish nationalism; and Graham in his parliamentary years had supported Irish and Scottish nationalism in the name of socialism (cf. *Hansard*, vol. CCCXXXV, col. 97, 9 April 1889). Even after he had become President of the Scottish Home Rule Association, Graham supported this cause partly in the belief that internationalism could only be achieved after dependent nations had gained independence. If Poland could become free, so could Scotland: so he argued, overlooking some small distinctions... (R. E. Muirhead's MS notes on Graham's speech at Stirling, 23 June 1931; Graham's letter to Muirhead, 27 June 1934.)

32

⟨Station:—
Sandling Junction, S.E.R.

PENT FARM,
STANFORD,
Near HYTHE.⟩
26th Feb 99.

Très cher et excellent ami.

The portrait came. It is gorgeous. I like its atmosphere. It is a likeness too besides being a picture.

In a little while came the books. Vous me gâtez. I've read Vathek at once. C'est très bien. What an infernal imagination! The style is old and I do not see in the work that immense promise as set forth by the introduction. Chaucer I have dipped into, reading aloud as you advised. I am afraid I am not English enough to appreciate fully the father of English literature. Moreover I am in general insensible to verse.

Thereupon came the "Stealing of the Mare". This I delight in. I've read it at once and right through. It is quite inspiring most curious and altogether fascinating. I've written to your wife a few words in the language of the Franks about Fam: Port: which is a delicious bit. The tenderness of the idea and the feeling for the past have delighted me. C'est tout à fait dans sa note. The quality that made the extraordinary charm of Sta Theresa is in that short article as visible as in the great work. Ever Yours with infinite thanks Conrad.

PUBLICATION

LL, I, 273.

COMMENTARY

8 'Vathek': The most recent edition of William Beckford's exotic pseudo-oriental novel was that of Richard Garnett (Lawrence and Bullen, London, 1893), whose introduction extols *Vathek*'s 'undiminished vitality'.

11–14 Nevertheless Conrad used three lines from the *Franklin's Tale* as the epigraph to *The Rescue*; and cf. Conrad's remarks on poetry in 'The Ascending Effort' (*Notes*).

15–17 Abu Zaid, *The Celebrated Romance of the Stealing of the Mare*: tr. Lady Anne Blunt and 'done into verse' by Wilfrid Scawen Blunt (Reeves and Turner, London, 1892). Graham told Garnett that it was 'in its way excellent, though not I believe a classic. The supernatural in it is so foolish as to repel but little.' (15 Feb. 1899.)

17–22 Gabriela Cunninghame Graham's essay 'Family Portraits' was eventually included in the volume *The Christ of Toro* (Nash, London, 1908). The tone of this characteristic exercise in nostalgia and melancholy is perhaps fairly exemplified by the following description of the figures in the portraits:

'They smile wistfully, as if they would tell me in a whisper none can hear but myself that effort is fruitless and ends in annihilation, not of the effort, but the individual, and that they are full of pity for the struggler who shall perish, glad of the effort which may live. Of death they speak not; they have known no death.' (P. 196.)

Conrad's letter congratulating Gabriela on this piece had been written on 24 February. He said:

'Quand j'ai levé mes yeux de dessus la page, c'est avec le sentiment très vif d'avoir vu non seulement la longue ligne des portraits mais encore la beauté de l'idée profonde et tendre qui éclairait pour vous tous les visages peints.....' (*LFR*, p. 37.)

33

⟨Station:—
Sandling Junction, S.E.R.

PENT FARM,
STANFORD,
Near HYTHE.⟩
17 Ap. 1899.

5 Très cher ami.

Your letter this morning made me feel better. It is possible that you like the thing so much? Well, you say so and I believe you but—do you quite believe it yourself soit dit sans vous offenser. The element of friendship comes in. But still I am willing, even
10 eager, to believe in your scrupulous literary honesty. And in any case my blessing on your intention.

I hold "*Ipane*". Hoch! Hurra! Vivat! May you live! And now I know I am virtuous because I read and had no pang of jealousy. There are things in that volume that are like magic and through
15 space through the distance of regretted years convey to one the actual feeling, the sights, the sounds, the thoughts; one steps on the earth, breathes the air, and has the sensations of your past. I knew of course every sketch; what was almost a surprise was the extraordinarily good, convincing effect of the whole. It is not always so
20 with a collection. The style grows on one from page to page. It is as wonderful in a slightly different way as the Morocco book. How do you do it? How? I do not say which I like best. I like best the one I happen to be reading. I think the sequence of the sketches has been arranged very well.

I have read it already three times.   25

I am cursedly tonguetied. Not only in my own work but when
I want to talk of a friend's work too. From a full heart nothing
comes. A weariness has laid its hand on my lips—I ask myself at
times whether it is for ever. Then I ought to die. However one is 30
never sure, and thus one hangs on to life. Can there be anything
more awful than such an incertitude and more pathetic than such
hanging on?
Shall I see you before you leave for the Sahara O Fortunate Man?
I'll come to town 'a-purpose' you know!   35
Jess sends her kindest regards   Ever Yours
                                                      Conrad.

PUBLICATION

LL, I, 275.
12 'Vivat': Aubry reads 'Viva'.
18–19 'extraordinarily': 'extraordinary'.
27 'cursedly': 'cursed and'.
28 'From': 'And from'.
35 'a-purpose': 'on purpose'.

TEXT

13 'know I': inserted.
28 'From': an alteration of 'Of'.

COMMENTARY

7 'the thing': Aubry identifies this work as *Lord Jim*: but *Lord Jim* was
   not serialised before October 1899 (in *Blackwood's Magazine*), and was
   not published in book form until October 1900. In any case, Conrad
   had not finished writing it on 19 December 1899 (see letter 35, lines
   9–12), and Graham wrote to praise it towards 3 March 1900 (letter 39,
   lines 4–5). The 'thing', therefore, is almost certainly 'The Heart of
   Darkness', the last instalment of which had just appeared in *Blackwood's Magazine* for April. Graham had written in February his
   comments on the first instalment, and Conrad had then warned him
   to wait until he had read the whole tale before judging it (letter 31,
   lines 3–13). On 7 April Graham had asked Garnett if part 3 of the tale
   had yet appeared.
12–25 Graham's volume of sketches, *The Ipané*, had been published
   in April. Most of the material had previously appeared in *SR* and
   Badminton Magazine.
21 'the Morocco book': *Mogreb-el-Acksa*.
34 Graham was due to set sail on 11 May (Graham to Garnett, 1 [?]
   April 1899).

34

5 Très chèr ami.

I was just wondering where you were when your dear letter arrived. I mean, dear—precious. Well! Vous me mettez du cœur au ventre; and that's no small service for I live in a perpetual state of intellectual funk. I only wish I knew how to thank you.

10 Shall I see you on your return from Madrid? The book that's gone to Heinemann is the "History of the Jesuits" I suppose—and I should think for next year. Now with this idiotic war there will be a bad time coming for print. All that's art, thought, idea will have to step back and hide its head before the intolerable

15 war inanities. Grand bien leur en fasse. The whole business is inexpressibly stupid—even on general principles; for evidently a war should be a conclusive proceeding while this noble enterprise (no matter what it's first result) must be the beginning of an endless contest. It is always unwise to begin a war which to be effective

20 must be a war of extermination; it is positively imbecile to start it without a clear notion of what it means and to force on questions for immediate solution which are eminently fit to be left to time. From time only one solution could be expected—and that one favourable to this country. The war brings in an element of in-

25 certitude which will be not eliminated by military success. There is an appalling fatuity in this business. If I am to believe Kipling this is a war undertaken for the cause of democracy. C'est a crever de rire. However, now the fun has commenced, I trust British successes will be crushing from the first—on the same principle

30 that if there's murder being done in the next room and you can't stop it you wish the head of the victim to be bashed in forthwith and the whole thing over for the sake of your own feelings. Assez de ses bêtises.

Borys wears the heart every day and says Gram-ma has given it to

35 him. Jessie's kind regards. We must be in town in Nov^{er} for your Wife's play. Rappelez moi a son bienveillant souvenir.

Drop me a line to say when you return.

Ever Yours Conrad

PUBLICATION

LL, I, 284–5.

34–5 (from 'Borys' to 'him.'): omitted by Aubry.

TEXT

18 'it's': *sic.*
18 'it's first': inserted.
29 'will be': written after the cancelled words 'would be'.

COMMENTARY

11 '"History of the Jesuits"': i.e. Graham's *A Vanished Arcadia: Being some account of the Jesuits in Paraguay, 1607 to 1767*, which was not published by Heinemann until September 1901.
12–32 For Graham, the Boer War was yet another sordid aspect of 'the base struggle to partition Africa' (*Hernando de Soto*, 1903, p. 36). While Conrad shared some of Graham's scepticism about Britain's motives, his hostility to Germany enabled him partly to defend the war as 'a struggle against the doings of German influence' (*LL*, I, 288).
26–8 Conrad is probably referring to the letter by Kipling which had appeared in *The Times* that morning (14 Oct. 1899, p. 9). In it, Kipling had claimed that the British Government would demand
    'equal rights for all white men from Cape to the Zambesi,.....the establishment of a Republic instead of an oligarchy.'
34 'the heart': described in *JEC*, p. 58.
35–6 'your Wife's play': probably *Don Juan's Last Wager*, Gabriela Cunninghame Graham's translation of *Don Juan Tenorio*, by José de Zorilla y Moral. This production did not open, however, until February 1900 (see letter 39, note 9–13).

35

⟨Station:—
Sandling Junction, S.E.R.

PENT FARM,
STANFORD,
Near HYTHE.⟩
19ᵗʰ Dec 99

Cher et excellent ami.   5

I was so glad to hear from you. Borys got his card the day after. You are emphatically a *nice man*.

This country does not want any writers; it wants a general or two that aren't valorous frauds. I am so utterly and radically sick of this African business that if I could take a sleeping draught on   10 the chance of not waking till it is all over I would let *Jim* go and take the consequences.

As it is—in the way of writing I am not much more good than if I were sleeping. It is silly of me to take a thing so much to heart but as things go there's not a ray of comfort for a man of my
15 complex way of thinking, or rather feeling.

It would do me good to hear you talk. I don't know why I feel so damnably lonely. My health is tolerable but my brain is as though somebody had stirred it all with a stick.

Allah *is* careless The loss of your MS is a pretty bad instance;
20 but look—here's His very own chosen people (of assorted denominations) getting banged about and not a sign from the sky but a snowfall and a fiendish frost. Perhaps Kipling's Recessional (if He understood it—which I doubt) had offended Him?

I should think Lord Salisbury's dying nation must be enjoying
25 the fun.

I can't write sense and I disdain to write Xmas platitudes so here I end. My wife and I send you unconventional greetings and as to Borys he *has* said you are a *nice man*—what more can you want to be made happy for a whole year? When do you return?
30 Shall I see you here before you go north? I am vexed about the preface. Your prefaces are so good! It is quite an art by itself. Well. This time I am really done.

Ever Yours

Jph Conrad

PUBLICATION

LL, 1, 287–8.
4 '19th Dec 99': Aubry reads '10th Dec. '99.'.

TEXT

23 'it': inserted.

COMMENTARY

8–9 Cf.:

'I had Kitchener on the nerves.....I daresay Buller is no Archangel either, but I pin my faith on him.' (*LL*, 1, 286, 26 Oct. 1899.)

'I am very glad Roberts is going,—or gone. To Kitchener by himself I would not have liked to pin my faith.' (*LL*, 1, 289, 28 Oct. 1899.)

9–12 Cf.: 'This imbecile war has just about done for me.' (*EGL*, p. 163, 15 Jan. 1900.)

12–15, 20–2 General Buller's forces had just suffered a surprising defeat. See *The Times* (16 Dec. 1899), p. 7; and cf. Conrad to Meldrum [17 Dec.]:

'I have been so upset by the turn of this war as to be hindered in my work.' (Blackburn, p. 77.)

19 'The loss of your MS': perhaps of 'Cruz Alta' (Garnett to Graham, 17 Aug. 1899); or perhaps a preface for *Thirteen Stories* or *A Vanished Arcadia* (lines 30–1).

22 'Recessional': Kipling's prayer to the 'Lord God of Hosts' had first appeared in *The Times* (17 July 1897), p. 13, and was first collected in *Recessional and Other Poems* (no imprint), London, 1899.

24–5 On 4 May 1898, at the Albert Hall, Lord Salisbury had said: 'From the necessities of politics or under the pretence of philanthropy—the living nations will gradually encroach on the territory of the dying.....It is not to be supposed that any one nation of the living nations will be allowed to have the profitable monopoly of curing or cutting up these unfortunate patients (laughter).....We shall not allow England to be at a disadvantage in any re-arrangement.....' (*The Times*, 5 May 1898, p. 7.)

At the time of this letter, Conrad and Hueffer were completing *The Inheritors*, with its judgement on political cynicism of this type.

36

⟨Station:—
Sandling Junction, S.E.R.

PENT FARM,
STANFORD,
Near HYTHE.⟩
4th Jan 1900   5

Cher ami

I just write a word to thank you for putting a little heart into me. I was glad to know You are back. And what of the affair?

I am pretty miserable—nothing new that! But difficulties are as it were closing round me; an irresistible march of blackbeetles 10 I figure it to myself. What a fate to be so ingloriously devoured.

I think the historian is quite right. It's a pity my style is not more popular and a thousand pities I don't write less slow. Of such that do is the Kingdom of the Earth. I don't care a damn for the best heaven ever invented by Jew or Gentile. And that's a fact. 15

And if the Kg^{om} of Earth were mine I would forthwith proceed to London to waylay you for a talk. As it is it shall not be—alas! Borys is not well. Heavy cold. He sends his How do you do. Ipsissima verba.

Jessie's kind regards   20
Weather beastly.

Ever yours
    Jph. Conrad.

PUBLICATION

This letter is unpublished.

COMMENTARY

7 'the affair': perhaps the sale of Gartmore (see letter 22, note 5–23).

9–11 Cf. Conrad to Sanderson (28 Dec. 1899):

'I am at work, but my mental state is very bad,—and is made worse by a constant gnawing anxiety. One incites the other and vice versa. It is a vicious circle in which the creature struggles.' (*LL*, I, 289.)

Part of this anxiety arose from the difficulties with *Lord Jim*, which he had hoped to complete by the end of September 1899 (*LL*, I, 278–9) but which was not finished until mid-July 1900.

12 'the historian': probably H. G. Wells, who had previously criticised the prolixity of Conrad's style. (*SR*, LXXXI, 509–10, 16 May 1896.)

37

Pent Farm.
19 Jan. 1900.

Très cher ami.

It's worse than brutal of me not to have answered your letter
5 sooner. To say the truth I haven't the heart to write either MS or letters; but now since I received the Sat Review I've something to write about. The German Tramp is not only excellent et bien tapé but it is something more. Of your short pieces I don't know but this is the one I like best. The execution has a vigour—the right
10 touch—and an ease that delight me. It is wonderful how you perceive and how you succeed in making your perception obey and bend to your thought. The *gold fish* the escaped Indians sketch and this one stand in a group by themselves waiting for more with just that easy probing touch which no one but you can give. There
15 is nothing in these that the most cantankerous caviller could pronounce out of focus. They are much more of course than mere Crane-like impressionism but even as impressionism these three sketches are well nigh perfect.

Well, I want to know—you know, so you should write to me.
20 I would write to you too if it were not for shame of having nothing to write. Out of that a good letter could be concocted but my mind

is not enough at ease for such exercises. And I don't think you would care to get a mere exercise in vacuo from me.

The leaden hours pass in pain but the days go in a flash; weeks disappear into the bottomless pit before I can stretch out my hand 25 and with all this there is an abiding sense of heavy endless drag upon the time. I am one of those who are condemned to run in a circle. Now and then only I have an illusion of progress but I disbelieve even illusions by this time. And where indeed could I progress! 30

Of course there is a material basis for every state of mind, and so for mine. Fame is a fraud—and, scurvy thing as it is at best, it is beyond my reach. Profit I do not get—since you did ask whether that was the matter. There may be the illusion of being a writer—but I had the honour to remark that I no longer believe 35 in illusions. This particular one I leave to my friends—it's something to have even this to give.

The fact of the matter is things go badly with me, and nobody can help—not even you unless you could invent something to make me write quicker. Palliatives won't do. And yet in the fourteen 40 months I've been at the Pent I've written upwards of 100000 words—that's a fact too—including of course some unutterable bosh for the unfinished *Rescue*. But I have lost all sense of reality; I look at the fields or sit before the blank sheet of paper as if I were in a dream. Want of mental vigour I suppose—or perhaps it is all 45 the fault of the body? I am discouraged and weary and

Satis! Send me everything you publish. When is Heinemann going to 'produce' your book?

Presentez mes devoirs a Madame Votre Femme. Jessie sends you her kind regards and Borys wishes to know whether you are 50 coming to-morrow. And I wish you were. Ever Yours JConrad.

PUBLICATION
This letter is unpublished.

TEXT
11 'succeed' follows the cancelled word 'know'.

COMMENTARY
7–12 Graham's sketch, 'In a German Tramp', had just appeared in *SR*, LXXXIX, 41–4 (13 Jan. 1900), and was later included in *Thirteen Stories*, in *Thirty Tales and Sketches*, and in *Rodeo*.

12 'The Gold Fish' had first appeared in *SR*, LXXXVII, 201–3 (18 Feb. 1899), and was later published in *Living Age*, CCXXI, 133–8 (8 April 1899), in *Thirteen Stories*, in *Thirty Tales and Sketches*, in *Rodeo*, and in *The Essential R. B. Cunninghame Graham* (ed. Paul Bloomfield).

12 'the escaped Indians sketch': i.e. 'A. Hegira', first published in *SR*, LXXXVIII, 160–4 (5 Aug. 1899), and later included in *Thirteen Stories*, in *Thirty Tales and Sketches*, in *Rodeo*, and in *The Essential R. B. Cunninghame Graham*.

14–16 Cf. Conrad's criticisms of 'Bloody Niggers': letter 18, lines 11–17.

16–18 Conrad, of Crane:

'His thought is concise, connected, never very deep—yet often startling. He is *the only* impressionist and *only* an impressionist.' (*EGL*, p. 107, 5 Dec. 1897.)

'He had indeed a wonderful power of vision . . . . . His impressionism of phrase went really deeper than the surface.' ('Stephen Crane' [1919], in *Notes*, p. 50.)

24–46 Cf. the depression of Conrad's letter to Sanderson, *LL*, I, 281–4.

48 'your book': probably *A Vanished Arcadia* (1901) (see letter 34, lines 10–12); perhaps *Thirteen Stories* (September 1900): both published by Heinemann.

38

⟨Station:—
Sandling Junction, S.E.R.

PENT FARM,
STANFORD,
Near HYTHE.⟩
13 Febr 1900.

5 Cher Ami.

Je me suis collété avec la mort ou peu s'en faut. However not this time yet it seems. I've been ill since the 26th of Jany. and have only tottered downstairs yesterday.

Malaria, bronchitis and gout. In reality a breakdown. I am better
10 but I've no sense of *rebound* don't you know; I remain under the shadow.

Ma pauvre femme est exténuée. Nursing me, looking after the child, doing the housework. She could not find a moment to drop you a line of thanks for Borys' purse. He was delighted with it,
15 and she wanted badly to write and tell you so. I suppose it isn't so much want of time but weariness that prevented her. I am afraid she'll break down next and that would the end of the world. I wish I could give her a little change but—quelle misère.

I think that to-morrow I'll be able to begin writing again. What

132

sorry stuff it'll be devil only knows. Moi aussi je suis extenué. 20
Il faut se raidir. Pardon this jeremiad Ever yours

Jph Conrad.

PUBLICATION

LL, I, 292–3.

TEXT

17 'that would the end': *sic.*

COMMENTARY

6–13 Cf. letter 40, lines 25–7; and Blackburn, p. 84.
13–15 Borys's birthday was on 15 January.
19–20 Conrad was then writing *Lord Jim*, which had been appearing
as a serial in *Blackwood's* since October 1899; he finished it in mid-July
(Blackburn, pp. 103–4; letter 40, line 13).

39

The Pent.
3 March

Très cher ami.

Just a word to thank you for your letter. Vous me mettez du
cœur au ventre though I can't possibly agree to your praises of Jim. 5
But as to *Buta* it is altogether and fundamentally *good*; good in
matter—that's of course—but good wonderfully good in form and
especially in expression.

I am sad we don't meet but I couldn't come to town for the play
as I very much wished to do. No doubt managers are as stupid as 10
the majority of publishers. I don't see the papers only the Standard.
It had a rigmarole but not even an attempt at any sort of appreciation so I don't know how Don Juan went. Is it going to be printed?

I am trying to go on with my work. It is hard but damn it all
if it is only *half* as good as you say then why groan? Have you seen 15
the last *vol* of Mrs Garnett's Turgeniev? There's a story there
Three Portraits really fine. Also *Enough*, worth reading.

Mes devoirs très respectueux a Madame Votre Femme. Jessie
sends her kindest regards. Borys is very fat and unruly but wears
the heart you've given him round his neck and thinks no end of it. 20
Poor little devil; if he had a decent father he would come to
something perhaps.

Ever Yours Jph Conrad.

LL, I, 293.

2 '3 March': Aubry reads '3 March 1900.' (Internal references amply confirm that the letter was written in 1900.)

COMMENTARY

4–5   The serialisation of *Lord Jim* was proceeding in *Blackwood's Magazine*. Graham, in his Introduction to the eventual Everyman edition of the novel (Dent, London, 1935), claimed that to Conrad *Lord Jim* and *Nostromo* 'were, perhaps, the favourite books of what may be called his second manner'; continuing:

> 'They were not so spontaneous as were those creations of his youth, *Almayer's Folly* and *An Outcast of the Islands*. *Lord Jim* has not the beauty of that miracle of prose, *The Mirror of the Sea*, or the intensity of some of his short stories. When Conrad wrote *Lord Jim* he had come to his full powers. His experiences in the Eastern Seas had settled themselves in his mind, and from his stores he was able to handle and select.' (P. vii.)

As Don Quixote led Cervantes, so Tuan Jim led Conrad, says Graham; adding that Conrad's work is likely to endure because, like Shakespeare, 'he does not write of types, but of humanity.' (P. vii.)

6–8   Graham's tale 'Buta' had appeared that morning in *SR*, LXXXIX, 262–3 (3 March 1900). It was later included in *Hope* (1910). Graham uses the oblique narrative form for his criticism of British hypocrisy in sexual and commercial matters (perhaps he was influenced by Conrad's methods in 'Heart of Darkness'): at nightfall on a riverside, an Arab tells a group of Europeans the tale of Buta's downfall; and his account is ironically interspersed with references to the hearers and the natural background.

9–13   *Don Juan's Last Wager* (Mrs Cunninghame Graham's translation of *Don Juan Tenorio*, by José de Zorilla y Moral) had opened at the Prince of Wales Theatre, London, on 27 February 1900, and its run ended on 31 March. The principal actor (and the manager) was Graham's acquaintance, Martin Harvey, who describes the disastrous production in *The Autobiography of Sir John Martin-Harvey* (Sampson Low, London, 1935), pp. 242–5.

The *Standard*'s critic was unenthusiastic ('the whole business has an artificiality about it not to be disguised') and censured the translation. (*Standard*, 28 Feb. 1900, p. 5.) The *Speaker* was severely critical of the acting and of Mrs Cunninghame Graham's 'formless' adaptation. (I, 591, 3 March 1900.)

14   'my work': probably *Lord Jim*, which was not finished until July (see letter 40, line 13).

15–17   *The Jew*, which Conrad had received from Edward Garnett in January (*EGL*, p. 163), was the fifteenth and final volume of Mrs Garnett's translation of *The Novels of Ivan Turgenev* (Heinemann, London, 1894–9). 'It is really you that ought to have had the task of translating him', she had once told Conrad. (See G. Jean-Aubry (ed.), *Twenty Letters to Joseph Conrad*, First Edition Club, London, 1926). He had later written to her husband:

> 'I told C. Graham to get Mrs Garnett's translation of Turgeniev. He admires T. but only read the French rendering.' (*EGL*, p. 131.)

Conrad pays tribute to Turgenev in *EGL*, pp. 108–9 and 268–70, and in his Introduction to Edward Garnett's *Turgenev: A Study* (Collins, London, 1917).

In a letter to Graham (28 Dec. 1905), Garnett recommended Turgenev's *Sportsman's Sketches* as a model for the expression of Graham's 'autumnal wistfulness'.

20 'the heart': see *JEC*, p. 58.

40

⟨Grand Hôtel de la Plage
DIGUE
KNOCKE-SUR-MER

———————

Propriétaire   5
Louis Baeyens = Van Tomme⟩

In A hurry to catch post
Belgium.
28 July 1900
Très cher ami   10

Yesterday I dispatched a letter to Morrocco, with apologies and news and a lot of loose chat which is no loss to you.

Jim finished on the 16ᵗʰ inst. At last. It is going to appear in book form (by itself). in October.

I started upon a small holiday at once even before the last instᵗ of 15 Jim had been typed and corrected. I shall do that here.

Youth, Heart of darkness and some story of the same kind which I shall write before long are to form a vol of Tales which (unless forbidden) it is my intention to dedicate to You.

My brain reduced to the size of a pea seems to rattle about in 20 my head. I can't rope in a complete thought; I am exhausted mentally and very depressed.

Pity I miss you. It would have done my heart good to see and hear you—you the most alive man of the century.

I am awfully sickened by "public affairs". They made me 25 positively ill in Febrʸ last. Ten days in bed and six weeks of suspended animation.

135

Drop me a line here. We return to the Pent on the 15th of August. I *must* see you when you come to London again. Jessie's
30 kindest regards. Borys (who's grown very ugly) remembers you perfectly and still wears the heart. Ever Yours Conrad.

PUBLICATION
This letter is unpublished.

TEXT
11 'Morrocco': *sic.*
14 '(by itself).': inserted.
17 'of the same kind': inserted.

COMMENTARY
1–3, 15–16   Conrad, with his wife and Borys, had travelled to Bruges shortly after 16 July. After meeting F. M. Hueffer and his wife they had proceeded to Knocke, whence the Conrads returned towards the end of August (*LL*, I, 295–6: *JEC*, p. 71).

13–14   After its serialisation in *Blackwood's Magazine*, *Lord Jim* was published in October 1900 by Blackwood, London.

17–19   The correspondence about this dedication illustrates the circumspection with which Conrad approached his relationships with friends and publishers.

Originally William Blackwood and Conrad had intended *Youth*, 'Heart of Darkness' and the then unfinished *Lord Jim* to appear as one volume. On 12 February 1899, Conrad had written to Blackwood:

'Re volume of short stories. I wished for some time to ask you whether you would object to my dedicating the Vol: to R. B. Cunninghame Graham. Strictly speaking it . . . . . is a matter between the dedicator and the other person, but in this case—considering the imprint of the House and your own convictions I would prefer to defer to your wishes. I do not dedicate to C. Graham the socialist or to C. Graham the aristocrat (he is both—you know) but to one of the few men I *know*—in the full sense of the word—and knowing cannot but appreciate and respect—abstractedly as human beings. I do not share his political convictions or even all his ideas of art, but we have enough ideas in common to base a strong friendship upon. Should you dislike the notion I'll inscribe the *Rescue* to him instead of the Tales.' (Blackburn, pp. 51–2.)

Conrad's 'apologia' for 'Heart of Darkness' (*ibid.* pp. 36–7) had previously shown his anxiety not to offend Blackwood's conservatism. Blackwood now asked David Meldrum for advice, and on 15 February Meldrum reported:

'*Cunningham Grahame* [*sic*]. I think it could do nothing but good to the book to have it dedicated to so brilliant a writer as Cunningham Grahame, as Conrad proposes . . . . .' (*Ibid.* p. 57.)

But when *Youth: A Narrative; and Two Other Stories* appeared in November 1902, it bore the dedication 'TO MY WIFE'; and eventually it was the volume *Typhoon* which was dedicated to Graham: partly because *Typhoon* was published by Heinemann, to whom Conrad was less beholden than to Blackwood, and also, perhaps, because the idea for *Typhoon* may partly have been prompted by Graham (see letter 6, note 53–5).

Conrad showed similar circumspection in writing to Meldrum about Garnett:

'Whatever his political and social opinions may be.....his attitude towards literature is, one may say, aristocratic. This obviously is not the same thing as conservative—still.' (Blackburn, p. 109, 1 Sept. 1900.)

When *Blackwood's Magazine* had rejected an item by Garnett, Graham had commented (unjustly) that Blackwood was 'the Puritanic holder up of patronage for those who are in no need', remarking 'There *is* no Blackwood. It is the sole blot on Conrad's otherwise blameless literary career.....' (Graham to Garnett, 17 April 1899.)

41

<Station:—
Sandling Junction,
S.E.R.

PENT FARM,
STANFORD, near HYTHE,
KENT.>
10th Oct 1900.

Très cher ami.   5

I know I am a beast. I've read Cruz Alta four days ago. C'est tout simplement *magnifique*. I knew most of the sketches, in fact nearly all, except Cruz Alta itself.

I shall write you about them in a few days. I am oppressed by the sense of my scoundrelism. This is only to let you know that   10
I am writing by this post to P telling him to send me 20 pounds which I shall forward to you at once as soon as I get the cheque.

I've been in bed ill and hopeless. Now I am tottering about and trying to write.

Don't cast me out utterly—but anyhow ever yours   15

J Conrad

PUBLICATION
This letter is unpublished.

TEXT
15 'utterly': appears to be an alteration of 'bitterly'.

137

6–9 Graham's tale 'Cruz Alta' was part of the volume *Thirteen Stories*, which had just been published (Heinemann, London, September 1900, *ECB*). Several of the items in the volume, but not 'Cruz Alta', had previously appeared in the *Saturday Review*. A few references in the tale may have contributed to *Nostromo* (see Introduction above, p. 38).

11 'P': probably Sydney S. Pawling of Heinemann's.

42

⟨THE BUNGALOW,
WINCHELSEA, Nr. RYE,
SUSSEX.⟩
New Year's Eve 1901

5 Très cher ami.

We have been here since the 24th and your letter did not reach me till yesterday, sent on by my wife who has gone home. I remain here to work up the last of our coll^{on} stuff.

I was under the impression that neither your wife nor yourself were in London—or even in England. So we only sent a card. For the same reason I did not write of the *Vanished Arcadia*

I am altogether under the charm of that book, in accord with its spirit and full of admiration for its expression. My very highest appreciation of your work (your written work—your lived work) can not be news to you. To word it efficiently I can not. The more one likes a book the less there seems to be in our power to say it. I haven't the vol here. Hueffer lent his copy. I should like to write to you with the book at my elbow. There are supreme places—but the *evenness* of inspiration feeling and effort is amazing

Ever Yours Conrad.

20

My best wishes to you both for the coming year.

You are very good to commend typhoon so much. It causes me the greatest pleasure. If you can see N^{os} of Ill^{d} Lond: News for the *14th 21st 28th* Dec^{er} there is a story of mine—Amy Foster. J'ai des doutes là dessus. Dites moi ce que Vous en pensez.

PUBLICATION
This letter is unpublished.

6–8, 17   As the letterhead shows, Conrad and his wife had been spending Christmas at the home of F. M. Hueffer.

8   'coll^on stuff': Since 1898 (cf. *LL*, I, 252–3) Conrad had intermittently been collaborating with Hueffer on *The Inheritors*, which had been published in July 1901 by Heinemann, and on *Romance* (née *Seraphina*), which was eventually published by Smith and Elder in October 1903 (*ECB*). A later product of the collaboration, 'The Nature of a Crime', appeared in the *English Review*, II, 70–8, 279–301 (April and May 1909), and was issued in book form by Duckworth in 1924.

9–10   Graham had been in Tangier earlier in the year, but by December he had returned to London and was staying at 7 Sloane Street (letter of 2 Dec. 1901 from Graham to McIntyre, NLS).

11–19   Graham's *A Vanished Arcadia: being some account of the Jesuits in Paraguay, 1607 to 1767* had been published by Heinemann, London, in September 1901.

In this history, one of Graham's main purposes is to make a contrast between on the one hand the relatively humane treatment of the natives in the Jesuit missions, where work proceeded in, he claims, a 'half-Arcadian, half-communistic manner' (p. 179), and on the other hand the exploitation of the natives by present-day European colonisers in other parts of the globe:

'It is easy to understand that the Spanish colonists, who had looked on all the Indians as slaves, were rendered furious by the advent of the Jesuits, who treated them as men.

To-day the European colonist in Africa labours less to enslave than to exterminate the natives; but if a body of clergy of any sect having the abnegation and disregard of consequences of the Jesuits of old should arise, fancy the fury that would be evoked if they insisted that it were as truly murder to slay a black man as it is to kill a man whose skin is white. Most fortunately, our clergy of to-day, especially those of the various churches militant in Uganda, think otherwise, and hold that Christ was the first inventor of the "colour-line".' (P. 53.)

22   'typhoon': Either Graham had read this tale (or part of it) before publication, or else the January number of the *Pall Mall Magazine* had appeared at the end of December, and he had just read the first part of *Typhoon* there. (It was serialised from January to March 1902. The first London edition was not issued until 1903 by Heinemann.) Graham claimed that *Typhoon* was 'the greatest of Conrad's battling sea pieces' (MS. inscription in a copy of the book: Yale).

23–4   'Amy Foster' had been serialised in 1901 in the *Illustrated London News* on the dates that Conrad gives here; it was later included in *Typhoon and Other Stories*.

43

Très cher ami.

Many thanks for your good and friendly letter. You have lost
5 no time in cheering me up. I however have been thinking of many
enthusiastic things to say of *Success* and written none of them.
Indeed when trying to talk of your work I am afraid to show myself
unintelligent in expression and that's the secret of my taciturnity.
But *Success* is a success—there's no doubt of it. The thing is
10 "telling" all along, from the first sentence of your preface. Your
prefaces are wonderful.

I feel so dull and muddle-headed that I daren't even attempt
to give you now an idea of the effect the little volume had produced
on me. One can only feel grateful to you; and, after all I am so
15 much in accord with your sentiment (ne pas confondre avec "senti-
mentalisme") that I can't say anything illuminating as to my
feelings. As to any critical remarks, that, from me to you, is impossible; I accept you without reservations; you express yourself
too consummately for anything else to matter even if I were stupid
20 enough not to *feel* your logic.

There may be a fallacy somewhere in your view of the world.
There may—it's of no consequence. For myself I see with you;
your talent has for me the fascination of deeper truth while with
others I fall under the spell of your brilliance which is as genuine,
25 I believe, as anything in letters since the invention of printing.
Mille amitiés

Tout à vous J.Conrad

PUBLICATION

This letter is unpublished.

TEXT

14 'so': written above the cancelled word 'too'.
16 'anything': follows the cancelled word 'much'.
24 'is': an insertion.

COMMENTARY

5–25 Graham's volume *Success* had been published by Duckworth,
London, in October 1902 (*ECB*). It was reissued by Duckworth in
1912 (twice), in 1927 and in 1936; and an American edition was pub-

lished by Stokes, New York, in 1917. It includes 'The Impenitent
Thief', on which Conrad had commented at length in letters 8 and 9.
The preface is a humorous attack on patrons, critics and the 'respectable
public' in general.

In a discussion of Conrad's accentuation, Ford Madox Ford
remarks that Conrad

'would talk of Mr. Cunninghame Graham's book *Success* alternately
as *Suc*cess and Suc*cess*, half a dozen times in the course of a conversation about the works of that very wonderful writer.' (*Joseph
Conrad: A Personal Remembrance*, Duckworth, London, 1924,
p. 201.)

44

19 Mch 1903
Pent Farm.

Très cher ami.

I hope you've forgiven my long silence. It is not, on reflection,
a very great transgression; seeing that the best of us have but a   5
few thoughts and that of these the best worth saying have a trick
of being unutterable—not because of their profundity but because
there is a devil that tangles the tongue or hangs to the penholder
making its use odious and the sound of words foolish like the
banging of tin cans.   10

With this exordium—c'est le mot, n'est ce pas?—I approach
you with the offering of my book whose title-page proof I've just
sent back to the Yahudi. It is to appear on the 22ᵈ of April (not on
the *first* as the War office Army Corps do) and the exordium above   15
is a sort of explanatory note upon the brevity of its dedication.

I have been reading again the Vanished Arcadia—from the
dedication, so full of charm, to the last paragraph with its ironic
aside about the writers of books "proposing something and con-   20
cluding nothing"—and its exquisite last lines bringing out the all-
resuming image of travellers "who wandering in the Tarumensian
woods come on a clump of orange-trees run wild amongst the
urundéys."

A fit beginning and a fit note to end a book for which I have the   25
greatest admiration wherein profound feeling and the poor judg-
ment of such reason as Allah deigned give me are in perfect accord.
Not for me are such beginnings and such endings. I should like to

draw your attention therefore to the austere simplicity of the " *To*
30 *R. B. Cunninghame Graham*" and nothing more—if my conscience
didn't whisper, what you will see without any pointing out, that
this is not austerity—but barrenness and nothing else—the awful
lack of words that overcomes the thought struggling eagerly
towards the lips.
35

Et voilà! It is poor, poor: the dedication saying nothing and the
book proposing something, wherefrom no power on earth could
extract any kind of conclusion; but such as they are, and worth
less than one single solitary leaf in the wilderness of the Taru-
40 mensian woods, they are yours.

Je vous serre la main

Tout à vous

Jph. Conrad.

PUBLICATION

LL, I, 311–12.
27 'deigned give': Aubry reads 'deigned to give'.

TEXT

19 'paragraph': follows the cancelled word 'phrase'.
37 'wherefrom': above a cancelled word, possibly 'with'.

COMMENTARY

12–16 *Typhoon and Other Stories* was issued by Heinemann, London,
in April 1903 (*ECB*), with the following dedication: 'TO / R. B.
CUNNINGHAME GRAHAM'.
14 'Yahudi': (Heb.) 'Jew'.
14–15 'not on the *first*.....': Lord Grenfell was to take command of the
4th Army Corps on 1 April, as part of a scheme which was meeting
strong parliamentary opposition (*Annual Register* for 1903, p. 27).
18–28 Cf. letter 42, lines 11–19.

45

⟨Station:
Sandling Junction,
S.E.R.

PENT FARM,
STANFORD, near HYTHE,
KENT.⟩
1903
9 May   5

Très cher ami.

Don't let your dedicatory obligation interfere with your peace of mind. Frankly, I am more than repaid by the satisfaction of seeing your name at the head of my book. It is a public declaration of our communion in more, perhaps, than mere letters and I don't 10 mind owning to my pride in it.

And if you will mettre le comble a Vos bontés you may render me a service by coming to see me here. (I speak not of heartfelt pleasure—cela va sans dire). I want to talk to you of the work I am engaged on now. I hardly dare avow my audacity—but I am 15 placing it in Sth America in a Republic I call Costaguana. It is however concerned mostly with Italians. But you must hear the *sujet* and this I can't set down on a small piece of paper.

Shall I send your copy of *Typhoon* to the club at once or may I keep it here till you find time to run down to my wretched 20 ranche in the wilderness. Tout a vous

Conrad.

PUBLICATION

LL, I, 314–15.

TEXT

21 'ranche': *sic*.

COMMENTARY

7–11 Graham later dedicated *Progress* (1905) to Conrad, and thus repaid the 'obligation' for the dedication of *Typhoon*.
12–18 See Introduction, above pp. 37–42.
19 'the club': probably the Devonshire.

46

<Station: PENT FARM,
Sandling Junction,   STANFORD, near HYTHE,
S.E.R.   KENT.>
                                                              1903
5   21 May
Très cher ami.

thanks for your good letter. I am glad you like the shorter stories
but je me berce dans l'illusion that *Falk* is le clou of that little show.
Of course: Gambusino. I ought to have corrected my proofs
10 carefully.
The book (Maison du Peché) has arrived and is now half read.
Without going further my verdict is that it is good, but is not "fort".
For that sort of thing *no matter how good* I always feel a secret
contempt for the reason that it is just *what I can do* myself—
15 essentielment. Fundamentally I believe that sort of fiction (I *don't*
mean the *subject* of course) is somehow wrong. Too easy. Trop
inventé; never *assez vécu*. There is a curse on the descriptive
analysis of that sort.
Kindest regards from us both. Always yours
20   Jph.Conrad.

PUBLICATION

LL, I, 314.

TEXT

5 Although this date is indistinct, the alternative reading ('2 May')
   may be dismissed because this letter clearly follows that of 9 May,
   when Graham had yet to receive *Typhoon*.
7 'shorter': inserted.
15 'essentielment': *sic*.

COMMENTARY

7–8 *Typhoon and Other Stories* (Heinemann, London, 1903) included
     'Falk', 'Amy Foster' and 'To-morrow'.
9   'Gambusino' (a Mexican term for 'roving prospector, fortune-
     seeker or adventurer') had been mis-spelt as 'Gambucino' in 'To-
     morrow' (*Typhoon*, pp. 297–8).
11–18 Marcelle Tinayre's *La Maison du Péché* had been published by
     Calmann Lévy, Paris, in 1902. This conventionally romantic treat-
     ment of sexual and psychological conflict brings far more readily to
     mind Mrs Cunninghame Graham's *Genara* than any of Conrad's tales;
     though it may perhaps be worth noting that the name of Marcelle
     Tinayre's unscrupulous egoist, Barral, recurs in *Chance*.

47

8 July 1903

Très chèr ami.

Your delightful enthusiasm for les Trois Contes positively refreshed my mind jaded with a sort of hopeless overwork.

I forward you the effigy (executed by Jacob Artiste Photographe) of your humble friend and servant. You are not however expected to compromise yourself by keeping it in a prominent place.

Trèves des plaisanteries! I am dying over that cursed Nostromo thing. All my memories of Central America seem to slip away. I just had a glimpse 25 years ago—a short glance. That is not enough pour bâtir un roman dessus. And yet one must live.

When it's done I'll never dare look you in the face again. Meantime (and always)

tout à vous

J. Conrad.

Presentez mes devoirs a Mme votre femme. What of the novel? When is it coming out? I admit I've been struck and excited by your mere hint of its subject.

PUBLICATION

LL, I, 315.

COMMENTARY

6 'les Trois Contes': Aubry identifies them as *Typhoon and Other Stories*. However, as that volume contains four tales, the reference here is to *Youth: a Narrative; and Two Other Stories* (Blackwood, London, 1902), which Conrad had thought of entitling

'"Three Tales" by Joseph Conrad. Flaubert (mutatis mutandis) published Trois contes.' (Blackburn, p. 55.)

13 'a glimpse': Conrad claimed to have spent about three days ashore at La Guayra and twelve hours at Puerto Cabello, 'on that dreary coast of Venla.' (*LL*, II, 321–2.)

19 'the novel': presumably Gabriela Cunninghame Graham's *Genara*, which was never published. (According to Graham's note on the flyleaf of the typescript, it was written in the period 1901–2.)

21 'its subject': The novel describes a disrupted love-affair between the quarter-Spanish, three-quarters-Scottish aristocrat, Evan Gordon, and his Spanish servant-girl, Genara. After a brief idyll in Spain the lovers

are separated through the machinations of Evan's mother and her friends. Evan returns to Scotland, and, being falsely informed that Genara has married, himself marries a girl of high birth who deserts him. He travels again to Spain, finds that Genara has entered a convent, and begs her to elope with him. At this moment she is dragged away by 'something—a shadow—a gigantic form', and the novel ends as follows:

'A swift hand drew the curtains to, and he was left alone in the silence of the empty Church. His eyes fell on the pale Christ. The features seemed to him to be writhed in an ironical smile. He raised his hand: he cursed it. He went swiftly towards the altar. He would spit upon it, drag it from its pedestal; he sawed the air with clenched fists in impotent frenzy like a madman; then he waved them help-lessly—uncertainly above his head as if to guard against some appalling menace—some awful danger. He was no longer conscious what he did. A slight froth whitened his lips. And then something in his brain seemed to burst. He felt his senses wavering; a thin trickle of blood ran from his mouth and he fell prone, face forwards on the Altar steps under the shadow of the Christ!'

Beside and beneath the last two lines of typescript is the following comment in Edward Garnett's hand:

'To get rid of the slight over-dramatic touch—Make a new sentence here, in which the idea is expressed more subtly, & quite simply,—as "His head lay on the corner of the Altar steps where struck the shadow of the Christ."'

The novel is breathlessly romanticised autobiography; Evan, his mother, and Genara being remotely based on Graham, Mrs Bontine, and Gabriela respectively, and with Gartmore providing the background for the Scottish scenes, Vigo the background for the Spanish scenes.

If Conrad ever saw her book, Gabriela's treatment of the romantic-aesthetic hero would probably have convinced him of his wisdom in abandoning *The Sisters*.

48

⟨Station: Sandling Junction, S.E.R.

PENT FARM, STANFORD, near HYTHE, KENT.⟩ Tuesday.

5 Très chèr ami.

Your Saturday Review fling is first rate. Nothing I liked more since the gold-fish carrier story

As to Rothenstein's proposal I am infinitely flattered to be drawn by him—and to be drawn in such company.

The question is whether he would find my personality sufficiently interesting. 10

Après tout, even admitting I *am* deserving, it is not every deserving person that is worth drawing from the artist's point of view—qui est sacré. The other question is: would he consent to come here for a day in a bohême spirit as a sort of wild pic-nic. 15 May I venture to ask him? For—I appeal to our loved Hudson— the wild beast should be studied and figured in its "habitat". Is it not so. Pray advise me on that point.

My wife joins me in kind regards

Borys has been 7 days in bed but is up now. Tout à vous 20

Jph Conrad.

PUBLICATION

This letter is unpublished.

COMMENTARY

4 'Tuesday.': This letter may be ascribed to 1903, and more tentatively to 25 August or one of the Tuesdays in September 1903, for the following reasons: Rothenstein first visited Pent Farm in late September or early October 1903 (note 8–16). As the letter was written before this visit, and as 'pic-nic' (line 15) suggests that the time of writing was the summer, it may be ascribed to August or September 1903. During those two months, only two 'flings' by Graham appeared in *SR*. These were published on 22 August and 19 September. Tuesdays after 22 August fell on 25 August and 1, 8, 15, 22 and 29 September.

6 'Your Saturday Review fling': perhaps 'Faith' in *SR*, XCVI, 230 (22 Aug. 1903); or 'The Laroch' in *SR*, XCVI, 357 (19 Sept. 1903).

7 'the gold-fish carrier story': i.e. 'The Gold Fish', published in *SR*, LXXXVII, 201–3 (18 Feb. 1899), which Conrad had praised in letter 37, lines 12–14.

8–16 The artist William Rothenstein (1872–1945) was a friend of Graham's, and had travelled in Morocco with him. His account of Graham is given in *Men and Memories*.....*1872–1900* (Faber, London, 1931), 215–24; *Men and Memories*.....*1900–1922* (Faber, London, 1932), pp. 18–19, 44; and *Since Fifty*..... (Faber, London, 1939), pp. 270–2. He visited and drew Conrad at the Pent on a weekend in October 1903: an event which marked the beginning of his friendship and correspondence with Conrad; and the letter from Conrad to Rothenstein praising the portrait made during the recent visit is dated 13 October 1903. (See *Men and Memories*, 1932, pp. 39, 41–3. A reproduction of one of his sketches of Conrad at this period faces p. 42.)

16 'our loved Hudson': W. H. Hudson (1841–1922), the novelist and

ornithologist whom Conrad epitomizes in letter 79, was another of
Rothenstein's subjects. Rothenstein's *Twenty-four Portraits* (Allen and
Unwin, London, 1920) includes a drawing of Hudson, an unsigned
essay on Hudson by Graham, and an essay on and portrait of Conrad.

49

Cher Ami.

I snatch this piece of MS paper first of all to thank you for
remembering the boy at this festive (?) season. Next to tell You
that H. de Soto is most exquisitely excellent: your very mark and
spirit upon a subject that only *you* can do justice to—with your
wonderful English and your sympathetic insight into the souls of
the Conquistadores. The glamour, the pathos and the romance of
that time and of those men are only adequately, truthfully, con-
veyed to us by your pen; the sadness, the glory and the romance of
the endeavour together with the vanity of vanities of the monstrous
achievement are reflected in your unique style as though you had
been writing of men with whom you had slept by the camp fire
after tethering your horses on the treshold of the unknown.

You have an eye for buried jewels! The Pizarro going about
mournfully with his hat pulled down on his ears after the death of
Atahualpa is new to me. He is made unforgettable at last. "C'est
énorme d'humanité" as the great Flaubert would have yelled to the
four winds of heaven. What a touch. Behold in this Conquistador
my long lost brother together with those others: the Indio gentile
hombre shouting insults underneath his tree and the thirty lances
riding on to the sea, some of them already with death sitting on
the pillion behind; to be received with the question: "Have you
seen any signs of gold in the country?" One seems to hear the very
voice. C'est la verité même! Its the most amazingly natural thing
I've ever read; it gives me a furious desire to learn Spanish and
bury myself in the pages of the incomparable Garcilasso—if only
to forget all about our modern Conquistadores.

Their achievement is monstrous enough in all conscience—but not
as a great human force let loose, but rather like that of a gigantic

and obscene beast. Leopold is their Pizarro, Thys their Cortez and their "lances" are recruited amongst the souteneurs, sous-offs, maquereaux, fruits-secs of all sorts on the pavements of Brussels and Antwerp. I send you two letters I had from a man called Casement, premising that I knew him first in the Congo just 12 years ago. Perhaps you've heard or seen in print his name. He's a protestant Irishman, pious too. But so was Pizarro. For the rest I can assure you that he is a limpid personality. There is a touch of the Conquistador in him too; for I've seen him start off into an unspeakable wilderness swinging a crookhandled stick for all weapons, with two bull-dogs: Paddy (white) and Biddy (brindle) at his heels and a Loanda boy carrying a bundle for all company. A few months afterwards it so happened that I saw him come out again, a little leaner a little browner, with his stick, dogs, and Loanda boy, and quietly serene as though he had been for a stroll in a park. Then we lost sight of each other. He was I believe Bsh Consul in Beira, and lately seems to have been sent to the Congo again, on some sort of mission, by the Br Gov^t. I have always thought that some particle of Las Casas' soul had found refuge in his indefatigable body. The letters will tell you the rest. I would help him but it is not in me. I am only a wretched novelist inventing wretched stories and not even up to that miserable game; but your good pen, keen, flexible and straight, and sure, like a good Toledo blade would tell in the fray if you felt disposed to give a slash or two. He could tell you things! Things I've tried to forget; things I never did know. He has had as many years of Africa as I had months—almost.—

Another small matter. S. Perez Triana heard from Pawling of my longing to get away south (when possible) and has written me the kindest letter imaginable, offering information and even introductions. I am quite touched. But pray tell me whether he is Colombian Minister in Spain and if it behoves me to *lui donner de l'Excellence on the envelope*. I don't want faire une *bévue* and after all I know him very little. And à propos what do you think of the Yankee Conquistadores in Panama? Pretty, isn't it? Enfin. Veuillez presenter mes dévoirs les plus respectueux à Madame Votre Femme. Borys instructed me to send his love to you. Jessie's kind regards. Tout à vous

Jph Conrad.

PUBLICATION

LL, I, 324–6.

17 'The Pizarro': Aubry reads 'Pizarro'.

TEXT

14 'of': apparently superimposed on 'on'.
15 'treshold': *sic*.
29 'Garcilasso': *sic*.
50 'been' follows the cancelled words 'had a'.
51 'by' follows the cancelled word 'from'.

COMMENTARY

6 'H. de Soto': Graham's *Hernando de Soto: together with an account of one of his captains, Gonçalo Silvestre* had been published by Heinemann, London, in December 1903.

13–15 Graham's Spanish ancestry, his appearance and his spectacular career, later encouraged his biographers West and Tschiffely to compare him with the Conquistadores.

17–22 *Hernando de Soto*, pp. 36–7.

22–3 *Ibid*. pp. 223–5.

23–6 *Ibid*. pp. 236–7.

28–9 One of Graham's four main sources for *Hernando de Soto* had been *La Florida* by Garcilaso de la Vega.

28–34 Conrad here echoes and endorses one of Graham's barbed comparisons: see *Hernando de Soto*, pp. x–xi:

'The massacres in German Africa may be put beside the worst deeds of Cortes, and the inhuman bringing in of basketfuls of human hands in Belgian Congoland excels the atrocities of any Spaniard in the whole conquest of America. That which the Spaniards did in the green tree three hundred years ago.....all Europe does to-day in the dry tree of modern Christianity and in full view of an indifferent world.'

34 'Leopold': King Leopold II of the Belgians, president of 'L'Association Internationale pour l'Exploration et la Civilisation en Afrique', which may have been in Conrad's mind when he chose to make Kurtz the representative, in 'Heart of Darkness', of 'The International Society for the Suppression of Savage Customs'.

Conrad and Hueffer appear to have based on the character of Leopold II their portrayal of the unscrupulous Duc de Mersch, who in *The Inheritors* is financier of 'a "Pan-European Railway, Exploration, and Civilization Company" that let in light in dark places' (Dent, 1923, p. 78). Certainly Hueffer later claimed that in *The Inheritors*

'the sub-villain was to be Leopold II, King of the Belgians, the foul —and incidentally lecherous—beast who had created the Congo Free State in order to grease the wheels of his harems with the blood of murdered negroes.' (Ford Madox Ford, *Joseph Conrad: A Personal Remembrance*, Duckworth, London, 1924, pp. 133–4.)

Conrad's final judgement on Belgian enterprise in the Congo was expressed as forcefully as any of Graham's: in 'Geography and Some Explorers' he described it as

'the vilest scramble for loot that ever disfigured the history of human conscience.....' (Last Essays, Dent, 1928, p. 17.)

And in the same essay (pp. 3–4 ff.) recurs the association of the Conquistadores with the Imperialists that is developed in this letter.

34 'Thys': Captain Albert Thys, acting manager of the Société Anonyme Belge pour le Commerce du Haut-Congo, with whom Conrad had had a successful interview in November 1889 after applying for a command of one of the company's steamers in Africa. (See LFR, pp. 25–30.) This experience with Thys doubtless contributed to the account of Marlow's interview in 'Heart of Darkness'.

Thys had written that on arriving at Matadi,

'on se croirait devant un pays maudit, véritable barrière qui semble créée par la nature pour arrêter le progrès. (Au Congo et au Kassaï, Brussels, 1888, p. 7, quoted by Aubry in Vie de Conrad, Gallimard, Paris, 1947, p. 158.)

37–49 Conrad had first met Roger Casement (1864–1916) at Matadi on 13 June 1890. He regarded the meeting as 'a positive piece of luck', and recorded of Casement: 'Thinks, speaks well, most intelligent and very sympathetic.' (Last Essays, p. 161.)

49–60 After consular service in Angola, Lourenço Marques, Durban, Capetown, Kinchassa and Boma, Casement had been asked by the British government in 1903 to report on the alleged atrocities in the Belgian Congo. The report, dated 11 December 1903, was published in February 1904; and its accounts of slave-dealings, mutilations, and other evils inflicted on the natives provoked an outcry in the press. See Accounts and Papers, LXII, 'Correspondence and Report from His Majesty's Consul at Boma respecting the Administration of the Independent State of the Congo' (H.M. Stationery Office, 1904).

Presumably the letters mentioned in line 37 contained a request that Conrad should help to publicise Casement's findings and should support the formation of the Congo Reform Association, which was publicly announced on the following 23 March. The previous quotation from Hernando de Soto has shown that Graham was already concerned to draw attention to the allegations; and on 1 January he had a meeting with Casement, who spent 3 January with the Conrads at Hythe. (René MacColl: Roger Casement, Hamish Hamilton, London, 1956, p. 42; and JEC, pp. 103–4. Mr MacColl tells me that his source was no. 2 of Casement's notorious diaries.)

In 1928 Graham wrote to H. W. Nevinson about Casement:

'He was presumably a brave man, and did splendid work both in the Congo and on the Putumayo. The abnormality of his private life, which I hear from Conrad, from Englishmen who had known him in Paranagua and Rio de Janeiro, did not weigh with me at the least.....it is not a disease that is catching.....

He died like a brave man, and for that I respect him, as I respect the consistent courage that he showed throughout his life.' (Letter of 27 November, quoted in *AFT*, pp. 391–3.)

52 'Las Casas': In *Hernando de Soto*, pp. x–xi and 193, Graham had praised Bartolomé de las Casas for being one of the few Spaniards to treat the Indians as human beings and to protest against their exploitation by the conquerors.

61–7 Don Santiago Pérez Triana (1860–1916), Colombian ambassador to Spain and England, diplomat, author, and editor of *Hispania*, reappears as Don José Avellanos in *Nostromo* and as 'the Minister of Costalarga' in Graham's 'A Belly-God' (see appendix 2, below).

61 'Pawling': Sydney S. Pawling of William Heinemann: a firm that published work by Conrad, Graham and Triana.

67–8 In November 1903 the United States had intervened in Panama, which was then Colombian territory, with the result that control of the Canal passed from Colombia to the United States. Both Graham and Triana were loud in their denunciations of this act of 'predatory imperialism'.

50

⟨Station:
Sandling Junction,
S.E.R.

PENT FARM,
STANFORD, near HYTHE,
KENT.⟩
18 May 1904

5 Très cher ami.

It is only from Pawling's letter today that I learn you are here. And first my thanks for the brass censer-cup (I call it) which I received some time ago. It is a thing I like—first with affection as coming from you and next from taste because it is brass for
10 which I have a fondness. The form is good too. Is it meant for embers to light one's pipe? Or is it for burning perfumes? Anyway it contains cigarettes now and stands at my elbow as I write or read.

Pawling's proposal of a joint article is fascinating. Whether it is practicable that is another affair. I desire it to come off. The
15 question hangs on your inclination and leisure. It would be jolly to have a day's sail, and a talk between sky and water: say starting from Deal in one of their galleys through the Downs and round Nth Foreland to Margate Roads. But I am afraid it would bore you to death. And in such promenades there is always too
20 much sun—or not enough: too little wind—or else a confounded, unnecessary blast. And yet, now and then, one falls upon a perfect day. Is your luck good? I mean that propitious Fortune of which

Sylla the dictator was the spoilt child. As to my luck I prefer to say nothing of it. I am absolutely ashamed to mention it; because if "Fortune favours the brave" I must be about the poorest sort 25 of coon on earth. Enfin.

Do let me know how you are. I presume you've been in Morocco. Rothenstein could not tell me—only the other day. Il est artiste celui là—et pas bête. N'est ce pas? Kindest regards from us all Tout à vous J Conrad. 30

PS m'est avis qu'il faut nous faire payer bien par ces gens là. Moi parcque j'en ai besoin et Vous par principe. Ce brave P. est vague sur ce point là.

PUBLICATION

LL, I, 329–30.
31–3   Omitted by Aubry.

TEXT

32   'parcque': *sic.*

COMMENTARY

6–8   Graham had probably been on one of his periodic visits to Morocco: his first *SR* article for two months appeared the following Saturday, and described village life in Angira, Tetuan and Tarifa. ('From the Stoep', *SR*, XCVII, 681, 28 May 1904.)

13–15, 31–3   S. S. Pawling was a partner of William Heinemann. Heinemann published work by both Conrad and Graham, and as Conrad had previously collaborated with Hueffer, the proposal of a joint article was understandable; but it seems to have been fruitless.

15–16   Graham came to visit Conrad before 2 July (see letter 51, lines 7–8).

23   'Sylla': L. C. Sulla, surnamed Felix, dictator of Rome from 82 to 79 B.C.; and celebrated by Plutarch for his good fortune.

28–9   See letter 48, note 8–16. Between 1904 and 1905 Rothenstein raised support to enable Conrad to receive confidentially an official grant of £500. (*LL*, II, 14–15; Rothenstein, *Men and Memories* . . . . . *1900–1922*, Faber, London, 1932, pp. 61–2.)

51

<Station: PENT FARM,
Sandling Junction,   STANFORD, near HYTHE,
S.E.R.   KENT.>

2 July 1904

5 Très cher ami.

Cigarettes came first and the two books followed. You are very good. Your too short visit has been a god-send. You've left me believing once more in the reality of things

Hudson's "Sparrow" is really first rate and just in the tone 10 I expected. C'est une belle nature, which never falls short in its domain. One can depend upon him.

The other vol^um I've been reading with a surprised admiration. It shall be an abiding delight—I see that much. But I don't pretend to have seen *everything* as yet. The sheer interest in themes and 15 workmanship stands as yet in the way of deeper appreciation. One must read oneself *into* the true quality of the book.

And so poor Watts is coming to the end of his august career. What a full and rounded life. And yet it seems poor in stress and passion which are the true elixirs against the majestic overpowering 20 tediousness of an existence full of allegoric visions. Dieu nous preserve de cette grandeur! Better be born a lord—a king—better die Arch priest of an incredible religion!

My wife sends her kind regards and Borys his love. The Cricket set is a great and solid success
25   Tout à Vous
           JphConrad.

Veuillez me rappelez au gracieux souvenir de Madame Votre Mère dont je n'oublierais jamais le bienveillant accueil.

PUBLICATION
LL, I, 331.
24 'solid': Aubry reads 'big'.

TEXT
14 'as': an insertion.

COMMENTARY
9–10 W. H. Hudson's nostalgic poem 'The London Sparrow' had been included in *Kith and Kin, Poems of Animal Life* selected by H. S. Salt

(Bell, London, 1901)—the book that Hudson had sent to Graham's mother (*WHH*, p. 65). Graham ironically described this poem as 'mischievous and Machiavellian' in *SR*, CVI, 393 (26 Sept. 1908).

12 'The other vol^{um}': perhaps Hudson's *Green Mansions*, which had been first published by Duckworth in February (*ECB*). On 3 April Hudson told Garnett:

'Mrs Cunninghame Graham wrote me a remarkable letter about *G.M.* a few days ago and said she wants to review the book in the *Saturday*, but she is too late.....' (E. Garnett (ed.), *Letters from W. H. Hudson to Edward Garnett*, Dent, London, 1925, p. 62.)

In December, Graham reviewed Hudson's *The Purple Land* (*SR*, XCVIII, 695–6, 3 Dec. 1904) and took the opportunity to praise both Hudson and Conrad for being distinguished among contemporary English writers by their cosmopolitan outlook.

17–22 G. F. Watts (1817–1904), the sculptor and painter celebrated for allegoric works like 'Mammon' and 'Death Crowning Innocence', had died on 1 July after a period of illness. G. K. Chesterton said of him:

'Here is a man whose self-depreciation is internal and vital; whose life is cloistered, whose character is child-like, and he has yet within such unconscious and colossal sense of greatness that he paints on the assumption that his work may outlast the cross of the Eternal City.' (*G. F. Watts*, Duckworth, London, 1904, p. 60.)

27–8 In the following month Conrad sent Mrs Bontine a copy of *Typhoon and Other Stories* as a token of gratitude for her interest in his work (*LL*, I, 317–18).

52

⟨Station:
Sandling Junction
S.E.R.

PENT FARM,
STANFORD near HYTHE,
KENT.⟩
7th Oct 1904

Très cher ami.

I forgive you (generously) the treacherous act of looking at a fragment of Nostromo. On your side you must (generously) forgive me for stealing and making use of in the book of your excellent "y dentista" anecdote.

The story comes out on Thursday next. Don't buy it. I'll send you a copy of—and in due—course. I expect as of right and in virtue of our friendship an abusive letter from you upon it; but I stipulate a profound and unbroken secrecy of your opinion as before everybody else. I feel a great humbug.

I am glad to hear you are in possession of your new house.

I wondered where you were. Hudson imagined you in Morocco. I met him the other day; dear as ever but a little depressed.

I notice there is no date yet to the adv^{ents} of your next (Duckworth) volume.

20 I don't suppose you'll remain very long now in the "Black North". We are contemplating a flight somewhere for the winter. Capri perhaps? Quien sabe? Don Pietro Canonico Ferraro, I hear, lets half his house and terrace with a south exposure above a grove of orange trees—and so on. It may be worth trying.

25 Our kindest regards. I am on the point of taking Jessie up to London to the doctors. C'est triste.

Ever affectionately yours
Jph Conrad.

PUBLICATION

LL, I, 336–7.

TEXT

8 'of.....of': *sic*.

COMMENTARY

6–7 *Nostromo* had been serialised in *T. P.'s Weekly* (London) from 29 January to 7 October 1904.

On 15 October Graham wrote to Garnett:
'Success has not spoiled Conrad. Why should it?
"Nostromo" is, as far as I have seen by bits of it (not a fair way to test a book), perhaps not quite his highest level. But his second best is better than most peoples' best.' (MS., University of Texas Library.) See, however, his verdict given on p. 214.

7–9 The 'y dentista' anecdote is used in *Nostromo*, pp. 444–5 (Dent, 1923). Cf.: 'Conrad tells me he has used a story I told him, in "Nostromo"' (Graham to Garnett, 15 Oct. 1904).

10–11 *Nostromo* was published by Harper's, London and New York, in October 1904.

11–14 See letter 53, lines 8–17.

15–16 After leaving Gartmore in 1900, Graham had stayed alternately, between journeys abroad, at 179 Bath Street, Glasgow, and 7 Sloane Street, London. In the summer of 1904 he had moved into Ardoch, his family's house at Cardross. (Letters to McIntyre, NLS.)

16 'Hudson': W. H. Hudson, whose correspondence with Graham extended from 1890 to 1922. See letter 79, note 6–14.

18–19 *Progress and Other Sketches* was published by Duckworth in February 1905.

22–4 Conrad had originally intended to stay at the Villa Sanfelice, a house on Capri owned by Canonico Pietro Ferraro. The location appears to have been suggested by Charles Davray (*LFR*, p. 68). Eventually Conrad preferred the Villa di Maria.

25–6   Bruce Clarke was to operate on Jessie's left knee (*MPL*, p. 105; *JEC*, pp. 89–91).

53

⟨Station: PENT FARM,
Sandling Junction   STANFORD near HYTHE,
S.E.R.   KENT.⟩
99ᴮ Addison Rᵈ
London W.   5
31 Oct 1904.

Très cher et bon ami.

Your letter was indeed worth having and I blush deeply as I re-read it both with pleasure and shame. For in regard to that book I feel a great fraud.   10

What is done with can not be mended. I know that you have made the most of my audacious effort; but still it is to me a comfort and a delight that you have found so much to say in commendation. Your friendship and good nature, great as they are where my person and scribbling are concerned, would not have induced you 15 to accept anything utterly contemptible—that I know. It is a great load off my chest. Now as to an explanation or two.

I don't defend Nostromo himself. Fact is he does not take *my* fancy either. As to his conduct generally and with women in particular I only wish to say that he is not a Spaniard or S. American. 20 I tried to differentiate him even to the point of mounting him upon a mare which I believe is not or *was not* the proper thing to do in Argentina; though in Chile there was never much of that nonsense. But truly N is nothing at all—a fiction—embodied vanity of the sailor kind—a romantic mouthpiece of "the people" which (I mean 25 "the people") frequently experience the very feelings to which he gives utterance. I do not defend him as a creation.

Costaguana is meant for a S. Amᶜᵃⁿ state in general; thence the mixture of customs and expressions. C'est voulu. I remembered but little and rejected nothing.   30

Mi alma is a more serious mistake. I've heard a little girl so address a pet small dog as they swung in a hammock together. What

157

misled me was this that in Polish that very term of endearment: "My Soul" has not the passionate significance you point out. I am
35 crestfallen and sorry.

Pasotrote I've heard somehow, somewhere, from someone—devil knows where. But the mistake is in the word *canter* which I wrote persistently while I really meant *amble*, I believe. I am appalled simply.
40 I am compunctious as to the use I've made of the impression produced upon me by the Ex^{im} Sr Don Perez Triana's personality. Do you think I have committed an unforgivable fault there? He'll never see or hear the book probably.

I end with a general apology for ever attempting a tale of this
45 kind; and with the renewed assurance of the great pleasure your good long letter has given me. It is a very magnificent sign of forgiveness on your part.

Tout à Vous de cœur

J. Conrad.

50 PS. My wife sends her kind regards. She is not at all well and I am very anxious. Borys too has been in bed a week now. Tonsilitis. The temperature went up to 103° on two nights. But he is mending I am glad to say. Rothenstein likes the book. He got hold of the inwards with an amazing intelligence. E. Garnett likewise wrote
55 me a most appreciative letter. As to the public it will turn its back on it no doubt. Ce sera un four complet. I don't care.

P.P.S. Are you likely to come to town this year? We are here till end of Nov^{er} at least.

PUBLICATION

LL, I, 337–8.

11 'done with can not': Aubry reads 'done cannot'.
35 'and sorry': 'and so sorry'.
43 'hear the book': 'hear of the book'.
57–8 Omitted by Aubry.

TEXT

15 'are': superimposed on 'is'.
28 'meant for': inserted.
29–30 (from 'C'est' to 'nothing.'): apparently inserted between the lines.
31 'heard' follows the cancelled word 'have'.
34 'not': inserted.

41 'me': inserted.
41 'Ex^{im}': ^{im} is indistinct. (This is presumably an abbreviation of 'Excelentísimo'.)

COMMENTARY

8–27 In a letter to Edward Garnett dated 31 October 1904 Graham remarked:

'Yes; "Nostromo" (a damned bad name; the book ought to have been called "Costaguana") is wonderful.

Certainly the last chapters are a mistake.

To me, the interest is in the affairs of Costaguana, & the monologue of the inimitable Captain Mitchell would have been a fit ending. I do not like either, the explanation of the end of Decoud.

Conrad seems to have been run away with "John Burns Nostromo, Esqr", whereas the book is "Costaguana".

All the same "Nostromo" is well done.'

(To Graham, John Burns, M.P. for Battersea from 1892 to 1918, was an example of a popular working-class leader who had betrayed his responsibilities. After his early days as a socialist agitator, during which he had once stood in the dock alongside Graham, Burns had become transigent and successful: from 1905 to 1914 he held office in the Liberal governments as president of the Local Government Board.)

A few days later, Garnett's review of *Nostromo* appeared in the *Speaker* (N.S. xi, 138–9, 12 Nov. 1904); and Garnett's chief adverse criticisms were in essentials the same as those made cursorily in Graham's letter. After praising at length Conrad's skill in conveying the 'psychology of scene' and the life and history of Costaguana as a whole, Garnett added:

'The psychology of certain characters, as Charles Gould, Decoud, and Nostromo himself, is indeed not always clear and convincing ..... We regret that the last two chapters describing Nostromo's death are included in the novel. Their touch of melodrama does violence to the evening stillness of the close. The narrative should have ended with the monologue of Captain Mitchell and the ironic commentary of Dr. Monygham on the fresh disillusionment in store for the *régime* of "Civilisation" planted by European hands on the bloodstained soil of the Republic of Costaguana.'

31 '*Mi alma*': Don José Avellanos addresses Mrs Gould as 'Emilia, my soul' (*Nostromo*, Dent, 1923, pp. 86 and 141).

36 '*Pasotrote*': 'he had come this moment to Costaguana at his easy swift *pasotrote*' (*ibid.* p. 48). The word means 'short trot'. Conrad could have seen it, spelt '*pasitrote*', in Páez's *Wild Scenes in South America*.

42–3 Most of Triana's letters to Graham at this period were sent from Seville.

50–1   Conrad was at this time in London in order to be near his wife while she underwent the operation on her knee.

53–4   Conrad had written to William Rothenstein, discussing *Nostromo*, on 3 September: see Rothenstein's *Men and Memories* . . . . *1900–1922* (Faber, London, 1932), pp. 61–2.

54–5   In his article in the *Speaker*, Edward Garnett said:
'Mr. Conrad. . . . . has a special poetic sense for *the psychology of scene*, by which the human drama brought before us is seen in its just relation to the whole enveloping drama of Nature around, forming both the immediate environment and the distant background. . . . . His method of poetic realism is, indeed, intimately akin to that of the great Russian novelists, but Mr. Conrad, inferior in the psychology of character, has outstripped them in his magical power of creating the whole mirage of Nature.'

57–8   The Conrads appear to have remained in London until 15 January 1905, when they set out for Capri. (*JEC*, p. 91; *LFR*, p. 68.)

54

Villa di Maria
Isola di Capri
(Napoli)
3ᵈ Febr 1905

5   Très cher ami.

This moment I receive Progress; or rather the moment (last night) occurred favourably to let me read before I sat down to write.

Nothing in my writing life (for in the sea life what could
10   approach the pride of one's first testimonial as a "sober and trust-worthy officer"!) has given me greater pleasure, a deeper satisfaction of innocent vanity, a more distinct sense of my work being tangible to others than myself—than the dedication of the book so full of admirable things, from the wonderful preface to the slightest
15   of the sketches within the covers.

My artistic assent the intellectual and moral satisfaction with the truth and force of your thought living in your prose is unbounded without reservation and qualification. And with every masterly turn of phrase masterly in picturesque vision and in
20   matchless wording my pride in the dedication grows, till it equals —nay—almost surpasses—the pride of that long ago moment, in another existence, when another sort of master of quite a different craft vouched with his obscure name for my "sobriety and trust-

worthiness" before his fellows well able to judge and amongst whom I believed my life was destined to run and end. Tout a vous, 25 de cœur

Jph. Conrad

PS Jessie who is progressing favourably sends her kindest regards.

PUBLICATION
LL, II, 10.
20 'my pride in the dedication grows': 'my pride grows'.
25 'to run and end': 'to run to the end'.
28 omitted by Aubry.

TEXT
4 '3ᵈ': indistinct; may be '2ᵈ'.

COMMENTARY
6–15 Graham's *Progress and Other Sketches* (Duckworth, London, Feb. 1905) bore the dedication 'TO JOSEPH CONRAD'.
9–11 Conrad's first voyage as an officer was on the 'Loch Etive', on which he served as third mate from 21 August 1880 to 24 April 1881 (Certificate of Discharge, Yale University Library).
'I will confide to you coyly.....that these suggestive bits of quarter-deck appreciation one and all contain the words "strictly sober".' (*A Personal Record*, Dent, 1923, p. 111.)

55

16 Febr. 05
Villa di Maria
Capri.
Italy
5

Cher Ami.

Your letter is delightful. As to your sea people and their manoeuvres (in *Progress*) You've confounded nothing either in form or in the substance. You seem to know more of all things that I thought it possible for any man to know, since the Renaissance swells (who knew everything about everything) perished by 10 sword, dagger, poison pest (and too much 'doune') in the glorious yesterday of the world.

Vous—Vous êtes né trop tard. The stodgy sun of the future —our early Victorian future—lingers on the horizon, but all the

15 same it will rise—it will indeed—to throw its sanitary light upon
a dull world of perfected municipalities and WC's sans peur et
sans reproche. The grave of individual temperaments is being
dug by GBS and HGW with hopeful industry. Finita la commedia!
Well they may do much but for the saving of the universe I put
20 my faith in the power of folly.

Do come over if you go south our way. A steamer leaves Naples
at 9 am and 3 pm every day. Arrives at Capri noon and six pm. We
can't, Alas! offer to put you up as we are pigging it in 3 rooms of an
inferior villa. But the Hotel de Capri is a place where one can hang
25 out well enough for a small ransom. Of the questions you start in
your "Polish" letter I'll talk—but I don't trust myself to write. It
would scandalise you if I did. Jessie and Borys send their regards.
Tout à vous

Jph. Conrad.

PUBLICATION

LL, II, 12.

TEXT

8 'that': *sic.*
11 "doune": possibly "donne".

COMMENTARY

6–8 Graham's *Progress and Other Sketches* (1905) includes the tale
'McKechnie *v.* Scaramanga', in which many nautical and nautical-
legal terms are employed.

8–12 Cf.:

'A dreamer with a passion for action, one whose dreams are action,
yet whose actions are certainly for the most part dreams, Cunninghame Graham brings a touch of the Elizabethan spirit into contemporary life, urgent, unpractical, haughty, at war with the world,
yet loving the world for its own sake.' (Arthur Symons, *Notes on
Joseph Conrad*, Myers, London, 1925, p. 32.)

13 'The stodgy sun of the future': an image perhaps suggested by
Graham's wild preface to *Progress*, in which he draws an ironic contrast
between 'a sunless world' of a vaguely defined past century ('under an
eighteen-carat sky set with sham diamonds for stars') and the en-
lightened present age in which 'Progress is justified of works,... because
they say so, and all unite to glorify success.' (Pp. xiii–xiv.)

13–17 Cf.:

'Nothing can stand against success and yet keep fresh. Nations
as well as individuals feel its vulgarising power.....So many
hundred feet of sanitary tubes a minute or an hour, so many wage-

162

saving applications of machinery.....Yet those who fail, no matter how ingloriously, have their revenge on the successful few, by having kept themselves free from vulgarity, or by having died unknown.' (*Success*, 1902, p. 8.)

'No doubt, in modern towns, the poor enjoy the doubtful blessings of improved sanitation, gas, and impure water.....; but, on the other hand, they have but little sun, either external or internal, in their lives, and know their misery by the help of the education which they pay for through the rates.' (*Mogreb*, pp. 131–2.)

'This leads me to consider whether, if all the world were regulated by a duly elected county council.....and all men went about minding each other's business.....they would be happier upon the whole than are the unregenerate Moors, who lie and steal, fight, fornicate, and generally behave themselves as if blood circulated in their veins and not sour whey?' (*Mogreb*, pp. 68–9.)

18 'GBS and HGW': Unlike Shaw and Wells, Graham never became a Fabian—largely because of the simple romantic primitivism exemplified above. Shaw's admiration for Graham was eloquently expressed in the Notes to *Captain Brassbound's Conversion*, which repaid Graham for his account of *Mrs Warren's Profession* as 'the best play which has been written in the English language in this generation' (*Daily Chronicle*, 28 April 1898, p. 3—as much an attack on the Censor as a tribute to Shaw). Wells, on the other hand, understood Graham 'only partly' (*LL*, I, 256).

Conrad's perplexed relationship with Wells—and his highly perplexed encounter with Shaw—is described in *Experiment in Autobiography* (Gollancz, London, 1934), II, 615–23, in which Wells writes:

'I think he found me Philistine, stupid and intensely English..... The frequent carelessness of my writing, my scientific qualifications of statement and provisional inconclusiveness, and my indifference to intensity of effect, perplexed and irritated him.'

25–6 A few weeks previously, on 27 January 1905, Garnett had written to Graham:

'I dont think there's so much *life* here, (in England,) as you say. Turgenev, of course, was *an inheritor* of Russian racial depths—& I always feel that where Hudson & you, & Conrad are handicapped is that there's nothing much to *inherit* now!.....I ought to be an Irishman—of the 17th century system—Conrad in Poland—& you in the Scotland of the 14 & 15th Centuries.'

Perhaps these speculations had been mentioned in Graham's 'Polish' letter.

56

⟨Station:
Sandling Junction
S.E.R.

PENT FARM,
STANFORD near HYTHE,
KENT.⟩
4 Oct 1906

5 Très cher ami.

Incredible as it may appear to you the paper you sent was the first news of your loss.

Rest assured of our most heartfelt sympathy. We would be very glad to hear how you are.

10 No matter how deeply one feels it is difficult to say the right thing; and for the conventional condoling phrases I have no heart. If you think of coming south it would be good to see you.

With my wife's kindest regards

Affectionately yours

15 J. Conrad

P.S. In a few days I'll be sending you a little book of mine just about to be published. I intend also to forward a copy to your brother to whom if he is still staying with you please remember me cordially.

PUBLICATION

This letter is unpublished.

COMMENTARY

6–7   Graham's wife, Gabriela, had died on 8 September 1906, aged forty-five.

12   Graham was then at Ardoch, Dunbartonshire.

16–17   *The Mirror of the Sea* was published in October by Methuen, London.

17–18   'your brother': Charles Cunninghame Graham.

57

31 Dec 1906
Riche Hotel.
Montpellier.

Très cher ami.

5 Your letter reached us here and no proof of your friendship could have been more welcome.

I ran away here from the Pent in a sort of panic before the menaces of the winter. A horrid almost suicidal depression sent me off in search of sunshine. We have found it here. The weather is cold, calm dry brilliant. I hope I will be able to work and don't want to get back with less than half a book.

And à propos of book. In December Edward Garnett said to me "I'll give you Cunninghame Graham's book—but I suppose he will send it to you."—I said: "Don't give me his book. I prefer having it from him."—
    The question is:
    Where is the book?
This however is no reproach. It simply explains why I haven't read it yet. Mudie is under instruction to send it on to me here. When it arrives I shall swallow it up at a sitting and then write to you.

We have been thinking much of you this year end. It is sad to think of you feeling your loneliness at this season—though you certainly are a man round whom many affections must be centred, many admirations and even some enmities. To you life must keep its value to the last, and the words you have written the perfect expression of your rare personality shall be read in the far future with the *disinterested* admiration they deserve. Your magnanimous indignations and your human sympathies will be perceived as having made their mark on their time. Words worthy of you, uncompromising and sincere shall be your descendants and the servants of your memory more faithful than any child could be— for alas our children are but men like ourselves with short memories and but an imperfect fidelity to the spirit that has animated our own existence. Exceptional natures are fated to remain alone, but when they possess the gift of noble expression they have and keep a family of their own from generation to generation. Je vous serre bien tendrement les mains. Yours

                                                        Conrad

My wife's love and also love from Borys who has religiously preserved with a special care everything you have ever given him from his very babyhood.

PUBLICATION

LL, II, 40.
5 'us': Aubry reads 'me'.
23 'end': omitted by Aubry.
41-3 also omitted.

COMMENTARY

5-6 Graham's letter probably complimented Conrad on *The Mirror of the Sea*, which had been published in book form in October 1906 (*ECB*): see note 13-16 below and p. 214.

7-8 The Conrads had set out for Montpellier on 16 December 1906 (*LFR*, p. 80). They went from Montpellier to Geneva in the following May, stayed there during June and July, and returned to England by September (*LL*, II, 47-55).

10-11 While at Montpellier, Conrad revised the French translation of 'Karain' (*LL*, II, 39), wrote 'The Duel' and worked on *Chance* (*LL*, II, 41).

13-16 Graham's recent collection, *His People*, had been published in November 1906 (*ECB*) by Duckworth, the firm for which Edward Garnett had worked since leaving Heinemann in 1901 (G. C. Heilbrun, *The Garnett Family*, Allen and Unwin, London, 1961, p. 72). On 30 October 1906 Garnett wrote to Graham:
'Dear Amigo,
    They say that "His People" is printing off, but dont know the exact dates when sheets will reach printer. [*sic*]
    Personally, I should much prefer it to wait over Xmas, as the rush of Xmas books will swamp it—& I I [*sic*] believe it will be reviewed & all better in January than in Nov. or Dec.
    However this is a matter for you & Duckworth to settle.
    Binding will be identical with *Progress*.
    Yes isn't *The Mirror of the Sea* splendid. There is a precision about Conrad's thought, & a hidden music in the phrasing of each sentence, also a flow, & pause, & flow of delivery that is like antique oratory. It is a book for us all to be proud of—*we* the audience.
    I dont think that *Initiation* is equal to *Youth* myself—but still it is magical.
    I much rejoiced in your mother's talk. I feel very near her. I wish I had got near her earlier—it was my fault—but I always feared to intrude. ————
    Yes. Time is like the atmosphere—now a flash of lightning, & now a drifting fog.
    How splendid *His People* (the first story) is. I like it more & more.
        You ought to read
            Les Frères Karamazov—
                By *Dostoievsky*.
            translated by Bielstok.

I have written another play—a modern one—I call it *Seduction*.
I wonder how it would strike you.

     Affectionately   Edward Garnett.'

20 'Mudie': Mudie's Select Library and chain of bookshops, then
controlled by A. O. Mudie.

20–1 See letter 58, lines 5–8.

23–38 Graham had been a widower for three months, and was childless.

34–6 Cf. *LL*, I, 292:
  'I always intended to write something of the kind [an account of
Conrad's ancestors] for Borys, so as to save all this from the abyss
a few years longer. And probably he wouldn't care. What's Hecuba
to him.....?'

58

14 Jan. 1907
Riche Hotel
Montpellier

Très cher ami.

I've read your book with the usual delight and more than the 5
usual admiration. You are incomparable in the consistency and
force of your vision, in the sustained power of expression—and
You are the Great Preface Writer of the Time.

Three times I've gone through your pages so vigorous, so
personal and so exquisite. What a *Return of the Native* you have 10
given us! *His people* is a wonderful piece of description and an
amazing feat of analysis.

And so is each one of these sketches—though I don't know
whether *Sketches* is the right name.

As a matter of fact a new name should be invented for the form 15
of the gems you have given to our literature. They are revelations
of the uncommon in feeling and expression. But that's a poor
definition and I feel I could accumulate words upon words without
coming anywhere near to the line of your peculiar distinction. On
the whole your quality so distinct in effect is in its essence elusive. 20
It is not a superficial gift of brilliance, of wit, of picturesque phrase.
It can't be touched by the critical finger because it lies deep. Its
origin rests in the "sens profond de la vie" characterised by irony
that is gentle and by a fierce sympathy.

Borys charges me to thank you infinitely for the book which 25
arrived safely the other day. He's very delighted with it. But upon

the whole that boy is not a reader. On the other hand he would spend his day on horseback if he were allowed. Just now he seems to live exclusively for riding. We went in search of a Camargue
30 saddle. Not a single one to be found in Montpellier. Arles, the riding master tells me, is the nearest place where I could see one. Our love to you. Yours always   Conrad.

PUBLICATION
This letter is unpublished.

COMMENTARY
5 'your book': *His People*.
10–12 The title-story of the book is a melancholy study of a Spaniard's homecoming.
       The reference to *The Return of the Native* is important because Baines (p. 144) records: 'It is not known whether Conrad ever read Hardy.' Graham knew Hardy personally and had visited him at Dorchester at least once. (Graham to Garnett, 20 Jan. 1899; Hardy to Graham, 12 May 1909, unpublished.)
25–6 Borys Conrad's ninth birthday was on the following day.

59

TUesday

Très chèr ami
   What a pity this cannot be published. The story has all the characteristic excellence of your work, and the missionary is
5 elaborated with judicious effect. Clearly this was the only way; but this is a way nobody has except you.—
   I send it back regretfully; I should have liked to freeze to it. Don't destroy the copy. The time may come when the good lady could be induced to take off the embargo. Her objection is inept.
10 The man is your creation and an entity while the person she imagines she has met somewhere is probably nobody at all.
                              Toujours a vous   Conrad
PS
My wife's kindest regards. Don't spoil her with books—tho' she
15 is on ne peut plus fière of your attention.
   Borys had the grammar read to him. Listened with attention and went away thoughtfully to dig. Not a word of comment.

168

PUBLICATION

This letter is unpublished.

TEXT

1 'TUesday': *sic.*

COMMENTARY

I put this letter in its present position because a comparison of lines
16–17 with letter 58, lines 25–8, suggests that both belong approximately
to the same period. The story discussed here remains obscure.

60

⟨Station: PENT FARM,
Sandling Junction,   STANFORD near HYTHE,
S.E.R.   KENT.⟩
                  7th Oct 1907
                  Someries   5
                  Luton
                  Beds.

Très cher ami.

I am sorry you've left town already. We have just got into this
new house and were anxious to see you under its fairly weather-   10
tight roof. It is very accessible from London: many trains and
some under 40 minutes and only 2½ miles from Luton. Its a farm-
house on the Luton Hoo Estate belonging to that Knight errant
Sir Julius Wernher. A flavour of South Africa and Palestine hangs
about our old walled garden—but it is not intolerably obtrusive.   15

I am glad you like the *S Agent* Vous comprenez bien that the
story was written completely without malice. It had some importance for me as a new departure in *genre* and as a sustained
effort in ironical treatment of a melodramatic subject—which was
my technical intention.   20

Mr Vladimir was suggested to me by that scoundrel Gen:
Seliwertsow whom Padlewski shot (in Paris) in the nineties Perhaps
you will remember as there were peculiar circumstances in that
case. But of course I did him en charge.

Every word you say I treasure It's no use: I can not conceal my   25
pride in your praise. It is an immense thing for me however great

the part I ascribe to the generosity of Your mind and the warmth of your heart.

But I don't think that I've been satirizing the revolutionary
30 world. All these people are not revolutionaries—they are Shams. And as regards the Professor I did not intend to make him despicable. He is incorruptible at any rate. In making him say "madness and despair—give me that for a lever and I will move the world" I wanted to give him a note of perfect sincerity. At the
35 worst he is a megalomaniac of an extreme type. And every extremist is respectable.

I am extremely flattered to have secured your commendation for my Secretary of State and for the revolutionary Toddles. It was very easy there (for me) to go utterly wrong.
40 By Jove! If I had the necessary talent I would like to go for the true anarchist—which is the millionaire. Then you would see the venom flow. But it's too big a job.

I have been thinking of your empty house. We must steel our hearts Living with memories is a cruel business. I—who have a
45 double life one of them peopled only by shadows growing more precious as the years pass—know what that is. I have had the new ed of Sta Teresa sent down for a leisurely re-reading. It seems no end of years since I read first this wonderful book—the revelation for the profane of a unique Saint and a unique writer. Tempi passati!
50 My wife sends her affectionate regards. We had a most atrocious time abroad—both children ill and Borys very seriously too. He is at a little preparatory school in Luton now. Do let me know when you are coming south again. Toujours à vous de cœur

J. Conrad.

PUBLICATION

LL, II, 59–60.
49 'the profane': Aubry reads '"*un profane*"'.
52 (from 'He is' to 'now.'): omitted by Aubry.

TEXT

1–3 The letterhead has been cancelled in ink.
21 'Gen:': inserted.
22 'Seliwertsow': the last two letters are an alteration of 'of'.
38 'Toddles': *sic*.

COMMENTARY

9–11 The Conrads had moved to Someries in September (Baines, p. 345).

12–15 Sir Julius Wernher (1850–1912) had been a diamond-buyer at Kimberley and had supported Rhodes in Africa. The tone of Conrad's reference is perhaps explained by *EGL*, p. 223:

> 'If I had made money by dealing in diamond shares like my neighbour here Sir Julius Wernher, of Hamburg, I would be a baronet of the U.K. and provided both with a language and a country.'

This may also explain Conrad's remarks on 'the millionaire' in lines 40–2: which in turn anticipate the study of de Barral in *Chance*.

16 *The Secret Agent* had been published by Methuen, London, in September 1907.

17 'without malice': i.e. towards Graham, who had advocated social revolution, aided if necessary by assassination (*DG*, p. 119); and whose acquaintances included the assassin and Nihilist, Stepniak, whose career appears to have provided elements of *Under Western Eyes* (see *Notes and Queries*, CCXI, 410–11, Nov. 1966). Perhaps Conrad had read Graham's defence of revolutionaries in the introduction to I. A. Taylor's *Revolutionary Types* (Duckworth, London, 1904).

21–4 Hints for both *The Secret Agent* and *Under Western Eyes* may have been provided by reports of this case, and by the comments in the press at the time on the assassination of General Mesentsow in the street, on the clandestine activities of the Nihilists, and on the fanaticism of Russian refugees.

General Seliwertsow (spelt variously in *The Times* as Seliverstroff, Seliverskoff and Seliverstoff) had been shot by the Nihilist, Stanislas Padlewski, in Paris on 18 November 1890. The 'peculiar circumstances' which the reporters mentioned were: (*a*) the fact that Padlewski had gained easy access to the General, shot him and walked away without attracting attention at the time; (*b*) the fact that although Padlewski had left his name with the General's valet, he managed to elude arrest; (*c*) the conjectures that Seliwertsow was connected with the Russian secret police in France; and (*d*) the doubts about whether Padlewski had shot the General as a private revenge or as part of a systematic Nihilist programme. The general opinion appeared to be that Seliwertsow had been a director of the secret police, had been responsible for recent arrests of Nihilists in Paris, and had therefore been killed on orders from the 'Central Nihilist Committee' (*The Times*, 19 Nov. 1890, p. 5; 20 Nov. 1890, p. 3; 21 Nov. 1890, p. 5; 22 Nov. 1890, p. 7; 24 Nov. 1890, p. 5 and 25 Nov. 1890, p. 5).

31–6 Conrad's defence of the Professor, and in particular the words 'He is incorruptible.....And every extremist is respectable', recall Conrad's earlier defence of 'les êxtremes anarchistes' in letter 31, lines 48–55, and perhaps also his banter to Garnett in 1897:

> 'An explosion is the most lasting thing in the universe. It leaves disorder, remembrance, room to move, a clear space. Ask your Nihilist friends.' (*EGL*, p. 79.)

33–4 The phrasing of the Professor's slogan echoes Archimedes' 'Give me but one firm spot on which to stand, and I will move the world' and anticipates the claim examined by Conrad in 'A Familiar Preface':

'Give me the right word and the right accent and I will move the world.' (*A Personal Record*, Dent, 1923, p. xiv.)

46–9 Gabriela Cunninghame Graham's *Santa Teresa* had just been issued in a new edition with a new preface by her husband (Nash, London, September 1907; *ECB*). Graham had sent Conrad a copy of the 1894 edition in December 1897 (see letter 5, lines 41–8).

50–1 See *LL*, II, 48–53.

61

⟨SOMERIES,
LUTON, BEDS.⟩

Wednesday.

Très cher et excellent ami.

5   The *Dark night* was received yesterday and the the *Wonderful Life* of the Wonderful saint came this morning. I am very much touched by you giving me these two books. I hope that by the force and depth of my appreciation I am worthy of the gift.

Your short and to us so delightful visit has done me an infinity
10 of good. Do not forget that we are to see you once more before you leave for the north. And many thanks from us both for the book for Jackolito—tho' arriving in the morning and being delivered to him in his bed it was a cause of a great and rebellious uproar when the time came to leave it for the bath.

15   Tout a vous
                                                              J. Conrad

PUBLICATION

This letter is unpublished.

TEXT

5   'and the the': *sic.*
11 'the book': 'the' is an insertion.

COMMENTARY

3   The date. This letter may tentatively be ascribed to July–August 1908, for the following reasons:

(*a*) It must have been written after that of 7 October 1907. (Compare lines 9–10 with letter 60, lines 9–11.)

(*b*) Conrad was at Someries until early March 1909 (*LFR*, p. 97).

(*c*) One of the works mentioned in line 5 appears to have been first published in 1908, and Graham distributed copies of it to his friends in July 1908.

(*d*) On 25 July 1908 Graham was in London, but by 16 September he was home again in Ardoch. (Heads of letters to *SR*, CVI, 145, 366.) The reference in lines 10–11 to Graham's impending return to the north would tally with these dates if the letter were written in the period July–August 1908.

5 'The *Dark night*': i.e. *The Dark Night of the Soul*, Mrs Cunninghame Graham's translation of *La Noche Oscura del Alma* by St John of the Cross. The second edition was published in 1922 by Watkins, London. I have been unable to find a copy of the first edition, or an official record of it; but certainly Graham sent copies of it to friends in July 1908, and one of Masefield's letters says that it, too, had been issued by Watkins (letters to Graham from John Masefield, 6 and 8 July 1908, and from Fitzmaurice Kelly, 15 July 1908, ASA).

5–6 'the *Wonderful Life*': another copy of Mrs Cunninghame Graham's *Santa Teresa*.

12 'Jackolito': John Conrad.

62

Aldington
N^r Hythe
Kent.
8 Jun 1909.   5

Très cher ami.

It is really good of you to have sent *Faith*. Your magic never grows less; each of your prefaces is a gem and my enthusiasm is roused always to the highest pitch by your amazing prose. I have already read (the book arrived but two hours ago) *the Idealist* and *The Saint*. Admirable in conception and feeling are these two   10
sketches. Strange that I should have pitched on these two at first. I suppose the titles seduced me. This afternoon I shall sit down with the book and forget my miseries in the delight of your art so strong and human. I envy it to you with affection.

Ever Yours J. Conrad   15

PUBLICATION
This letter is unpublished.

TEXT
7 'of your': inserted.
11 'at first': inserted.

1   The Conrads had moved to Aldington early in March 1909 (*LFR*, p. 97).

6–10   Graham's latest collection of tales, *Faith*, which includes 'An Idealist' and 'A Saint', had been published by Duckworth in March 1909.

63

<Telegrams:—⎞ Conrad.
   Station:— ⎠ Hamstreet.

CAPEL HOUSE,
ORLESTONE,
Nᵣ ASHFORD.>
13 July 1910.

5 Très Cher Ami.

It is most kind of you. The cigarettes arrived yesterday evening but I was finishing an article for the *Dly Mail* (I am supposed to have a column every Saturday) and put off my thanks till this morning when, behold, Jackolito's boïna was duly delivered. He is

10 immensely fascinated by it and I see him in it outside my window devastating the flower-bed. He's a little devil but the red cap suits him exceedingly and charms his mother very much. That really good woman (tho' she doesn't want a vote) is delighted with the cabue cloth. You are spoiling us no end And it is so exceedingly

15 nice to be spoiled by you that I have no heart to protest. Le gentil menage was extremely gratified at having met you. You see, to so many young men you are not only a great stylist but also a great romantic figure. No man of genuine talent, (and Gibbon is that) can remain unmoved by what you write and indifferent to what

20 you say.

Don't forget the visit in the autumn. We won't talk of dates. A word from you to say you are coming is always most welcome here. And as the days will be well shortened by then you ought really let us put you up for the night. Enfin—Vous ferez ce qui

25 Vous conviendra le mieux.

Well—so long—as they say in Australia.

Yours affectionately
J. Conrad.

Pray remember us and give our duty to your Mother. We were so

30 glad to hear she was well.

PUBLICATION

LL, II, 113–14.

14 'cabue': Aubry reads '*cabuya*'.

TEXT

1 'Conrad.': This word has been inserted in Conrad's hand as an addition to the printed letterhead.

COMMENTARY

7 'an article': probably 'In My Library. The Life Beyond' (*Daily Mail*, 16 July 1910, p. 8: a review of J. B. Hunt's *Existence After Death Implied by Science*); or possibly 'In My Library. A Happy Wanderer' (*ibid.* 23 July 1910, p. 8: a review of C. B. Luffmann's *Quiet Days in Spain*).

9 'boïna': (Sp.) 'flat, round woollen cap'. John Conrad was then nearly four years old.

13 '(tho' she doesn't want a vote)': Among Graham's speeches advocating female suffrage are those reported in the *Glasgow Herald* (3 Nov. 1906), p. 7, and (28 Jan. 1914), p. 11. Since 1897 Graham had lent support to the Social Democratic Federation, whose programme demanded female suffrage.

14 'cabue': (Sp.) 'sisal or hemp cord'.

15–20 Perceval Gibbon (1879–1926), novelist, poet and journalist, had become a frequent visitor of the Conrads (*JEC*, pp. 132–4).

29–30 Mrs Bontine was then eighty-two years old: she lived until 1925.

64

⟨Telegrams:—⎫
Station:— ⎰Hamstreet.

CAPEL HOUSE,
ORLESTONE,
Nʳ ASHFORD.⟩
2 June 1911

Très cher ami. ⁵

Thanks very much for the books. You are indeed very good to me. Hudson's vol is fine, very fine, infinitely loveable and, as one reads on, one feels one's affection increase at every page. And as mere writing it is remarkably harmonious, nothing too much, the right note of humanity, the right tone of expression, a sort earnest ¹⁰ quietness absolutely fascinating to one's mind in the din of this age of blatant expression. He is a delight—absolutely individual.—It is as if some very fine, very gentle spirit were whispering to him the sentences he puts down on the paper. A privileged being. Give him my love when you write to him. ¹⁵

François is quite good. Very genuine touches all along and quite telling bits here and there...I am grateful to you.

I send back His Excellency's letter. I wish I could read Spanish so as not to miss the smallest crumbs of your prose of which I have
20 been enamoured for years, with a passion I imagine to be inextinguishable since your pages give me the same emotion as years ago, haunt my mind with the same persistence, bring in their train the same delight.

Well no more just now. I've been writing late last night and feel
25 slack and stupid this morning

Jessies Kind regards

Yours ever
J. Conrad.

PUBLICATION

LL, ii, 129–30.

TEXT

7 'loveable': *sic.*
10 'a sort earnest': *sic.*

COMMENTARY

7 'Hudson's vol': probably W. H. Hudson's *The Purple Land*, which had been reissued by Duckworth in March 1911 (*ECB*). This title was included in the catalogue of Hodgson & Co. for the auction of Conrad's library on 13 March 1925. Graham later wrote a prologue to the Spanish translation, *La Tierra Purpurea* (Sociedad General Española de Libreria, Madrid, 1928), in which he said: 'I am proud that I was one of those who wrought on Hudson to republish his interesting and charming Uruguayan idyll.' (Quotation from the English text of the Prologue, in H. F. West (ed.), *Three Fugitive Pieces*, Westholm, Hanover, N.H., 1960, p. 33.)

16 'François': A remote possibility is George Sand's *François le Champi*; but in view of Graham's devotion to (and Conrad's respect for) Maupassant, and because Conrad's comments would apply more aptly to a tale than to a novel, I think that 'François' may perhaps refer to Maupassant's short story which had had an English publication by C. W. Daniel (London, 1906) under the title *Françoise: Tolstoy's Adaptation of a Story by Guy de Maupassant.* Its plot is paralleled in Graham's 'Christie Christison'.

18–19 'His Excellency': Don Santiago Pérez Triana, the Colombian ambassador mentioned in letters 49 and 53. Graham had been corresponding with him since 1899. The letter from Triana evidently contained a request that Graham should write for *Hispania: Política, Comercio, Literatura, Artes y Ciencias*. This magazine, which was due to appear on 1 January 1912, was owned and edited by Triana, and it was published monthly in London, in Spanish, for distribution to Spanish-speaking countries. The first issue contained Graham's tale 'El Gaucho', translated by Triana (I, 9–11). Graham was a frequent contributor to *Hispania* during the following four and a half years of its existence.

65

⟨Telegrams:—Conrad, Hamstreet.
    Station:—Hamstreet, S.E.R. & C.R^y

CAPEL HOUSE,
ORLESTONE,
N^r ASHFORD.⟩
14 Ap. '12

Très cher Ami.   5
        Charity! Charity!
    You understand these exclamations. I know I need it—from my friends: the charity of judgement; but you are the man who of all men has most of that virtue. Elle deborde gloriously in the volume which on my first visit to London in many months I carried off   10 home. From the first word of the wonderful preface to the last short sketch of the Pampa as it was, it has been one huge delight. Of course some of these stories—gems—I've read (The incomparable Aurora a long time ago first) but the cumulative effect is magnificent in its pictorial force and emotional power. Comme   15 c'est bien vous! You don't change! You don't weaken! Neither heart, nor mind, nor art. You are unique and everlasting as man and as a stylist. Our love. Yours ever Joseph Conrad.

PUBLICATION
This letter is unpublished.

COMMENTARY
6   Graham's volume *Charity* had been published by Duckworth, London, in March 1912.
11   'the first word': The Preface begins:
     'Hope has been said to be the quality of youth, and faith of middle age.
         Therefore, it ought to follow, that the old should cling to charity
         as the best antidote to avarice, their chief besetting sin.'
11–12 'the last short sketch': 'La Pampa'.
13–14 Conrad had first read 'Aurora la Cujiñi' in July 1898 (see letter
     21). Most of the other sketches in *Charity* had been first published in
     SR and the *English Review* between 1910 and 1912.

66

⟨Telegrams:—Conrad, Hamstreet.   CAPEL HOUSE,
 Station:—Hamstreet, S.E.R. & C.R^y ORLESTONE,
            N^r ASHFORD.⟩
             23 Jan '14

5 Très cher ami.

I celebrated the publication of Chance after the time-honoured custom, by a beastly bout of gout which laid me up for a week. That's why I did not write to thank you for your book (and the Ranee's) as soon as I ought to have done. Upon my word it's
10 a marvellous volume. It's absurd to say that its the best you have done—you are always your own unique self. Il n'y a que Vous!

But it's a fact that there is in this latest book something not other or new but as it were a particular intensity and vibration of feeling a vitality of impression—as though you had lately taken a
15 draught out of the Fontaine de Jouvence—renewed your invincible youth in some mysterious way.

It's impossible to say what I like best. Every single page has given me the old, the certain, the ever-welcome delight. Everything in you, the undimmed eye, the unjaded sentiment, the ever-ready
20 responsiveness and the very technique have the quality of a gift from the gods. I ask myself if it is honest or even proper to envy you—and I conclude that it is at least excusable. But no one can deny that there is that in you worthy to receive and fit to use those gifts—your universal humanity, the undiscouraged love of man-
25 kind, greater even than the pity, the scorn and the poetry of your pages reflecting the infinite variety of its fate.

        Ever yours, admiring J. Conrad.

PS Many thanks for your letter. I am glad you find Chance tolerable I don't.
30 The Ranee's book is delightfully ladylike but her sentiment for the land and the people is so obviously genuine that all her sins of ommission shall be forgiven her.

PUBLICATION

This letter is unpublished in book form but was included in my article 'Joseph Conrad and the Ranee of Sarawak', *Review of English Studies*, N.S. xv, 404–7 (Nov. 1964).

TEXT

10 'its': *sic*.
13 'or new': inserted.
19 'eye': an alteration of 'eyes'.
20 'the quality': 'the' appears to be superimposed on 'a'.
32 'ommission': *sic*.

COMMENTARY

6 *Chance* was published by Methuen, London, in January 1914.
8 'your book': Graham's most recent collection of tales was *A Hatch-ment* (Duckworth, London, November 1913).
9 and 30–2 'The Ranee's book': *My Life in Sarawak*, by the Dowager Ranee of Sarawak (Lady Margaret Brooke), was published by Methuen, London, in November 1913. Conrad later wrote to her, stating that her book had provided material for *The Rescue*: see appendix 3 below.

67

⟨Telegrams:—Conrad, Hamstreet.   CAPEL HOUSE,
  Station:—Hamstreet, S.E.R. & C.R^y   ORLESTONE,
                                      N^r ASHFORD.⟩
                                      25 Febr '15

Très cher Ami.   5

Ever since we came home (from Galicia) I have been laid up with gout in various joints in my miserable carcass—and feeling beastly ill with it too. Of course we were there amongst friends but that (you'll understand me) made the mental and nervous strain rather worse. The sheer despair of these people seeing nothing but ruin 10 and ultimate extinction whatever would happen was very hard to bear. In addition to that the affair in the West looked disastrous at first from that side. We had the greatest difficulty in keeping up some show of confidence. Ultimately the Austrians let us go; but only a week after our departure from Vienna an order was issued 15 to detain us to the end of the war. Too late. We had escaped into Italy and we came from Genoa to London in a Dutch steamer.

The first thing almost I read was a par in some paper stating that you had gone to Sth:Am: as president of a commission to buy horses. Well! One man, at any rate, in the right place! 20
I regretted you were gone. I could have poured my distressful tale into your ears—and it would have eased my trouble, for, I am sure, you would have understood it as nobody here can. Enfin!

But generally this looks to me a very ugly business from which
25 no satisfaction commensurate with the efforts and sacrifices can be
expected. This is not pessimism—I have unbounded confidence in
the country—but a calm and reasonable view of the issue. A
miserable affair, no matter how much newspapers may try to
write it up.

30 But as to the fighters themselves its another thing. They are
splendid. I do envy you the sight of the Glasgow and her crew of
bearded pirates. Ones heart warms up to them; and I hope they will
succeed in bringing to account these German ships which are
dodging "down there" or "up there somewhere".

35 When can one expect to see you? I hope it is not till you have
swept up all the horses of Uruguay and Argentina into your net!
That will be a long time—too long. It would do me good to see you.
For apart from my affection for your person I've always felt that
there are certain things which I can say to you because the range
40 of your feelings is wider and your mind more independent than
that of any man I know.

Today I saw a good review of your book in the Dly Chr. by some
woman. I am going to get the vol forthwith. Wife and the boys
send their love.

45 Tout à vous de cœur   J. Conrad.

PUBLICATION

This letter was not included in *LL*, but lines 18–23 and part of paragraph
6 were quoted in *AFT*, p. 370.

TEXT

21 'my': an alteration of 'a'.
30 'its': *sic.*
32 'Ones': *sic.*
35 'it is': inserted.
41 'that': inserted.

COMMENTARY

6–17   In August 1914 the Conrads had been staying at Cracow. War
broke out between Britain and Austria on 12 August. With the help of
Frederic Penfield and J. B. Pinker, among others, the Conrads managed
to return to England via Genoa, and arrived in England on 9 November
(see Wit Tarnawski (ed.), *Conrad Zywy*, Swiderski, London, 1957,
pp. 253–6; *KRZ*, pp. 126–32; *LL*, II, 158–63; and *Notes*, 'Poland
Revisited' and 'First News').

18–20   Cf. *Glasgow Herald* (4 Nov. 1914), p. 6:

> 'The War Office has appointed Mr R. B. Cunninghame Graham head of the Commission which is about to sail for South America to buy horses for the Government.'

Graham had sailed for Montevideo towards the end of November 1914, and worked in Uruguay, selecting horses to be transported to the battlefields of Europe. In March he wrote to his mother:

> 'To-day a man was missing, and so I had to lazo all day.....
> *Quite by accident* I got on a buck-jumper, but sat him all right.....'

He returned to England at the end of May 1915. (*AFT*, pp. 361–71.)

24–9   Cf. letter 34, lines 13–32. In the war, Conrad had at first envisaged a limited German victory which would still leave Britain in control of the sea (*KRZ*, p. 124).

31–2   In December 1914, H.M.S. 'Glasgow', a light cruiser, had distinguished herself by her part in the action which resulted in the sinking of the German warships 'Scharnhorst', 'Gneisenau', and 'Leipzig'.

32–4   One product of Conrad's interest in this aspect of the war was 'The Tale', which Graham later helped Richard Curle to select for *Tales of Hearsay*.

42–3   Graham's *Bernal Diaz del Castillo* was published by Nash, London, in February 1915, and was reviewed by Agnes Herbert (*Daily Chronicle*, 24 Feb., p. 4). She praised the book's 'grace and style' and remarked that 'Mr. Cunninghame Graham removes the reproach that no one has yet written of Bernal Diaz with sympathy and understanding'.

68

⟨Telegrams:—Conrad, Hamstreet.   CAPEL HOUSE,
Station:—Hamstreet, S.E.R. & C.Rʸ   ORLESTONE,
                                        Nʳ ASHFORD.⟩
                                        15 Sept '15

Trés cher ami.   5

I send these few lines at once to tell you that thanks to your good offices Borys has obtained a commission in the A.S.C. The order from the W.O. has arrived this moment. He has got to join the Res: Depot of Mechanical Transport A.S.C at Grove Park, Lee, on the 20th of this month.   10

The boy himself and we his parents are infinitely grateful to you. Without your recommendation he wouldn't have had the ghost of a chance on the score of his age alone.

He will have to fly round for the next 2 days to get equipped, as

15 Sat: is "no day" and on Mond he will have to join. I told him I am writing to you and he will write after he has joined.

I've been anything but well (mentally) for the last 2 months. We expected before this a note from you announcing your most desired visit.   Yours ever

20   J Conrad.

Love from all the house.

PUBLICATION

This letter is unpublished.

COMMENTARY

6–13   The one known absentee from the sequence of letters is an unpublished letter, bearing no date, which Conrad sent to Graham in the summer of 1915. It has not been possible to trace the present owner of this manuscript. There Conrad, noting that Borys had been the subject of conversation between Graham and J. B. Pinker, and confirming that seventeen-year-old Borys was impatient to serve in the Royal Army Service Corps (if possible as an officer, if necessary even as a stretcher-bearer), hinted that Graham might be able to help in the matter.

In 1914 Graham had gained employment with the War Office as an honorary colonel, after having initially been rejected on the grounds that at sixty-two he was seventeen years over the age-limit (Graham's letter to McIntyre, 17 Aug. 1914, NLS).

Borys, after being commissioned, served in the army for the remainder of the war, was gassed and suffered shell-shock during the Second Army's advance on the Menin Road, and was in hospital at Le Havre when the Armistice was signed (Jessie Conrad: *Personal Recollections of Joseph Conrad*, privately printed, London, 1924, p. 79; and *LL*, II, 211).

17–19   Graham, accompanied by Mrs Dummett, visited Conrad in October (*LL*, II, 169–70).

69

⟨Telegrams:—Conrad, Hamstreet.   CAPEL HOUSE,
    Station:—Hamstreet, S.E.R. & C.R^y   ORLESTONE,
                                                                N^r ASHFORD.⟩

My dear friend

5   Jessie and I are very grateful to you for your kindness to our young officer. He left us yesterday to join the Depot at Grove Park looking very well, very happy and most determined to do his

utmost to show himself worthy of your recommendation. He was 17y 9m and 4d old. He will be the baby of the A.S.C officers, I imagine. Tempus fugit très cher ami. You saw him first when he was an infant of 4 months. And now you have given him his heart's desire.

I shall send him your check to morrow and convey to him your good wishes.

I've never seen Jessie more touched than by your friendly thought. I may say the same of me.

Tout à Vous de cœur.

J. Conrad.

PUBLICATION
This letter is unpublished.

TEXT
13 'check': *sic.*

COMMENTARY
The date of this letter:

Borys was born on 15 January 1898, according to the birth certificate in the name of Alfred Borys Conrad Korzeniowski at Somerset House. This confirms the date of letter 7's postscript, and confutes the alternative date, 17 January, given in *LL*, I, 224. Therefore if Conrad's arithmetic in line 9 were correct, the date of this letter would be 20 October 1915.

However, as Borys joined the depot on Monday 20 September 1915 (letter 68, lines 8–10; confirmed by the 'Tuesday' caption in *RCL*, p. 27), he must then have been 17 years 8 months and 5 days old: therefore the date of this letter is Tuesday, 21 September 1915.

6–8 Borys was eventually attached as a second lieutenant to the 594th Company of the Mechanical Transport Corps (*LFR*, p. 132).

70

⟨Telegrams:—Conrad, Hamstreet.
Station:—Hamstreet, S.E.R. & C.R^y

CAPEL HOUSE,
ORLESTONE,
N^r ASHFORD.⟩
28 Oct '15

Très cher ami.

I've just finished B Diaz.

The terminal pages of the preface are just lovely with their irrestible reference to the tempi passati. As to the book itself no personal friend of the old Conquistador could have put it together with greater skill and more tender care.

You have given us there a series of vignettes en suite set off by your most characteristic prose and coloured by your invincible indignations and most lofty prejudices.

At least so the world would call them. Prejudices!

I am not feeling bright at all. Cette guerre a été bien mal engagée. Enfin!

A vous de cœur

                        J. Conrad

PUBLICATION

LL, II, 170–1.
9 'the old': Aubry reads 'one old'.

TEXT

8 'irrestible': *sic.*

COMMENTARY

6 'B Diaz': Graham's *Bernal Diaz del Castillo: being some account of him, taken from his True History of the Conquest of New Spain* (Eveleigh Nash, London, 1915).
7–8 On pp. xiii–xiv of the preface, Graham claims to be well equipped to understand the Conquistadores, because he has endured similar hardships in his youth:
> 'I too have heard the Indians striking their hands upon their mouths as they came on, swaying like centaurs on their horses and brandishing their spears......'
8–10 The same opinion was expressed by the reviewer in the *Nation* (XVII, 150, 1 May 1915).
14 Perhaps his chief 'prejudice' is indicated on p. xi:
> 'They thought themselves the instruments of God, just as we think ourselves the instruments of progress, and it may be that both they and ourselves have been deceived......'
15 Cf. letter 67, lines 24–9.

71

⟨Telegrams:—Conrad, Hamstreet.   CAPEL HOUSE,
    Station:—Hamstreet, S.E.R. & C.R^y   ORLESTONE,
                                           N^r ASHFORD.⟩
                                           3d Jan '17

Très cher ami   5

    I thought I could run up to say goodbye—but my swollen foot does not improve and I can just crawl across a room and no more. So these lines go to you—avec mon cœur—to wish you a safe journey and the success of the "entreprise" the forestalling of the yanks and fine galloping days in the Sta Marta valley.   10

    Your protégé Borys is expected on leave about the 15th. We haven't heard from him for more than 10 days which is unusual—but I don't suppose it means anything. Still Jessie is worried. She sends you her love and best wishes for your journey.

    I can't say I've been very much bucked-up by the change of the   15 government. The age of miracles is past—and the Yahudi God (Who rules us) seems seems to develop Central European affinities. He's played out as a patron. Why not turn over the whole Establishment and the Non-Conf^st organisations to the Devil and see what'll happen. Nothing short of that will put this pretty business we're   20 engaged on right. Et encore! Ever affect^ly yours

                                    Joseph Conrad.

PUBLICATION

LL, II, 181.
9–10 'the forestalling of the yanks': omitted by Aubry.
16–21 (from '—and the' to the end): omitted.

TEXT

11 'Your': an alteration of 'Our'.
17 'seems seems': *sic*.
18 'over': inserted.

COMMENTARY

8–10 Graham landed in Cartagena on 17 February, and until 31 March he remained in Colombia, conducting a survey of the cattle resources there in order to advise the British government on the possibility of expanding the export-trade between South America and Britain (see Graham's 'Report.....on the cattle resources of the Republic of Colombia', published in *Three Fugitive Pieces*, Westholm Publications, Hanover, N.H., 1960).

9–10 'the forestalling of the yanks': Cf.:

> 'I found the chief cattle breeders and the people in general much opposed to private enterprise, as they have suffered much from the tricky dealings of certain powerful neighbours in the north of their country.
>
> On the other hand, they would welcome with enthusiasm any move on the part of the British Government.....' ('Report', *Three Fugitive Pieces*, p. 26.)

11–13 Borys had been serving with the 34th Artillery Brigade at Armentières (*LFR*, p. 135).

15–16 Asquith had resigned on 5 December 1916, and Lloyd George had been asked to form a new Cabinet on 6 December.

16–21 Cf.:

> 'The year 1916 closed in gloom for the Entente. The simultaneous offensive on all fronts, planned a year before, had misfired, the French army was at a low ebb, the Russian still lower, the Somme had failed to produce visible results.....' (*Encyclopaedia Britannica*, XXIII (1961), 766).

72

⟨Telegrams:—Conrad, Hamstreet.
Station:—Hamstreet, S.E.R. & C.R^y

CAPEL HOUSE,
ORLESTONE,
N^r ASHFORD.⟩
17. Jan '17

5 Cher Ami

Thanks for your good letter and enclosure for the officer—of your creation, really.

I am glad and more than glad to hear that he has produced a good impression on you. I've heard he has "the respect of his
10 seniors". His friends amongst his Contemporaries are not a few. There is a sort of quiet enthusiasm about him—et il a naturellement des idées de gentilhomme, combined with a deep democratic feeling as to values in mankind. Indeed he might have sat at your feet except for Your divine indignation which is a gift of the gods
15 to you especially—and which in any case is not of his age—and certainly not in his mentality. Car il n'est pas brilliant.—All good luck go with you très cher ami and whatever happens pray believe in my inalterable and admiring affection

Yours J Conrad.

PUBLICATION
This letter is unpublished.

6–7 'of your creation': see letter 68, note 6–13.

16–18 Graham, who was then sixty-four years old, arrived in Colombia
on 17 February.

73

⟨Telegrams:—Conrad, Bishopsbourne. OSWALDS,
Station:—Bishopsbourne, S.E. & C.R. BISHOPSBOURNE,
KENT.⟩
22.II.19.

Dearest Don Roberto 5
I am just fresh from the second reading of your vol. My
dear friend the track of your unshod hores may be faint but it is
imperishable.

There is a tone, a deep vibration in these latest pages of yours
which has moved me profoundly 10

In this great wealth of things grown precious with time it is hard
to say on which the heart is set especially. Wonder goes with one
as one turns the pages; in the Park or on the Pampa you have the
gift of drawing the reader with you into the very core—the central,
the imponderable—of your own experience; so that unless he be 15
dead to all truth he looks at the lands of this earth (on which you
have travelled so much) with your own eyes—the eyes of wanderer,
of a horseman and of a très noble gentilhomme.

Los Pingos—Bopicuà which of them, or of any one between, do
I like best? When I read you I identify myself so completely with 20
your words, your sensations and as it were the very soul of your
vision that I'll never be able to answer that question to myself.

A Vous de cœur
Joseph Conrad

PUBLICATION
LL, II, 235–6.

TEXT

7 'hores': *sic.*
11 'is': inserted.
15 'he': inserted.
17 'of wanderer': *sic.*
20 'best': follows an apparently cancelled 'the·

6 'your vol.': *Brought Forward* (Duckworth, London, 1916) includes the tales 'Los Pingos' and 'Bopicuá'.

7–8 At the end of the preface to *Brought Forward*, Graham says:
'Tis meet and fitting to set free the horse or pen before death overtakes you.....I would have you know that hardly any of the horses that I rode had shoes on them, and thus the tracks are faint.' (Pp. x–xi.)

74

⟨Telegrams:—Conrad, Bishopsbourne.   OSWALDS,
Station:—Bishopsbourne, S.E. & C.R.   BISHOPSBOURNE,
KENT.⟩
15. 4. '20.

5 Très cher et excellent ami.

The photograph arrived this morning and is a great joy to me and a great acquisition for my study. Now I consider its fitting out as completed and not a single object, picture or effigy will be allowed to enter it after this. I am extremely proud to have you
10 both—I mean you and your kind and wise-looking friend with the white face. He looks most worthy of a place in your heart.

Ever so many thanks too for the *Life and Miracles* which I have just read for the second time. There is no one but you to render so poignantly the pathetic and desperate effects of human credulity.
15 It is a marvellous piece of sustained narrative and of intensely personal prose. Your large treatment makes the story intelligible both in its social origins and in its absurd and tragic psychology. Very fine—very frightful too by the sort of reflections that only your writings have the power to suggest

20 ——————————

Jessie is going on very well. She sends her love and reminds you earnestly of your promise to visit us again before long. I expect to be able to move her home in about a week.

Mes devoirs les plus respectueux a Mme Votre Mère.
25 À Vous de cœur
Joseph Conrad.

PUBLICATION
This letter is unpublished.

TEXT

17 'social': inserted.
18 'sort of': inserted.

COMMENTARY

10 'your kind and wise-looking friend': probably Graham's horse, 'El Chaja'.

12 'the *Life and Miracles*': Graham's *A Brazilian Mystic, Being the Life and Miracles of Antonio Conselheiro* (Heinemann, London, 1920).
Conselheiro led a band of primitive millenarians in Brazil of the nineteenth century. The vagrant members of his sect or cargo-cult awaited the return of the Spanish king on a Doomsday when they would attain salvation and glory. Graham mocks the absurdity of the doctrines—

'This millenarianism, curiously enough, in the face of all his preaching chastity and the duty of not continuing the race by breeding sinners to be damned eternally, furthered the practice of free love. It mattered little what men did as the world was to last so short a time, and thus salvation was assured by faith, without the mere formality of works' (p. 83);

but he nevertheless sympathises with Conselheiro, firstly because his faith was at least passionate and virile compared, say, with conventional Christianity:

'"Repent, and sin no more" is a sort of moral fire insurance. No such ideas entered the heads of the Jagunços who sang their hymns with fervour, passed hours in church, and fornicated briskly, drinking as much raw rum as they could come by (for there was no fast on the drink), and waiting patiently for the destruction of mankind' (p. 111);

secondly, because the sect practised a primitive communism; and thirdly, because Conselheiro was fighting a hopeless battle against modern civilisation as typified by the Brazilian army, which with its Whitworth and Krupp guns in 1897 exterminated the sect. On the eve of the final battle:

'Once again, lost in the heart of the Sertão, was the stage set for the old contest between the forces representing law and order, and the old world, in which each man was a law unto himself—the world of myths and portents, prophets and miracles. The old and new stood face to face before Canudos, one savage, brutal, but not the least ashamed; the other painted in bands of parti-coloured hue, with Progress, Humanity, and Toleration writ large upon them.' (P. 205.)

And when the Brazilian troops had found Conselheiro's corpse:

'Some of the faithful had placed some withered flowers upon his breast. His body lay upon a ragged piece of matting, and both his eyes were full of sand.' (P. 238.)

21–3 Jessie Conrad, who had been having further operations on her knee, returned from the nursing home on 20 April (*LL*, II, 237–9).

189

75

⟨Telegrams:—Conrad, Bishopsbourne.   OSWALDS,
    Station:—Bishopsbourne, S.E. & C.R.   BISHOPSBOURNE,
                                                KENT.⟩
                                          23. 12. 20

5   Très cher Ami.

What to me—an old friend for whom your prose (with your poetry) and your friendship, have been an inherent part of daily existence for so many years—seems most wonderful in the Carthagena book is its inextinguishable vitality, the unchanged strength of
10   feeling, steadfastness of sympathies and force of expression. I turned the pages with unfailing delight (only regretting that there were so few of them) recognising at every turn the eye, the voice, the hand of the Captive of Kintafi. As to the soul You and I cher ami, are too honest to talk of what we know nothing about. Still,
15   after all these years, I think I may venture to say to you this: that if there is such a thing, then yours Don Roberto is a very fine one, both in what it receives from the world and in what it gives to it. May you ride, firm as ever in the saddle, to the very last moment, et la lance toujours en arrêt, against The Enemy whom you have
20   defied all your life!

He is a multitude—for who can count the follies and meannesses of the suffering mankind? He is probably invincible. But what of it! Could I wish you a better fate? Je vous embrasse

                              Yours   Joseph Conrad.

25   Veuillez présenter mes devoirs les plus fidèles et les plus re-spéctueux a Madame Votre Mère.
Give my most affectionate good wishes to Mrs Dummett with my thanks for her letter.

PUBLICATION
LL, II, 251–2.

TEXT
13   'the soul': 'the' may be 'his'.

COMMENTARY
6–7 'your poetry': As Graham is not known to have written any verse, this is amost certainly a complimentary reference to his prose.

8–9 'the Carthagena book': Graham's *Cartagena and the Banks of the
   Sinú* (Heinemann, London, 1920).
13 'the Captive.....' :In October 1897, Graham had been held captive
   by the Caid of Kintafi: see *Mogreb-el-Acksa*.
18–20 As Hudson had told Graham in 1900:
   'You are rather like an Arthurian Knight abroad in the great forest
   of the world in quest of adventures & ready at a moments [*sic*]
   notice to lower your lance & joust at any evil-minded person that
   may turn up.' (Letter of 2 Dec. 1900, ASA.)
27–8 Three of Conrad's letters to Mrs Elizabeth Dummett were included in *LL*, II. She was a close companion of Graham in his later
   years, and according to Tschiffely her acquaintances included Max
   Beerbohm, H. G. Wells, Axel Munthe and John Lavery (see A. F.
   Tschiffely's *Bohemia Junction*, Hodder and Stoughton, London, 1950,
   p. 249). In 1927 Graham dedicated *Redeemed* to her.

76

⟨Telegrams:—Conrad, Bishopsbourne.   OSWALDS,
   Station:—Bishopsbourne, S.E. & C.R.   BISHOPSBOURNE,
                                 KENT.⟩
                              6. Dec 21

Très cher ami

I ought to have written to you long before this to thank you
for the letter you sent me from Scotland. You must forgive me for
not telling you at once how deeply I felt every word of it. It would
not have been an easy task and I do not know that I can do it at all.
Ever since I saw You in London I have been seedy and often in
pain; which I would not mind much but for the depression (conse-
quent on the inability to work seriously)—which I can not somehow shake off. Your letter so full of friendship and appreciation
was a great moral tonic. I am glad that those two early works had
kept enough of their quality to bring me such a letter from you.
Their existence is just as old as our friendship; and I can assure
you that I never wrote a book since without many mental references
to you of whom alone almost amongst my readers I always thought
that *He* will understand.

You have been one of my moral supports through my writing life;
and this latest letter I had from you made me happy in a particular
way. To write it was a true friend's thought. Yours with the greatest
affection J Conrad

191

PS Jessie sends her love and begs you to give her love to Mrs
25 Dummett in which I humbly associate myself.

PUBLICATION
LL, II, 263.
24–5 omitted.

COMMENTARY
12 'inability to work seriously': At this period, Conrad was working
   on *The Rover* and *Suspense* (*LL*, II, 240, 264 and 297).

77

⟨Telegrams:—Conrad, Bridge.   OSWALDS,
  Station: Bishopsbourne, S.E. & C.R.   BISHOPSBOURNE,
                               KENT.⟩
                             28.6.22
5 Dear Don Roberto.
I would have written to you before about my delight in the
Conquest of Granada if it had not been for the beastly swollen
wrist which prevented me holding the pen. G.J.Q. is the most
sympathetic of them all, no doubt about it; and you give a fine
10 portrait of him. The display of perseverence and endurance is
marvellous and worthy of admiration tho' as an edifying instance
it fails, for reasons I need not point out to you. You make the most
of it, in a way that is touching in the earnestness of its sympathy
and the sober force of its language. A fine performance in which
15 I seem to detect an under-note of wistfulness. But then, très cher
ami, I believe that you have missed by a mere hairsbreadth of
400 years being a Conquistador yourself. We are looking forward
eagerly to your visit on Sunday with Mrs Dummett to whom pray
give my duty. Ever most affectionately Yours J Conrad.

PUBLICATION
This letter is unpublished.

TEXT
16 'you' precedes the cancelled word 'yourself'.
17 '400': superimposed on '300'.
17 'years' precedes the cancelled word 'from'.

6–17   Graham's *The Conquest of New Granada: Being the Life of Gonzalo Jimenez de Quesada* had been published by Heinemann, London, in June 1922. As in his previous histories, Graham was concerned to draw parallels between the barbarities of the Conquistadores and those of present-day Imperialists:

> 'That they were cruel is a truism; but not more cruel than were other conquerors at the time when they lived, or than are conquerors today.....
>
> In most of the republics they left Indians who today are citizens, and who have risen in some instances to the highest offices of state. How many, the Indians in the United States or Canada? In what Valhalla suitable to them are the inhabitants of Tasmania, or the Australian blacks? An enlightened Anglo-Saxon Protestantism has allowed them to be exterminated' (pp. 87–8).

In Quesada Graham finds, if not a Quixote, at least a brave, adventurous and relatively humane conqueror; and with the account of the Chibcha Indians (chapter 9) Graham finds another temporary resting-place in his perennial imaginative hunt for the lost Arcadia:

> 'How happily they passed their lives, in spite of human sacrifices and the barbarities that seem incidental to all primitive communities! Eden perhaps was still more innocent; but not Arcadia, for in that land beloved of poets they had wars and crimes and shed the blood of animals, just as the Chibchas killed their prisoners at the feasts Piedrahita tells of in his Chronicle. Still, they were happy in their own way' (p. 104).

As is usual with Graham's histories, the work is an unscholarly but interesting assemblage of conjecture, fact, romanticised nature-descriptions, lengthy extracts from the Spanish chronicles, and polemical asides.

78

⟨Telegrams:—Conrad, Bridge.   OSWALDS,
  Station:—Bishopsbourne, S.E. & C.R.   BISHOPSBOURNE,
                                          KENT.⟩
                                        7. 7. 22

Très cher Ami.   5

We will be delighted to lunch with Mrs Dummett and you at Claridge's on Sunday. 1.15.

I can't tell how grateful I am for your Kind wise and patient attitude to B.

I hope I received the shock with becoming fortitude. One does not   10
want to quarrel with one's son as long as one still keeps some

belief in him. It is a crippling affair for me. One could get the money by extra work but in this affair the element of time is important. A thing like that must be settled as quick as possible by
15 some arrangement of the sort that kind of citizen is used to.

Jessies love.
Ever yours
J. Conrad

PUBLICATION
This letter is unpublished.

TEXT
11 'want to': inserted.

79

⟨Telegrams: Conrad, Bridge.   OSWALDS,
    Station:—Bishopsbourne, S.E. & C.R.   BISHOPSBOURNE,
                               KENT.⟩
                            25.8.'22.

5   Très cher ami.
Pardon me not answering your letter before. I knew you would feel Hudson's death deeply. I was not intimate with him but I had a real affection for that unique personality of his with its, to me, somewhat mysterious fascination. If there was ever a "Child of
10 Nature" it was he; and he never grew older except, of course, in his body. You and I will miss that mortal envelope, but the rare spirit it contained will speak to the coming generations which may appreciate his truth and his charm perhaps better than the men of his own time.
15 Strangely enough I was more intimate with that other dead Northcliffe. How quickly that power was snuffed out! Strange lot, these Harmsworths—it is as though they had found Aladdin's Lamp. But N. himself was absolutely genuine. He had given me one or two glimpses of his inner man which impressed me: And he was
20 most friendly to us all. After all that fortune was not made by sweating the worker or robbing the widow and the orphan. Our love to you dear Don Roberto. Ever Yours J. Conrad

PS Borys got a post with the Daimler Co. in Coventry. Went to work about 10 days ago.

This letter is unpublished.

TEXT
17 'is': an alteration of 'was'.

COMMENTARY
6–14 W. H. Hudson (1841–1922), the novelist, short-story writer, poet and ornithologist, had died on 18 August.

Both Hudson and Graham had passed much of their early lives in South America and had drawn on these experiences in their books; and there were many points of contact between the two men. Their correspondence (see *WHH*) had extended from 1890 until Hudson's death; both men were for several years contributors to the *Saturday Review*, and had collaborated there in a campaign to protect the albatross from extinction (see *SR*, XCI, 49, 12 Jan. 1901); and like Conrad, both had early in their writing careers won the admiration and support of Edward Garnett. Graham had long regarded Hudson and Conrad as jointly outstanding modern writers (cf. *SR*, XCVIII, 695–6, 3 Dec. 1904; and CVIII, 662, 27 Nov. 1909); he contributed an essay on Hudson to William Rothenstein's *Twenty-four Portraits* (1920); and he later wrote introductions to some of Hudson's works as well as to some of Conrad's. On 8 September 1912 Graham said in a letter to Lady Margaret Brooke:

'Hudson's death is indeed a loss. He leaves a blank that nothing can fill. Men of his genius only appear very rarely in a century. Personally, as you know, he was one of the most lovable of men.

We were friends for about 30 years. Though we met too seldom, we always wrote at intervals, & there was no one I thought more highly of, as a man, or respected more as a genius.....

I last heard from him on the 31st of this July, when he talked of his new book & journey to Cornwall.....

Lord Grey of Fallodon & I are going to get together some of Hudson's friends in October to consult about a monument.' (MS. in the possession of Lady Jean Halsey. The 'monument' was eventually to be Epstein's controversial 'Rima' in Hyde Park.)

Although Conrad had little personal contact with Hudson (see *EGL*, p. 315, and *LL*, II, 275) he always referred sympathetically to him and his work, as letters 3, 48, 51, and 64 have indicated. In *Joseph Conrad: A Personal Remembrance* (Duckworth, London, 1924), p. 197, Ford remarks:

'Our greatest admiration for a stylist in any language was given to W. H. Hudson of whom Conrad said that his writing was like the grass that the good God made to grow and when it was there you could not tell how it came.'

15–21 Alfred Harmsworth, Lord Northcliffe, (1865–1922) had died on 14 August. He had written to Conrad in 1916, praising *The Nigger of* the 'Narcissus', and his acquaintance with Conrad appears to date from that period. (See R. Pound and G. Harmsworth, *Northcliffe*, Cassell, London, 1959, p. 504. A flattering letter from Conrad is given on p. 834.) His lively visits to Conrad are described in *RCL*, pp. 54–5; *JEC*, pp. 196–7; and *Cornhill Magazine*, LXVI, 25–6 (Jan. 1929). Eleven short articles and reviews by Conrad had first appeared in Harmsworth's *Daily Mail*.

Ford states that Northcliffe had been represented as one of the 'powers of evil' (evidently Fox) in *The Inheritors*. (Ford, *Joseph Conrad*, p. 139.)

80

⟨Telegrams:—Conrad, Bridge.   OSWALDS,
Station:—Bishopsbourne, S.E. & C.R.   BISHOPSBOURNE,
KENT.⟩
30 Mch 23.

5 Exmo Don Roberto, my dear friend.

I don't remember such a great pleasure for years than that your letter in praise of Gaspar Ruiz has given me. That story was written about 1905 and published in book form in 1908. I thought you had seen it a long time ago; and to receive such a testimony to
10 its general truth (of impression) *from You*, is the most gratifying thing that has happened to me in my career—of letters. But it is a longish story and you may not be so pleased with "la suite".

Still, even if no more than those few opening pages secure you commendation it is something to be proud of. I can't however let
15 you read it in French (in slow instalments, at that) and I am writing to Methuen to send me the vol: (Set of Six) which I will inscribe and forward to you. G.R. is the first story in it.

I found the seed of it in Capt Basil Hall RN. "Journal of the years 1820–21–22"; a work of which you may have heard. Hall was
20 a friend of Gen: San Martin. The original of G. Ruiz is a man called Benavides, a free-lance on the southern frontier of Chile during the wars of the revolution. Hall gives him a page or two— mostly hearsay. I had to invent all his story, find the motives for his change of sides—and the scenery of the tale. And now the very
25 writing of it seems like the memory of a dream!

I was about to write to you to tell you that I had a letter from Ibañez (which I answered at once) and also from his publishing house. As Pinker is gone to the US and I am going on the 21st

I asked both Ibañez and the publishing house to let us take up the
negociation early in June when Pinker will be back. I also expect   30
to be back by the 10th of that month. Mine is not a dollar hunting
expedition. I am going to stay with Doubleday at Oyster Bay and
see a few people. You'll hear from me in a few days as to my movements. We must meet if at all possible before I leave. Jessie sends
her love.   35

Ever Yours J. Conrad

PUBLICATION

LL, II, 299–300.
6   'than': Aubry reads 'as'.
13 'few': omitted by Aubry.
34–5 (after 'leave.'): omitted.

TEXT

13 'you': *sic.*
19 'of': inserted.
30 'negociation': *sic.*

COMMENTARY

7–8 'Gaspar Ruiz' had been first published in the *Pall Mall Magazine*,
XXXVIII (July–October 1906), and had been later issued in *A Set of Six*
by Methuen in 1908.

14–15 Evidently Graham had just begun to read the translation by
Philippe Neel in the *Revue de l'Amérique Latine*, année 2 (April–July
1923).

18–25 *Extracts from a Journal written on the Coasts of Chili, Peru, and
Mexico, in the years 1820, 1821, 1822*, by Captain Basil Hall, R.N.
(1788–1844), had been published by Constable, Edinburgh, in 1824.
Conrad's account of Gaspar Ruiz is based chiefly on volume 1,
chapter 8 of Hall's book. Hall's description of the pirate Vicente
Benavides provided much of the characterisation, and the name
'Gaspar Ruiz' is also given (3rd edition, I, 374). In some cases, Conrad
follows Hall remarkably closely: Conrad uses the incident in which
a sergeant slashes Benavides' neck as he lies feigning death (Hall,
Extracts from a Journal, pp. 322–3; 'Gaspar Ruiz', pp. 18 and 20,
Dent 1923 edn.); he repeats the exact arrangements for a secret meeting
between Benavides and San Martin (Hall, *Extracts from a Journal*,
pp. 323–4; 'Gaspar Ruiz', p. 43); and he repeats Benavides' final
speech of defiance (Hall, *Extracts from a Journal*, p. 370; 'Gaspar Ruiz',
p. 52).
The idea of Erminia's potent influence over her husband in 'Gaspar
Ruiz' may have been suggested by G. F. Masterman's descriptions of

197

Mrs Lynch's influence upon the Paraguayan dictator, Lopez, in *Seven Eventful Years in Paraguay* (Sampson Low, London, 1869), the book from which Conrad had drawn hints, at the same period of writing, for *Nostromo*.

Conrad has naturally made Gaspar a far more sympathetic character than was Benavides: Benavides was cunning and ruthless; Gaspar is well-meaning, basically docile, a victim of injustice and of the ambition of others.

20 'San Martin': José de San Martin, the liberator of Argentina, Chile and Peru, who was later to be portrayed in Graham's *José Antonio Páez* (1929).

26–30 The letter from Vicente Blasco Ibañez, the Spanish novelist, contained the proposal that Conrad's works should appear in a Spanish edition (see *LL*, II, 298; and Conrad's reply: *LFR*, p. 182).

28 'Pinker': J. B. Pinker, Conrad's literary agent.

31–3 F. N. Doubleday was Conrad's publisher in the United States. The journey is described in pp. 58–115 of *Joseph Conrad's Letters to his Wife*, edited by Jessie Conrad (privately printed, London, 1927).

81

⟨Telegrams:—Conrad, Bridge. OSWALDS,
Station:—Bishopsbourne, S.E. & C.R. BISHOPSBOURNE,
KENT.⟩
12. 12. '23

5 Très cher ami.

We are much relieved by your news. I curse myself for a dismal crock who can't go to see a friend in trouble.

I assume that the horse actually went down and that you alighted "parado".

10 I hope to goodness he didn't roll over you.

I shall hope for a line from you soon.

Mrs Dummett wrote me a most charming letter. So I see I am pardoned. Epstein I believe is going to operate on me now. I have been told that Tittle's drawing of you is good.

15 Jessie sends her love.

Ever Yours
J. Conrad

PUBLICATION

LL, II, 329–30.
14 'Tittle's': Aubry reads 'Title's'.

198

TEXT

12 'me': inserted.

COMMENTARY

6–10 Graham had sprained his back when his horse had stumbled (*Century Magazine*, New York, CVIII, 510, Aug. 1924).

9 'parado': (Sp.) 'on your feet'.

13 Jacob Epstein made a bust of Conrad at Oswalds in March 1924 (*LL*, II, 341; *LFR*, p. 196). Other accounts of his visit are given in *JEC*, pp. 236–8, and in *Epstein: an Autobiography* (Hulton Press, London, 1955), pp. 73–7. Epstein's book includes a character-study of Graham, who had also sat for him (pp. 88–9).

14 Walter E. Tittle had recently met both Conrad and Graham: his drawing and description of Graham appeared in *Century Magazine*, CVIII, 507–10; and in the same volume, pp. 641–5 (Sept. 1924), is his essay on Conrad.

Conrad died on 3 August 1924. The obituary essay by Graham is quoted in appendix 5 below.

Later in the year, Graham corresponded with Richard Curle about the preparation of *Tales of Hearsay*, which was published in 1925 with a preface by Graham.

APPENDICES

1 *Variant readings in two letters*

The numbers refer to the line-numberings in this edition.
LL italicised all the French, apart from the words marked here
with an asterisk.

LETTER 1

	MS.	LL
1	Aug	Aug.
2	Hope.	Hope,
4	R. B. Cunninghame Graham Esqr	[omitted]
7	signature —	signature, —
10	myself	myself,
10	These —	These, —
10	doubt —	doubt, —
11	see"	see."
11	and —	And, —
12	yourself;	yourself:
13	mine.	mine?
14	distinclty	distinctly
15	Your vision	your vision
16	value —	value, —
18	generations —	generations, —
20	little	*little*
22	squint;	squint:
22	all —	all, —
24	corner like	corner, like
26	anything tho'	anything, tho'
27	letter;	letter:
27	beliefs —	beliefs, —
29	pen it	pen, it
31	form —	form, —
36	most and	most, and
37	long —	long, —
38	and now I live	and I live
41	wilderness —	wilderness, —
42	If —	If,
42	circumstances —	circumstances,
45	sincerly	sincerely
47	moral, and	moral and
47	austere but	austere, but
48	*You*	you
49	indeed —	indeed, —
51–2	[from 'Believe' to 'Conrad']	[omitted, by editorial convention]

	MS.	LL
1	8 Feb[r] 99.	8th Feb. 1899.
2	Cherissime ami.	CHÉRISSIME AMI*,
3	heaven, to	heaven to
3	*H of D*	"H. of D."
6–7	You — even You! —	you, — even you! —
10	convictions —	convictions, —
11	episodes you	episodes, you
12	intention though	intention, though
14	toute c'est	toute, c'est
15	très-bien	très bien
16	in West. Gaz.	on West. Gar.
21	really)	really),
24	westerners	westerness [?]
25	I pensez-Vous?	Y pensez-vous?
26	can not	cannot
26	fraternity not	fraternity, not
28	sentiment the	sentiment, the
32	democratique	démocratique
33	phantôme, and	phantome, [*sic*] and
37	for and,	for, and,
39	Franchement what	Franchement, what
40	street. I	street, I
41	streets.	streets?
42	can be —	can be, —
42	thats	that's
48	mechanceté	méchanceté
49	nécéssaire	nécessaire
50	essentielment	essentiellement
50	criminelle —	criminelle, —
51	tout — absolument tout —	tout, — absolument tout, —
51–2	abhorrons tout	abhorrons, tout
53	êxtremes	extrêmes
54	generale" — Très	générale." Très
54	plus c'est	plus, c'est
55	ou	où
56	connait	connaît
57	crie — "Je	crie: "Je
57	sauvé!".	sauvé."
58	aporte	apporte
59	mort ça	mort, ça
60	eloquence	éloquence
60–1	par ce qu'elle	parce qu'elle
62	questions là	questions-là
62	sérieuses —	sérieuses, —

63–4	Vous—vous pouvez tout faire. Vous êtes	Vous, — vous êtes
64	essentielment	essentiellement
65	Fronde du reste	Fronde, du reste
65	Moi je	Moi, je
67	a une cause	à une cause
67–8	a une idée	à une idée
68	avénir	avenir
70	verité — une	vérité, — une
71	rien — je	rien, — je
71	rien car	rien, car
72	a ma personalité	à ma personnalité
73	egoisme	égoïsme
73	rationel	rationnel
73	moi même	moi-même
74	la dedans	là-dedans
74	Puis la	Puis, la
75	desespoir	désespoir
77	croiyez	croyiez
77	indifferent	indifférent
78	indifferent	indifférent
78	a ce qui Vous interesse	à ce qui vous intéresse
78	interet	intérêt
79	desire	désire
80	áme	âme
80–1	Comprenez Vous?	Comprenez-vous?
81	devouez	dévouez
82	a la	à la
83	dois —	dois, —
84	fidelité a	fidélité à
85	peux	puis
85	jété	jeté
85	a tous	à tous
85	ciel mais	ciel, mais
86	chose — c'est tout — ce	chose, — c'est tout, ce
86	rien —	rien, —
87	incoherente	incohérente
87–8	existence mais	existence, mais
88	pourtant —	pourtant, —
90	verité	vérité
96	It delights her.	It delights.
99	know — if	know, — if
99	If, if if!	If, if, if!

2   S. P. Triana

Santiago Pérez Triana (1860–1916) was the son of Dr Santiago Pérez, the Liberal president of Colombia from 1874 to 1876. In 1893 his father was banished, and he himself escaped by river to the coast, during a revolutionary upheaval. After a further change of government, Triana became 'Envoy Extraordinary and Minister Plenipotentiary for the Republic of Colombia' at London and Madrid. He was later a representative at the Hague Conferences, and a prolific writer on topical political issues; and in the obituary articles in *Hispania*, the magazine which he established, he is described as a man of immense culture, humour, imagination and integrity (see *Hispania*, London, v, 1615–22, 27 June 1916).

The narrative of his early flight from Colombia, *Down the Orinoco in a Canoe*, originally published in Spanish, was eventually issued by Heinemann, London, in 1902. (As it had a preface by Graham, Conrad may have been sent a copy.) In some of the more rhetorical passages, Triana expresses his love for Colombia and adds his hopes that European investment might lay the foundations of stable government there:

> 'Why should not the ideal of righteousness, of liberty, and of justice prevail? And the vast continent of South America, why should it not be the predestined home of a happy and regenerate humanity?' (P. 114.)

> 'In the midst of the daily turmoil and agitation and sanguinary struggle which constitutes the life of those democracies [Colombia and Venezuela], these [economic] problems, urgent and vital as they are, pass unheeded; and the more the pity, for in their solution lies the basis of a permanent peace. Prosperity begets abhorrence of internal revolutions.....The world begins to sicken at the very mention of the constant strife which converts into a positive hell those regions where Nature has shown herself prodigal beyond measure in all her gifts.' (P. 246.)

Yet while this liberal eloquence may certainly remind one of José Avellanos, who declared that her strife and disorder had made Costaguana ' "a reproach and a byword amongst the powers of the world" ', and who hoped that European investment would provide the key to her peace and prosperity (*Nostromo*, pp. 136–49); and while Avellanos's fervent belief that ' "Militarism is the enemy" ' (p. 136) tallies with Triana's view that

> 'Militarism is a form of exploitation of mankind which adds human blood to the ingredients productive of gold and power to others; it is nothing but an engine of plunder and of pride.....' (p. 204);

nevertheless there is among Triana's attitudes a nostalgia for the 'unspoilt', and a scepticism about a 'civilisation' built on commerce, that is perhaps more reminiscent of Graham's political pamphlets than of Avellanos's speeches:

'I thought, are these lands and this vast continent still virgin in the sense that humanity has not exploited them? are they to be the last scene of the stale criminal imposture now called civilisation?..... Far better were it that the mighty rivers should overflow their course and convert into one immense lake.....the vast plains, the endless mysterious forest.....' (Pp. 112–13.)

'Men have been led on, and are still being led on, to cut each other's throats.....Meanwhile the exploiters sit safe on their office chairs, pocket the shekels, and chuckle at the pack of fools, the smug middle-class flunkies, and the dirty, bamboozled millions.....' (P. 205.)

One of the greatest affronts to Triana's idealism appears to have been the seizure of Panama by the United States, which (as was mentioned in the Introduction, above, p. 40) he censured in his section of the *Cambridge Modern History* (1910). This event was uppermost in his mind in the period during which he was in touch with Conrad. On 29 November 1902 he had written to Graham:

'I sat and dictated about 9 to 10 thousand words, dotting the i's and crossing the t's in the question of the Panama Canal. I fear he [T. L. Courtney of the *Daily Telegraph*] will not publish, principally because as a Colombian and a lover and advocate of justice, I am anxious that the world should know the real inwardness of things. Of course that will not prevent the U.S. from abusing their powers and robbing Colombia, but, if that, as I fear, comes to pass it is well that they should appear, as what they will be, highway robbers and land thieves, and not be able to pose as redeemers.....I am indeed very much obliged to you for all your efforts on my behalf.'

Triana's other letters to Graham express a related contempt for the dominance of commercial motives in international affairs:

'The condition of affairs in intertropical America is hellish.....The Stock Exchange is the Mecca of all those governments. Its approval is the one coveted prize.....; and the S.E. says: you may rob, murder and oppress your people....., provided you pay the coupon, all shall be well, and our press shall cheer you.' (Letter of 9 March 1908.)

'Anglo-Saxondom reeks with deceit, and hypocrisy, regarding its "duty" to "inferior races".

What I like is your underlying thought, that humanity amounts to more than reforms, and the dominion of the alleged superior peoples.....

Our modern humbug par excellence is the chase for the dollar or the pound sterling; the new estimate of men is commercial. Because you stand for what is sound and healthy, because you have a keen sympathy for the under dog, you command the admiration of sensible and discerning men.' (24 March 1902.)

His article 'The Partition of South America' (*Anglo-Saxon Review*, x, 104–15, September 1901) gives further insight into Triana's preoccupations near the time of his introduction to Conrad. (Because Graham contributed to this magazine and kept copies of it at his home, it is conceivable that Graham brought the article to Conrad's notice: certainly most of Triana's ideas find treatment in *Nostromo*.) Thus on p. 106, Triana suggests that many of the old silver mines of South America are freshly exploitable, because previously only primitive machines were available. On pp. 110–12 he suggests that North America offers an insidious threat to the Latin-American states: as in Cuba, 'railways will be built, factories erected,' but

'that product of American civilisation which seems to be the highest evolution of American life—the self-made man, who worships only his maker, and in most cases is considered by outsiders as irredeemably self-conscious—is an importation which Latin Americans can hardly desire to make into their country from abroad. They have enough to bear with their own local political despots, and the change would not be desirable.' (P. 112.)

In the same article he criticises the role of the Catholic clergy, discusses the psychology of the Italian settlers in South America, and concludes that it is in British and Spanish, rather than in North American, investment that hope lies for the political stability and economic growth of the new republics.

Thus, in the absence of a direct parallel in Triana's published works to Avellanos's 'impartial and eloquent *History of Fifty Years of Misrule*' (that 'principal authority for the history of Costaguana' whose place was taken partly by the memoirs of E. B. Eastwick, G. F. Masterman and Ramon Páez), it seems possible that the liberal, rhetorical and optimistic side of Triana's nature, with its hopes of a Colombia rendered peaceful and prosperous by European commercial enterprise, may have contributed to Conrad's account of the character and function of Avellanos; while Triana's more pessimistic awareness of the modern 'commercial estimate of men', of the dangers of North American intrusions into Latin-American life, and of the fact that 'reforms' mean little without 'humanity', may partly have encouraged Conrad to develop the wider subjects of the novel. What is certain is that in referring to the use he had made of Triana's personality, Conrad had in mind Triana's opinions, and was not referring loosely to his physical appearance; for at the time of *Nostromo* Triana was a stout, genial man in his early forties, in the prime of active life, and little like the ageing, ailing, Elder Statesman of Costaguana.

It might be added that Triana also found his way into Graham's writings: he appears as 'the Minister of Costalarga' in the tale 'A Belly-God' (*English Review*, XII, 532–40, Nov. 1912). Graham pays tribute to Triana in the preface to *Down the Orinoco*, in *The Conquest of New Granada* (1922), p. 104, and in an obituary article (*Hispania*, v, 1617–19, 27 June 1916). In turn, Triana (who, as 'Triano', discusses Graham's work in Frank Harris's *Contemporary Portraits, 3rd Series*) was translator and editor of some of Graham's tales.

3   Conrad and the Dowager Ranee of Sarawak

A recognised landmark in Conrad scholarship was the essay 'The Rajah Brooke and Joseph Conrad' (*Studies in Philology*, XXXV, 613–34, Oct. 1938), in which John D. Gordan showed, on internal evidence alone, that Conrad had read widely among material about Rajah James Brooke of Sarawak and his dynasty, and had incorporated much of this material in works including *Lord Jim* and *The Rescue*. Gordan added, however, 'External evidence is lacking. Conrad wrote no essays about the English Rajah, did not refer to him in any published letter or mention his name in the novels and short stories.'

In a later essay entitled 'The Ranee Brooke and Joseph Conrad' (*ibid.* XXXVII, 130–2, Jan. 1940), Gordan offered a piece of external evidence to support his claim: a reference by Bertram Brooke to a letter sent by Conrad to Lady Margaret Brooke (the widow of Sir Charles Brooke, the second 'White Rajah' of Sarawak) acknowledging that he had drawn on her autobiography *My Life in Sarawak* for elements in *The Rescue*. Gordan was unable, however, to produce this letter, which would have clinched his argument.

Two letters in fact serve to complete the story of Conrad's borrowing from *My Life in Sarawak*. The first is the letter to Graham dated '23 Jan. '14' which acknowledges receipt of the book. Graham was one of the many celebrated writers who corresponded with the Ranee: others were Henry James, John Galsworthy, Edmund Gosse, F. M. Hueffer, Pierre Loti, Axel Munthe, H. W. Nevinson and H. M. Tomlinson. When *My Life in Sarawak* had first appeared, Graham had written to her to praise its 'great interest and charm';[1] and letter 66 (above, p. 178) indicates that she had given Graham an additional copy to pass to Conrad. Conrad evidently took more interest in it than his initial patronising comments might suggest.

He had practically abandoned *The Rescue* about the year 1899, when he ceases to mention it in correspondence; but he resumed work on it in 1918 (*LL*, II, 208) and it was finished in 1919 (*ibid.* p. 222). His receipt of *My Life in Sarawak* may conceivably have encouraged him to complete *The Rescue*: for the confrontation between a proud and cultivated young Englishwoman and the alien, exotic and primitive world of the Malay Archipelago had been the subject of the ranee's autobiography and the basis of Conrad's treatment of Mrs Travers; and the autobiography evidently reminded him of the Brookiana which had contributed to his

---

[1] Letter dated 'Jan 13/1913'. Presumably Graham had forgotten the change of the year, and '1913' should be '1914', because the Ranee's book first appeared in November 1913 (*ECB*).

previous Malayan books. Certainly pp. 3–4 of *The Rescue* (Dent, 1924) contain a clearly identifiable tribute to James Brooke, the 'disinterested adventurer' who was in some respects the prototype of Lingard.

When the ranee wrote to him in praise of *The Rescue*, Conrad replied with the following letter. Part of it was published in Sir Robert Payne's *The White Rajahs of Sarawak*, the relevant third paragraph being among the omitted portions. The complete text is given below.

⟨Telegrams:—Conrad, Bishopsbourne.   OSWALDS,
Station:—Bishopsbourne, S.E. & C.R.   BISHOPSBOURNE,
                                        KENT.⟩
                                        July 15th. 1920.

Madam

I am immensely gratified and touched by the letter you have been good enough to write to me. The first Rajah Brooke has been one of my boyish admirations, a feeling I have kept to this day strengthened by the better understanding of the greatness of his character and the unstained rectitude of his purpose. The book which has found favour in your eyes has been inspired in a great measure by the history of the first Rajah's enterprise and even by the lecture of his journals as partly reproduced by Captain Mundy and others. Even the very name of the messenger whom you so sympathetically appreciate was taken from that source. Jaffir, if you remember, was the name of the follower and favourite servant of Pangeran Budrudin, who brought to the Rajah his master's ring and his last words after that prince with Muda Hassim and others had been treacherously attacked and murdered in Bruni.

Your Highness is not mistaken as to my feelings towards the people of the islands she knows so well and has presented so intimately in the volume of her Life in Sarawak. It was never my good fortune to see Kuching; and indeed my time in the Archipelago was short though it left most vivid impressions and some highly valued memories.

It was a very great pleasure to read "My Life in Sarawak", recalling so many things (which I, myself, have only half seen) with so much charm and freshness and a loving understanding of the land and the people. I have looked into that book many times since. My thanks are due to Your Highness for the renewed pleasure of it, and also, more especially, for the Cage which I have lifted bodily from your palace in Kuching and transported on board the "Emma"—a great liberty; but I really had to do something to save Mrs Travers from mosquitos. Your Highness will see yourself that from the position of that old hulk, right against the edge of the forest and on a swampy shore, unless I had done something like this Mrs Travers would have been eaten alive long before the end of that bitterly romantic episode of her life. I hope I will be forgiven the liberty I have taken.

For all my admiration for and mental familiarity with the Great Rajah the only concrete object I ever saw connected with him was the old steamer "Royalist" which was still in 1887 running between Kuching and Singapore. She was a venerable relic of the past and the legend, I don't know how far true, amongst all the officers in the Port of Singapore was that she had been presented to Rajah Brooke by some great lady in London.

I have dictated this letter so far to inflict as little as possible of my horrible scrawl on Your Highness. I have had a gouty wrist for the last month, a very disconcerting thing to me for I agree with Your Highness as to the difficulty of saying things in "type".

With renewed thanks for the letter Your Highness has worded so charmingly and in such a kindly Spirit of appreciation I beg to subscribe myself Your Highness'

Most faithful and obedient Servant

Joseph Conrad.

The letterhead is printed, and apart from the word 'Madam' (in Conrad's hand) the letter is typed from the date to the end of the fourth paragraph; thereafter it is handwritten. The typed portion includes a number of small corrections and insertions by Conrad.

The work by 'Captain Mundy' is evidently Rodney Mundy's *Narrative of Events in Borneo and Celebes, down to the occupation of Labuan: from the Journals of James Brooke, Esq......* (2 vols., John Murray, London, 1848). Mundy tells the story of Jaffer's escape from ambush to deliver Budrudeen's ring to James Brooke in volume II, pp. 129–37. As Gordan first showed, Conrad's version of the same incident is given in *The Rescue*, pp. 372–9.

The 'Cage' discussed in paragraph 3 is mentioned in *My Life in Sarawak*, p. 82, and a photograph of it faces p. 136. Other possible borrowings from her book are discussed in 'The Ranee Brooke and Joseph Conrad'.

James Brooke's steamer 'Royalist' (named after his old schooner) was launched in March 1867. It had been bought with the proceeds from the sale of the steamer 'Rainbow'—a vessel for which, in 1860, Miss Angela Burdett Coutts (later Baroness Burdett-Coutts) had paid £4,100 on Brooke's behalf (see Norman Sherry's letter in *Review of English Studies*, N.S. XVII, 183–4, May 1966).[1]

[1] Most of this appendix was originally published in *Review of English Studies*, N.S. XV, 404–7 (Nov. 1964).

4 A leaf from one of Garnett's letters to Graham, written between 19 and 24 May 1898[1]

everyday, commonplace, exceptional, or vanishing human figures, the Gaucho on the plains, Mistress Campbell in Gart-na-Cloich, Heather Jock, or the Bristol Skipper, all remote from each other, all part of the great ridiculous common Human Family!—This is badly expressed—damnably so—but you catch my meaning—that a volume of such Sketches gives *through its very diversity*, (& through the author's strong Central point of view) a really connected harmonious picture of life—the *sketches fall into harmony*, & form an artistic whole. The wider the range, the more powerful artistically does the volume become—with each fresh atmosphere the reader yields more & more to the eyes that saw, to the spirit that interpreted. And it is largely for this reason—as well as for the "Overseas"—idea that I should like all the Sketches to be harmonious—& social & political papers to be put on one side for the moment.

I think you claim in your letter that you're not an artist! but you have committed yourself too far by writing "The Ipané & Un Pelado". You must get rid of the virus by writing a few more in that style. The critics will forgive you for making a clean breast of it, by saying—"If Mr Graham took pains, no doubt these unconvincing sketches could be—rendered—...respectable———...products of...Kipling...failures...short stories"—etc.

I missed your book of Tales altogether—but I am going to see Conrad in a few days, & will borrow the copy from him.

All you say about Conrad is very true. Apart from the personal side he is, I believe, all that the words—Polish genius—imply. There's a very good analysis of the Polish spirit in Lister's *Life of Chopin*—& it hits off all Conrad's characteristics in a remarkable degree. The greatest delicacy of feeling, the greatest subtlety of thought—each quality hidden & shadowed by a contradictory quality—giving strangeness depth charm & mystery—but I wont widen the analysis any further.

Just now Conrad seems in low health & worse spirits—he wants a change to active life—but "The Rescuer" & circumstances bar the way. No doubt as a friend you know this—anyway his friends ought to know it—as he is a very delicate instrument—& delicate instruments are easily broken.

Yours truly
Edward Garnett.

———

[1] See notes to letter 16, above, p. 86.

Will you then send me, or tell me, of any sketches you think do, or may, come into the province, sketched out, & secondly any 'advanced sketches' you have by you, for my own pleasure.

In his reply, dated 25 May 1898, Graham commented:

Before definitely arranging, I think we ought to meet & talk things over.....Yes, I know about Conrad, poor fellow. I think, he is far from strong, & as you say a delicate instrument soon breaks. He is in every way an intelligence elite. I enter now & for the past the present & the future my *protest* against the horrible title "Rescuer" it will hurt the book. I shall write to Conrad about it.

5 An extract from 'Inveni Portam: Joseph Conrad' by Cunninghame Graham[1]

All the dead man had written and had done welled up in my mind. 'Nostromo', with its immortal picture of the old follower of Garibaldi, its keen analysis of character, and the local colour that he divined rather than knew by actual experience, its subtle humour and the completeness of it all, forming an epic, as it were, of South America, written by one who saw it to the core, by intuition, amazed me just as it did when I first read it, *Consule Planco*, in the years that have slipped past. Then came 'The Nigger of the Narcissus', into which he put the very soul of the old sailing ships, and that of those who sailed and suffered in them, as he himself once sailed and suffered and emerged tempered and chastened by the sea. 'Youth' and 'Heart of Darkness', and then the tale of 'Laughing Anne', so deep and moving in its presentment of a lost woman's soul, all flitted through my mind. Lastly, 'The Mirror of the Sea', with its old Danish skipper who intoned the dirge of ships, past, present and to come, haunted my memory. So dreaming with my eyes wide open, all the long years of friendship rolled back again, and my lost friend appeared, as I remembered him. . . . .

His nose was aquiline, his eyes most luminous and full. It seemed his very soul looked out of them, piercing the thoughts of those whom he addressed; his beard trimmed to a point was flecked with grey a little and his moustache was full. His face of the dull yellow hue that much exposure to the tropic sun in youth so often causes, was lined and furrowed by the weather. His hair, dark and wiry, age had respected, except that it had grown a little thin upon the temples, leaving his forehead bare. His cheek bones, high and jutting out a little, revealed his Eastern European origin, just as his strong, square figure and his walk showed him a sailor who never seems to find the solid earth a quite familiar footing after a sloping deck. His feet were small and delicately shaped and his fine, nervous hands, never at rest a minute in his life, attracted you at once. They supplemented his incisive speech by indefinable slight movements, not gestures in the Latin sense, for they were never raised into the air nor used for emphasis. They seemed to help him to express the meaning of his words without his own volition in a most admirable way. Something there was about him, both of the Court and of the quarter-deck, an air of courtesy and of high breeding, and yet with something of command. His mind, as often is the case with men of genius—and first and foremost what most struck one was his genius—seemed a strange compact of the conflicting qualities, compounded in an extraordinary degree, of a deep subtlety and analytic power and great simplicity.

[1] This obituary essay was first published in *SR*, cxxxviii, 162–3 (16 Aug. 1924).

As he discoursed upon the things that interested him, recalled his personal experiences, or poured his scorn and his contempt upon unworthy motives and writers who to attain their facile triumphs had pandered to bad taste, an inward fire seemed to be smouldering ready to break out just as the fire that so long smouldered in the hold of the doomed ship in which he made his first voyage to the East suddenly burst out into flames. His tricks of speech and manner, the way he grasped both of your hands in his, his sudden breaking into French, especially when he was moved by anything, as when I asked him to attend some meeting or another, and he replied, "Non, il y aura des Russes," grinding his teeth with rage. England, the land of his adoption, he loved fervently, and could not tolerate that anything with which he had been once familiar should be tampered with, as often happens when a man adopts a second fatherland, for to change that which first attracted him seems a flat blasphemy.

As the car drew up at the cemetery gate with a harsh, grating noise upon the gravel, I wakened from my dream.

Index

Page-numbers in bold type indicate references within Conrad's letters to Graham; page-numbers in ordinary type refer to the editorial matter. Works are listed after their authors' names.

218

Globe Syndicate, 81
God, 50, 65, 67
Gordan, J. D., 209
Graham, Charles Cunninghame, 59,
    61, 71, 74, 164
Graham, Gabriela Cunninghame, 9–
    10, 51, 64, 88–9, 106, 111, 113,
    123, 123–4, 133, 145, 164, 170
Her works:
'Batuecas, The', 87
'Best Scenery I Know, The', 51,
    52
Dark Night of the Soul, The (tr.),
    172, 173
Don Juan's Last Wager (tr.), 126,
    127, 133, 134
'Family Portraits', 123; quoted,
    124
Father Archangel of Scotland, 87,
    88
Genara, 144, 145; quoted, 146
Santa Teresa, 51, 57, 65, 70–1,
    72–3, 74, 87, 88, 123, 170, 172;
    quoted, 73
'Vera de Plasencia, La', 87
'Will, A', 87
'Yuste', 87
Graham, Robert, 9
Graham, Robert Bontine Cunning-
    hame,
Political career, 4, 5, 9–18
Literary reputation, 27 ff.
Troubles with Gartmore, 64, 98, 99,
    100
War-time missions to South Ameri-
    ca, 179–80, 181, 185, 185–6
Letters to Garnett, quoted, 26–7,
    86, 92, 96, 98, 99, 104, 106, 120,
    123, 137, 156, 159, 213
His works:
'Animula Vagula', 30
'An Tighearna', 18
Aurora la Cujiñi, 94, 95–6, 103,
    177; Garnett on, 96, 104
Bernal Diaz del Castillo, 180, 181,
    183–4; quoted, 184
'Bloody Niggers', 28, 87, 88, 89,
    89–90; quoted, 89, 119
'Bolas, The', 87
'Bopicuá', 187
'Braw Day, A', quoted, 99
Brazilian Mystic, A, 188; quoted,
    189
'Bristol Fashion', 76, 77–8
Brought Forward, 187; quoted, 188
'Buta', 133, 134

Cartagena and the Banks of the
    Sinú, 190
Charity, 33, 177
'Christie Christison', 33
Conquest of New Granada, The,
    192; quoted, 193
'Cruz Alta', 137; quoted, 38
'Enemy, The', quoted, 4
Faith, 173
Father Archangel of Scotland
    (vol.), 46, 87, 88
'Father Archangel of Scotland'
    (tale), 87
'Glorious Memory of Captain
    Kidd, The', quoted, 39
'Gold Fish, The', 130, 146
Hatchment, A, 179
'Hatchment, A', 33
'Hegira, A', 33, 130; quoted, 31
Hernando de Soto, 41, 148–9,
    150, 152; quoted, 127, 150
'Higginson's Dream', 105, 106;
    quoted, 5
His People, 165, 166, 167
'His People', 167
'Horses of the Pampas', 87
'Idealist, An', 173
'Impenitent Thief, The', 59, 62,
    68, 69; quoted, 69
'In a German Tramp', 130;
    quoted, 33–4
Introduction to Lord Jim, quoted,
    6
'Inveni Portam: Joseph Conrad',
    quoted, 214–15
Ipané, The, 86, 103, 114, 115,
    124–5, 212–13
José Antonio Páez, 38
'Los Pingos', 187
'McKechnie v. Scaramanga', 162
Madonna of the Sea, The (tr.), 92
'Might, Majesty and Dominion',
    quoted, 33
Mogreb-el-Acksa, 33, 34–5, 77,
    79, 109–11, 112, 114, 115,
    124; quoted, 20, 34, 36, 163;
    Garnett on, 115; Preface ('To
    Wayfaring Men'), 100–1, 111;
    quoted, 102–3
Notes on the District of Menteith,
    46, 78, 79
'Pakeha, A', 116, 119
Pedro de Valdivia, 29
Portrait of a Dictator, 38
Preface to Tales from Mau-
    passant, quoted, 32

219